ADVANCE PRAISE

"The most common and difficult thing companies do is make decisions. In a world driven by continuous change, new technologies, and geopolitical unpredictability, leaders who can sense this change coming and react appropriately win. The Decisive Company provides the tactics and skills to do just that. This is required reading."

—JEFF GOTHELF, BESTSELLING COAUTHOR OF *WHO DOES WHAT BY HOW MUCH?*, *SENSE & RESPOND*, AND *LEAN UX*

"As a senior executive, getting up-to-date information to make decisions is an ongoing challenge. By the time data is gathered and discussed, the game has often changed. Plans and metrics are often stale by the time they are presented. Elliott delves into using AI and graph-driven context to connect the dots while building organizational memory. The potential to transform strategy execution presents a massive opportunity for tech-savvy leaders."

—TIM ARNOULT, FORMER GLOBAL HEAD OF TECHNOLOGY & OPERATIONS AT BANK OF AMERICA

"In today's environment of extreme uncertainty, relentless competition, and ever-increasing pace of change, Steve hits a nerve with this book. The Decisive Company offers a blueprint for operationalizing decision-making, boldly challenges the status quo, and presents a powerful perspective on decisiveness as a competitive advantage."

—JIM KELLY, FORMER GLOBAL CIO OF BANK OF AMERICA

"I spent four years at a leading product analytics company, working with countless teams across the industry. While data access and interpretation are often seen as the biggest challenges, I realized the real hurdle lies in how teams frame and make decisions. The best teams strike a balance between decision quality and velocity, creating a 'pull' for good-enough data. They operate as decision factories.

"In The Decisive Company, Steve tackles decision-making head-on, combining an entrepreneur's drive with a practical approach to a complex topic. He makes decision-making accessible and actionable, focusing on ingraining habits and rituals across the entire company—from top-down to bottom-up. Thank you, Steve!"

—JOHN CUTLER, PRODUCT MANAGEMENT THOUGHT LEADER, HEAD OF PRODUCT AT DOTWORK

"In The Decisive Company, Elliott makes a compelling case for why decisiveness is critical for large organizations today. His insights drive swift and effective decision-making across products, functions, teams, and capabilities."

—JOSH SEIDEN, BESTSELLING COAUTHOR OF *WHO DOES WHAT BY HOW MUCH?*, *SENSE & RESPOND*, AND *LEAN UX*

"I've seen firsthand how decisiveness can make or break an organization. Strategic, swift, informed decisions are paramount in complex business ventures and sports. Just as important as a good decision is aligning across the entire organization once a decision is made. The Decisive Company isn't just theory—it's a playbook for managing uncertainty and disruption. Steve delves into the importance of using data intelligence to inform decisions, effectively communicating those decisions, and tracking outcomes to help the organization learn. The Decisive Company contains the plays that can keep an organization agile and ready to compete in a rapidly changing world."

—JIM CRANE, OWNER AND CHAIRMAN OF THE HOUSTON ASTROS, CEO OF CRANE CAPITAL GROUP, CRANE WORLDWIDE LOGISTICS, AND CRANE FREIGHT AND SHIPPING

"In *The Decisive Company*, Steve tackles the challenge of making swift decisions in the chaos of running a complex business. His pragmatic approach helps leaders cut through the noise and make clear choices."
—CAMERON DEATSCH, BOARD MEMBER AT INTERCOM, FORMER CHIEF REVENUE OFFICER OF ATLASSIAN

"*The Decisive Company* explains why connecting strategy to execution is daunting in large companies and offers practical solutions. Steve's insights bridge the gap and streamline the strategic alignment process."
—ZUBIN IRANI, CEO OF CPRIME

"Elliott demystifies the intricate nature of decision-making, offering practical solutions for leaders. His book is a must-read for leadership teams looking to improve their decision-making skills."
—GREG STOCK, CEO OF ZENOSS

"Businesses everywhere want business agility. But that agility—that ability to adapt to change—assumes that decisions are happening effectively all the time, all across the company. In *The Decisive Company*, Steve focuses on how we make organizational decisions and how we can get better at them. Read this and you'll see that if you want to transform, you should start with your decision-making."
—STEPHANIE BAILEY, CMO OF PRAXIS LABS

"Maintaining a competitive edge can be challenging. *The Decisive Company* makes it less so. Emphasizing the value of coherent culture and clear messaging as the foundation for making smart and timely choices, Steve Elliott guides readers through the process of building a company for long-term success."
—ERIC RIES, BESTSELLING AUTHOR OF *THE LEAN STARTUP* AND FOUNDER OF LTSE

"Navigating the complexities of strategic alignment across a large organization can often feel like steering a ship through stormy seas. In The Decisive Company, Steve skillfully dissects the challenges of coordinating an organization to maximize results as it rapidly evolves. The emphasis on reducing the time lapse in decision-making is critical, and the strategies outlined here are invaluable for any leader aiming to foster organizational cohesion while increasing competitive advantage."

—LEE DITIANGKIN, DIRECTOR OF ENGINEERING
AND PRODUCT AT NVIDIA

"We all want our teams to make better decisions faster, but in today's complex and fast-paced environment, that can feel like an uphill battle. In this book, Steve shows us how to intentionally design a more decisive business and provides invaluable and actionable insight into how the best businesses make it happen."

—MARTIN ERIKSSON, CO-FOUNDER OF MIND THE PRODUCT

"The sheer number of decisions made and those that were merely contemplated can be staggering. The population and magnitude may be unknown to top executive teams. Elliott certainly explores how strategic operational intelligence will transform an organization's ability to consider more timely and effective critical business decisions. It is a fascinating read for our future-focused leaders."

—DOUG COGAN, FORMER PARTNER AT PwC

"Steve's The Decisive Company delivers a fresh and actionable approach to navigating the complexities of modern leadership and decision-making. What makes this book stand out is its focus on decision flow as a competitive advantage. Steve reframes decision-making as a dynamic, context-driven process rather than a series of isolated choices. His 'Wire for… (Context, Flow, Action)' chapters are particularly impactful, offering practical guidance for designing organizations that are wired for clarity, adaptability, and sustainable growth.

"Through innovative ideas like relational mapping of context and perspective, wiring for real-time insights, and empowering decisions at the right level, the section on strategic operational intelligence is intriguing. Steve gives leaders the tools to identify and mitigate blind spots, align priorities, and build systems that thrive in uncertainty. The inclusion of actionable tools—decision-rights matrices, self-revealing dashboards, and feedback loops—ensures that this isn't just a theoretical exploration but a practical guide for transformation.

"Steve's book is a must-read for leaders who want to build organizations that are not just resilient but proactive, using the power of strategic alignment and decision flow to drive success in today's fast-changing world."
—DENNIS STEVENS, FOUNDER OF ORGWRIGHT

"In a world where the speed of decision-making defines success, The Decisive Company offers a roadmap to overcoming the inertia that hinders many organizations. By diagnosing indecisiveness, aligning strategic goals, and leveraging AI-driven insights, this book equips leaders to transform their decision-making processes. Embrace decisiveness, and you'll not only navigate uncertainty but thrive in it."
—GREG COTICCHIA, SIX-TIME CEO, PROFESSOR
AT UNIVERSITY OF PITTSBURGH

THE DECISIVE COMPANY

THE
DECISIVE
COMPANY

How High-Performance Organizations Connect Strategy to Execution

STEVE ELLIOTT

HOUNDSTOOTH
PRESS

THE DECISIVE COMPANY
How High-Performance Organizations Connect Strategy to Execution

SECOND EDITION

ISBN   978-1-5445-4644-5   *Hardcover*
      978-1-5445-4643-8   *Paperback*
      978-1-5445-4645-2   *Ebook*

CONTENTS

PART 4: ACTIVATE STRATEGIC OPERATIONAL INTELLIGENCE

INTRODUCTION

In today's world, speed isn't optional—it's survival.

The pace of change has never been faster, and the cost of indecision has never been higher. Competitors are moving quicker. Customers are demanding more. Markets shift overnight. Leaders know they need to act, yet many organizations remain paralyzed.

Why?

Because the systems designed to support decisions are broken. Information is scattered. Context is missing. Processes are slow, and cultures favor consensus over clarity. As a result, decisions are delayed, diluted, or distorted.

And in a rapidly evolving world, that's deadly.

As Jeff Bezos once said: **"If you're good at course correcting, being wrong may be less costly than you think, whereas being slow is going to be expensive for sure."**[1]

This book is about fixing that indecision.

---

1   Jeffrey P. Bezos, "2016 Letter to Shareholders," Amazon News, April 17, 2017, https://www.aboutamazon.com/news/company-news/2016-letter-to-shareholders.

THE STAKES

The organizations that will thrive tomorrow act decisively today. They don't wait for perfect information. They don't get trapped in bureaucracy. They don't accept the status quo.

Take MySpace. It was the king of social media, with millions of users and a head start no one thought could be beat. Then, Facebook arrived—cleaner, faster, more focused. MySpace hesitated. They ignored user complaints about cluttered design, overbearing ads, and slow performance. Facebook listened, iterated, and grew. By the time MySpace tried to catch up, it was too late. The users were gone and so was their dominance. **Indecision comes at a cost: hesitation.** And often, that's the difference between winning and losing.

New systems that empower leaders to make smarter decisions are inevitable. Soon, these systems will seamlessly connect strategy with action, reduce friction, and turn complexity into clarity—all without disrupting existing workflows.

Decisiveness isn't a luxury—it's the difference between leading the market and being left behind.

The choice is simple: Improve how you make decisions, or fall victim to those who do.

THE CHALLENGE OF MODERN DECISION-MAKING

Organizations today are drowning in data yet starved for insights. Technology has made it easier to collect information but harder to connect it. Leaders are overwhelmed, teams are misaligned, and critical decisions lack the context they need.

The result?

- **Bias** clouds judgment.
- **Noise** scatters decisions.
- **Inertia** keeps the status quo alive.

It doesn't have to be this way.

This book provides a blueprint to fix decision-making at its core. From reducing bias and eliminating noise to embracing speed and clarity, the tools found here will help you transform your organization into one that decides smarter, faster, and better—every time.

WHAT TO EXPECT

Context drives clarity, and clarity drives action. You'll learn how to build a foundation of decision-making that gives your teams unshakeable purpose. Then, we'll tackle decisiveness—the art of cutting through uncertainty when others hesitate. You'll also discover tools like the context graph—a framework to map, streamline, and accelerate decision-making across your teams. This isn't just about making decisions; it's about making them stick through coherent action that aligns strategy with execution.

But great decisions need more than just speed; they need precision. We'll explore how to strip away bias and eliminate noise, creating systems that consistently produce smart outcomes. And as your organization grows, you'll discover how to activate strategic operational intelligence—a powerful framework that can help your company get smarter with every decision it makes.

Each chapter of this book transforms theory into practice. You'll find frameworks that have been tested in the real world, insights that cut through complexity, and examples that show you exactly how to implement these ideas in your organization—starting today.

WHY THIS MATTERS

Jean-Paul Sartre said it best: **"Man is defined as the choices he must make."**[2] The same is true for organizations. What kind of

---

2   Jean-Paul Sartre, *Existentialism Is a Humanism*, trans. Carol Macomber, ed. John Kulka (Yale University Press, 2007), 59.

organization do you want to be? One that hesitates—or one that leads?

Every decision—who to hire, what to build, where to invest—shapes your organization's identity and future. A great organization isn't just a collection of people. It's also a collection of decisions.

This book will help you make those decisions better.

Faster. Smarter. Sharper.

Your decisions today shape your tomorrow. Let's build an organization that doesn't just survive—it leads.

HOW TO GET THE MOST FROM THIS BOOK

As Benjamin Franklin wrote, "It is not only right to strike while the iron is hot, but that it may be very practicable to heat it by continually striking."[3] This book is your tool kit for decisive action—whether you are leading a team or scaling enterprise-wide transformation.

This book is for leaders at all levels who are ready to move their organizations forward—faster and smarter. Whether you are **an executive** steering strategy and growth, **a program or operational leader** turning plans into action, or **a product manager** driving roadmaps and innovation, you will find actionable insights to help you move faster, align your teams, and turn strategy into action.

HOW TO USE THIS BOOK

This book is both a compass and a tool kit. Like any powerful tool, its value multiplies with intentional use. Start with the **chapter summaries**—they are your quick-start guide to each major concept. They'll help you navigate directly to the solutions you need most.

But don't just read—engage. Share the frameworks you find here with your team. Challenge assumptions. Test ideas in your next meeting. The **Decision Points** at the end of each chapter aren't

---

3   William Morgan, *Memoirs of the Life of the Rev. Richard Price, D.D. F.R.S.* (London, 1815), 96.

just checkpoints—they're conversation starters. They'll help you spot the gaps between where you are and where you need to be.

Knowledge becomes power through application. So return to the **Knowledge Maps** in each chapter when you're facing a tough decision or hitting resistance. They're designed to be your rapid reference guides, helping you adapt these frameworks to your unique challenges. Remember: Decisiveness isn't about making perfect decisions every time—it's about getting better with every choice you make.

WHO IS SPEAKING TO YOU?

Over the last two decades, I've led large-scale transformations for Fortune 500 organizations. I've also built fast-moving companies from the ground up and been on the leadership teams of five successful startups. Through it all, I've seen how indecision stalls progress and decisiveness drives transformation. This book will show you how to **act decisively, align strategy with execution,** and build a culture where **every decision fuels progress**.

Organizations that act with speed, clarity, and conviction won't just survive uncertainty—they'll lead the future.

PART 1

DIAGNOSE YOUR DECISIVENESS DISORDER

Making fast, aligned decisions in a complex organization isn't easy. It's messy. It's chaotic.

Why? Because competing priorities, misaligned goals, and tangled processes create friction. Decisions stall. Momentum dies.

But it doesn't have to be this way.

In this section, you'll uncover the root causes of indecision—why alignment breaks down, why clarity feels out of reach, and why the status quo keeps winning. Most importantly, you'll learn how to diagnose your decision-making challenges and clear the path to better, faster results.

Let's pinpoint what's slowing you down—and fix it.

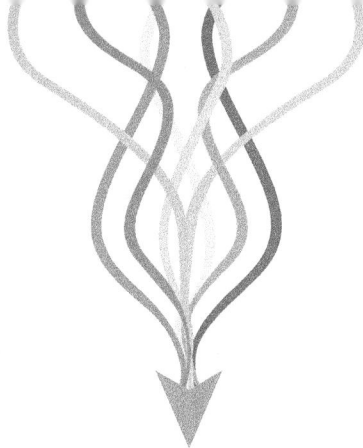

CHAPTER 1

IS YOUR ORGANIZATION INFECTED WITH INDECISION?

"Uncertainty is an uncomfortable position. But certainty is an absurd one."
—VOLTAIRE

Decisions are the heartbeat of success. But leaders today face a storm of complexity—data overload, shifting markets, and vanishing opportunities. The pressure to act swiftly has never been greater. Uncertainty is uncomfortable, but avoiding decisions doesn't solve them.

Indecision **paralyzes progress**.

Decisiveness is the ability to act quickly, choose confidently, and move forward even when the path ahead isn't perfectly clear.

And what about the leaders who hesitate? They miss opportunities. They amplify risks. Indecision doesn't just slow you down—it costs you. Innovations are delayed. Progress falters. The window for bold action slams shut.

The cost of indecision? It's steep.

Slow decisions waste time, resources, and morale. They create confusion, frustration, and—worst of all—missed opportunities. **Success favors the decisive.** It rewards those who move boldly and swiftly.

You might be wondering, "Aren't all companies at least a little slow and indecisive?" Let's examine a real-world example.

Two companies, same storm: **COVID-19.** Hertz flinched. Demand fell. It stalled. Competitors pivoted to curbside pickups, clean-car guarantees, and home deliveries. In May 2020, Hertz filed for bankruptcy.[4]

Chipotle moved fast. It doubled down on its drive-through "Chipotlanes," perfectly aligning with shifting customer needs.[5] In 2022, Chipotle opened its five hundredth Chipotlane.[6] And growth didn't stop there.

Decisions define organizations, but indecision infects them. It slows progress, clouds strategy, and frustrates teams.

Ask yourself:

- How are strategic decisions made here?
- How is strategy communicated? Where is it stored?
- How often do we track progress?

Now, dig deeper:

- Can we analyze past decisions to improve future ones?
- What is our decision velocity—and is it increasing?
- How do we balance speed, consensus, and alignment?

---

4   Niraj Chokshi, "Hertz, Car Rental Pioneer, Files for Bankruptcy Protection," *New York Times,* last modified November 3, 2021, https://www.nytimes.com/2020/05/22/business/hertz-bankruptcy-coronavirus-car-rental.html.

5   Nancy Luna, "Chipotle Mexican Grill Outlines Key Tactical Wins During COVID-19 Crisis," *Nation's Restaurant News,* September 18, 2020, https://www.nrn.com/fast-casual/chipotle-mexican-grill-outlines-key-tactical-wins-during-covid-19-crisis.

6   Alicia Kelso, "Chipotle Hits Its 500th Chipotlane Milestone," *Nation's Restaurant News,* November 16, 2022, https://www.nrn.com/fast-casual/chipotle-hits-its-500th-chipotlane-milestone.

When answers to these questions are unclear, indecision spreads. Confusion reigns. The result? A culture of hesitation over action.

Chaos, complacency, and bureaucracy don't just confuse teams. They erode trust. They stall progress. They make decision-making feel like trudging through mud—slow, exhausting, and murky.

The price of inaction? It's high.

It's missed opportunities. It's slow responses to changing markets. It's innovations that die in committee. And worse, it's the steady drip of frustration. Teams lose motivation. Leaders lose credibility. Momentum disappears.

So, what stands in the way?

The barriers to decisiveness are everywhere:

- **Chaos** that clouds clarity.
- Inertia that favors **the status quo** and smothers innovation.
- Hidden **biases** that distort judgment.
- The **consensus trap** that delays action.
- Layers of **bureaucracy** that weigh everything down.

Before you can fix these, you must face them head-on. First, let's dig into the real price of inaction—and what it means for your organization's future.

MOST ORGANIZATIONS ARE SUSCEPTIBLE TO INDECISION

The goals of decision-making are simple: **quality and speed.**

But most organizations struggle with both.

McKinsey research revealed a troubling truth: Only **37 percent** of leaders believe their organizations make decisions that are high in both quality and velocity.[7] Even worse? Just **20 percent** of

---

7   Iskandar Aminov et al., *Decision Making in the Age of Urgency* (McKinsey & Company, 2019), 5–6, https:// www.mckinsey.com/~/media/mckinsey/business%20functions/people%20and%20organizational%20 performance/our%20insights/decision%20making%20in%20the%20age%20of%20urgency/decision-making-in-the-age-of-urgency.pdf?shouldIndex=false.

organizations excel at quickly making and executing high-quality decisions relative to their peers.[8]

The impact is clear.

Leaders at decisive organizations were twice as likely to report their most recent decisions delivered financial returns of **20 percent or more.**[9] The data indicates a simple but powerful truth: The speed and quality of decision-making directly drive overall company performance.

And here's the surprising part.

Organizations that move quickly don't sacrifice quality—they enhance it. Fast decision-makers were **twice as likely** to make high-quality decisions compared to those who moved slowly.[10]

Why? **Because speed fuels clarity, and clarity drives outcomes.**

When you make decisions fast, you don't just act—you increase your odds of winning.

THE PRICE OF INDECISION

When big things go wrong, indecision is often to blame. It's not just a missed opportunity—it's a chain reaction of consequences.

What happens when indecision drags on for years? Bayer AG's story shows the devastating impact of prolonged indecision—and how decisive leadership can change the tide.

In January 2024, Bayer faced a sharp decline in share price and a staggering **$2.25 billion lawsuit payout** related to its Roundup

---

8   Aminov et al., *Age of Urgency*, 6–7.

9   Aminov et al., *Age of Urgency*, 7.

10 Aminov et al., *Age of Urgency*, 7.

weed killer.[11] Since acquiring Monsanto in 2018, the company's value had plummeted by **70 percent**.[12]

The reasons? Legal hurdles. Reputational damage. Regulatory scrutiny. Integration chaos. But above all: **slow decisions in the face of crises.**

The board was forced to step in and act. They hired Bill Anderson with a clear mandate: dismantle bureaucracy, empower frontline teams, and replace annual budgets with **ninety-day cycles**.[13]

Anderson knew slow decisions were fatal. So, he changed the system.

Lesson 1: Bureaucracy kills momentum. Streamline processes and empower frontline teams to act.

Lesson 2: Rigid annual planning stifles agility. Shorter cycles—like ninety-day plans—drive faster results.

Bayer offers a public example of the cost of indecision. But more often, the damage unfolds behind closed doors—leaders and teams paralyzed while trying to act decisively.

THE HIDDEN COSTS OF INDECISION

Indecision isn't harmless hesitation. It bleeds into every corner of an organization.

Indecision carries a steep price. Innovation stalls, progress grinds to a halt, and frustration builds. Teams lose morale, leaders lose trust, and flawed, rushed decisions damage long-term

---

11 Ludwig Burger and Patricia Weiss, "Bayer Shares Fall Nearly 6% on Court Order to Pay $2.25 Billion in Damages," Reuters, January 29, 2024, https://www.reuters.com/business/healthcare-pharmaceuticals/bayer-shares-drop-45-after-jury-verdict-over-225-bln-damages-2024-01-29/.

12 Brendan Pierson, "As Roundup Verdicts Pile Up, Bayer Bets Big on US Appeals Courts," Reuters, January 31, 2024, https://www.reuters.com/business/healthcare-pharmaceuticals/roundup-verdicts-pile-up-bayer-bets-big-us-appeals-courts-2024-01-31/.

13 Brian Buntz, "New Bayer CEO Bill Anderson's Move to Cut Management Mirrors His Roche Playbook," Pharmaceutical Processing World, September 18, 2023, https://www.pharmaceuticalprocessingworld.com/bayer-ceo-bill-anderson-roche-strategy/.

outcomes. The result? Competitors surge ahead while your organization falls behind.

The cost of indecision is real. What happens when indecision wins? History gives us plenty of cautionary tales.

Lessons from the Fallen

Why do organizations with everything to lose—and everything they need—still hesitate?

They have the data. They have the time. They see the shift coming. Yet, when decisive action is needed most, they falter.

Take Kodak.

Kodak invented the digital camera in 1975. But its leadership clung to film, convinced consumers wouldn't abandon printed photos. They had the technology, the data, and the time to pivot—but they didn't. In 2012, Kodak filed for bankruptcy.[14]

Or Blockbuster.

Once the king of video rentals, Blockbuster had a chance to adapt when Netflix introduced DVDs by mail and streaming. They waited. Consumer habits changed. Blockbuster didn't. The result? Irrelevance and bankruptcy.[15]

Or Toys"R"Us.

As e-commerce exploded, Toys"R"Us failed to build a competitive online presence. Sticking to its physical stores only, the company fell behind while competitors surged ahead.[16]

And then there's Yahoo.

In 2002, Yahoo could have bought Google and in 2006, Facebook. Twice, they hesitated. Twice, they passed. Missed opportunities,

---

14   Laura Ross and Melissa Epifano, "9 Companies That Failed to Adapt to Disruption and Paid the Ultimate Price," Thomas, January 16, 2025, https://www.thomasnet.com/insights/9-companies-that-failed-to-adapt-to-disruption-and-paid-the-ultimate-price/.

15   Ross and Epifano, "9 Companies That Failed."

16   Ross and Epifano, "9 Companies That Failed."

combined with internal missteps, led to Yahoo's steady decline and eventual sale to Verizon.[17]

Hesitation is the common thread.

Kodak. Blockbuster. Toys"R"Us. Yahoo.

Different industries. Different challenges. **Same story.**

Leaders saw the opportunities and had the resources but hesitated. The result? Inaction became their downfall.

These cautionary tales remind us that indecision isn't harmless. It's a choice—one with consequences.

TURNING UNCERTAINTY INTO OPPORTUNITY

The pace of technological disruption, global interconnectedness, and shifting markets has made managing uncertainty one of today's greatest leadership challenges. Change isn't slowing down—it's accelerating. Since the early 2000s, uncertainty has climbed to unprecedented levels, leaving leaders with harder decisions, higher stakes, and less predictable outcomes than ever before.

Uncertainty will disrupt your business—it's just a matter of when.

SIX FORCES DRIVING UNCERTAINTY

The business landscape is being reshaped by the following key forces:

- **Technological Disruption:** AI, cloud computing, and software advancements are transforming industries at breakneck speeds. Leaders must anticipate impacts, adopt new tools, and outpace competitors.
- **Workforce Shifts:** Remote work, the gig economy, and shifting employee expectations are challenging traditional leadership

---

17   Ross and Epifano, "9 Companies That Failed."

models. Organizations must adapt faster than ever to retain talent and maintain productivity.

- **Hyperconnectivity:** Global events—whether supply-chain disruptions, geopolitical conflicts, or market volatility—send ripple effects across industries. Everything is interconnected, compounding complexity.
- **Regulatory Disruption:** Shifting laws and compliance requirements demand constant adaptation. Slow responses can lead to costly fines, reputational damage, and competitive disadvantages.
- **Expectation Escalation:** Customers expect faster, better, and more personalized experiences. Organizations unable to deliver on these expectations will lose relevance to more agile competitors.
- **Data Explosion:** Leaders now have access to more data than ever, but sorting signal from noise is harder. Misinformation and analysis paralysis further cloud decision-making, stalling progress.

These forces are accelerating uncertainty in ways unimaginable decades ago. Take artificial general intelligence (AGI): once science fiction, now a reality. The race has begun, and hesitation could be fatal.

A MINI CASE STUDY: THE RACE TOWARD AGI

AI is transforming decisions, but AGI raises the stakes even further. Companies like OpenAI and Google are moving fast, betting billions on this technology. The implication is clear: Organizations that hesitate will be outpaced. Leaders must act decisively to experiment, integrate, and adapt—or risk irrelevance.

AI is already changing how business is done by automating tasks, generating insights, and improving efficiency. AGI, however, will go further—potentially learning, adapting, and solving complex problems across domains, much like a human. Beyond that lies **Super AGI**, which could surpass human intelligence entirely.

EXPECTED YEARS UNTIL LAUNCH OF A GENERAL ARTIFICIAL INTELLIGENCE SYSTEM (LOG SCALE)

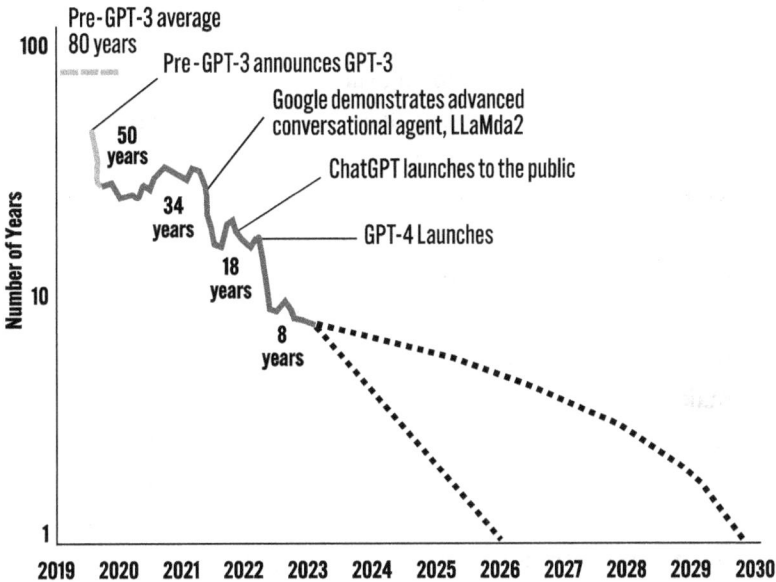

Source: ARK Invest, *Big Ideas 2024: Annual Research Report* (ARK Investment Management, 2024), 10, https://assets.arkinvest.com/media-8e522a83-1b23-4d58-a202-792712f8d2d3/ 8cea086f-21b4-47bf-8ac6-666b96a84a04/ARK-Invest_Big-Ideas-2024.pdf.

The timeline here is very uncertain, but the impact is inevitable. Businesses that hesitate to embrace AI risk being outpaced. Those who move early, experiment strategically, and integrate thoughtfully will gain a decisive edge.

The crucial question: This is just one of a dozen major disruptions on the horizon. Will your organization act now to prepare for this shift or wait until it's too late?

Transformation brings chaos—but also opportunity. Leaders who embrace change and leverage emerging trends can turn uncertainty into a competitive advantage.

Here are four transformative trends driving disruption:

- **Digital Transformation:** Technology is reshaping operations. Innovate or fall behind—it's that simple. For example, Rolls-Royce uses AI to monitor jet-engine performance in real time, reducing costs and improving safety.
- **Hybrid Work:** Managing distributed teams demands new approaches to leadership, culture, and collaboration. Flexibility isn't a perk anymore—it's a competitive differentiator.
- **Business Agility:** Markets shift rapidly. Organizations with agility in their DNA can adapt quickly, seize opportunities, and thrive amid disruption.
- **AI Integration:** Thoughtfully adopting AI can enhance decision-making, efficiency, and strategic insight. Leaders integrating AI today are building sharper, faster organizations that will outpace competitors.

Each of these trends represents uncertainty but also holds keys to building a more decisive organization. These disruptors are explored further in Appendices A–D.

Leaders who drive transformation while reducing uncertainty won't just survive disruption—they'll turn it into a catalyst for growth.

In 2023, a McKinsey survey highlighted the weight of disruption on businesses:[18]

- **Fifty-eight percent of CEOs** named disruptive digital technologies their top concern.
- They also cited fierce competition for talent, shifting work patterns, and macroeconomic instability as substantial disruptions.

Radical uncertainty is the new normal. To combat unpredictable forces, **62 percent** of leaders plan to invest in advanced analytics, recognizing its importance in managing uncertainty.[19]

Leaders who hesitate, waiting for perfect clarity, will fall behind. Those who embrace decisiveness—moving quickly, adapting continuously, and experimenting thoughtfully—will thrive.

Your ability to navigate uncertainty will define your success. The question is no longer **if** disruption will hit—it's whether you'll be ready **when** it does.

THE FIVE WARNING SIGNS OF INDECISION

Indecision doesn't spring up overnight—it creeps in, symptom by symptom, slowing progress and compounding frustration. Left unchecked, it infects teams, decisions, and strategies.

Let's examine the five biggest warning signs that indecision is creeping into an organization.

---

18 Tom Chapman, "McKinsey & Company: Top CEOs Reveal Priorities for 2023," *Business Chief*, March 16, 2023, https://businesschief.com/leadership-and-strategy/mckinsey-top-ceo-priorities-for-2023.

19 Chapman, "Top CEOs Reveal Priorities."

1. CHAOS

Chaos is indecision's natural habitat. Chaos thrives on volatility, uncertainty, complexity, and ambiguity.[20] Everyday market instability, tangled communications, and data overload paralyze organizational decision-making.

Organizations that thrive in chaos don't eliminate it—they navigate it with speed, focus, and decisive action.

2. THE STATUS QUO

Comfort can become a trap. Familiarity feels safe, but it smothers innovation. Leaders cling to what worked yesterday because change seems risky.

Why It Happens: Past wins breed complacency. Cultural norms reward stability. Short-term gains trump long-term strategy.

The Danger: The world moves on, but you don't.

Leaders must challenge norms before the market challenges them.

3. HIDDEN BIASES

Biases are mental shortcuts we all take—but they can distort decisions. Do any of these sound familiar?

- **Anchoring Bias:** Overrelying on old data or initial ideas.
- **Confirmation Bias:** Seeking information that supports your assumptions.
- **Authority Bias:** Deferring to titles instead of ideas.
- **Groupthink:** Prioritizing consensus over critical thinking.

---

20 Nate Bennett and G. James Lemoine, "What VUCA Really Means for You," *Harvard Business Review*, January–February 2014, https://hbr.org/2014/01/what-vuca-really-means-for-you.

Decisive leaders identify and challenge biases head-on, turning flawed judgment into clear, informed decisions.

4. THE CONSENSUS TRAP

Seeking input is good—until it becomes a bottleneck. Consensus feels safe, but overdoing it delays bold action. Teams avoid dissent. Ideas get watered down. Decisions slow to a crawl.

The solution: Balance inclusion with action. Ask, **"Is this a moment for input or a moment for decision?"**

A practical fix: Use **"Disagree and Commit."** Encourage teams to debate vigorously early on, make a decision, and ensure everyone aligns behind the outcome—even if they didn't initially agree with it. This fosters inclusivity without stalling progress.

5. EXCESSIVE BUREAUCRACY

Process often becomes a roadblock in large organizations. Bureaucracy suffocates speed under layers of approvals, meetings, and red tape.

The result? Progress stalls. Costs rise. Innovation dies.

Leaders must simplify processes so systems **enable decisions** instead of stall them. In a fast-moving world, speed wins.

IS YOUR ORGANIZATION SHOWING THESE SIGNS?

These five symptoms—chaos, the status quo, hidden biases, the consensus trap, and excessive bureaucracy—don't exist in isolation. They feed on each other, compounding friction and delay.

So, ask yourself:

- Are we navigating chaos, or are we overwhelmed by it?
- Do we challenge the status quo, or are we clinging to complacency?

- How aware are we of bias, and what steps do we take to combat it?
- Are we stuck in consensus-building when decisive action is needed?
- Do our processes enable speed—or do they slow us down?

Your answers reveal whether indecision is holding you back or you're ready to take action, lead boldly, and move ahead.

SUMMARY

Decisiveness drives progress. Chaos, complacency, bias, consensus traps, and excessive bureaucracy hold organizations back. Overcoming these barriers separates the leaders who thrive from those who falter.

Organizations that act quickly and confidently seize opportunities, spark innovation, and build momentum. Those that hesitate lose ground to missed opportunities, stalled progress, and weakened trust.

Here's what holds most organizations back:

- **Chaos:** Uncertainty and complexity overwhelm clarity and action.
- **The Status Quo:** What worked yesterday stifles what's needed tomorrow.
- **Hidden Biases:** Groupthink, anchoring, and overconfidence distort judgment.
- **The Consensus Trap:** Endless alignment delays bold decisions.
- **Excessive Bureaucracy:** Red tape smothers speed and suffocates innovation.

The solution? Simplify systems. Balance inclusivity with action. Challenge norms. Recognize that speed, clarity, and decisiveness are the real competitive advantages in today's world.

Because in a fast-moving market, hesitation isn't harmless—it's fatal.

DECISION POINTS

Consider This Scenario: At a critical executive meeting, leaders of a large organization confront an alarming report: Customers are leaving—fast. A major competitor's superior online services are pulling them away.

The VP of pricing and monetization speaks up: "We need to trial new pricing models. It'll boost competitiveness, but it could disrupt our six-month roadmap."

The room grows tense. New initiatives mean uncertainty. Trade-offs. Risks. Over the next few weeks, debate drags on. Leaders weigh the benefits of change against the comfort of the status quo.

WHICH PATH WOULD YOUR ORGANIZATION CHOOSE?
Path 1: Wait and Analyze

- Commission a detailed competitor-analysis report.
- Suspend any decisions until after the report delivers more data.
- Form a committee to review the existing packaging strategy and debate trade-off scenarios.

The Result: Time passes. Customers keep leaving.

Path 2: Act and Adapt

- Approve a **pilot project** to test new pricing models on a small customer segment. Measure real-time reactions, and establish a feedback loop to make swift adjustments.
- Develop a **comprehensive communication plan** outlining the challenge, hypothesis, desired outcomes, contingencies, and the project's impact on ongoing work.

- Broadcast the decision across all internal channels with a **full write-up, short video,** and **TL;DR** for quick access.

The Result: Decisions are made. Action is taken. Learning happens now, not later.

Your Turn: If this were your organization, would you wait, debate, and risk losing more customers with Path 1—or act decisively, learn quickly, and adapt in real time with Path 2?

Our Take: In fast-moving markets, indecision is a decision. Action creates momentum. Waiting creates losses.

KEY TAKEAWAYS AND DISCUSSION QUESTIONS
1. DECISIVENESS DRIVES SUCCESS

Decisiveness isn't optional—it's a competitive necessity. Organizations that act quickly and confidently seize opportunities, build momentum, and thrive. Indecision, on the other hand, comes at a cost: missed opportunities, stalled innovation, and weakened trust.

Discussion Questions:

- How do we measure the impact of indecision on our organization's performance (e.g., missed opportunities, delays, or inefficiencies)?
- Can we identify moments in our organization's history when indecision cost us progress? What did we learn?
- What cultural or structural barriers slow down decision-making in our organization? How can we dismantle them?
- Do our current processes encourage or inhibit decisiveness? What changes could help streamline decisions without sacrificing decision quality?
- How can we reward and reinforce decisive leadership while balancing thoughtful action and speed?

2. THE FIVE BARRIERS TO DECISIVENESS

Organizations face common obstacles that undermine decisive action: chaos, complacency, bias, consensus traps, and excessive bureaucracy. These barriers don't exist in isolation—they compound one another, creating friction and delays.

Discussion Questions:

- Where do we see symptoms of chaos (volatility, uncertainty, complexity, ambiguity) in our operations? How do we manage them today?
- Are we too comfortable with the status quo? How can we foster a culture that challenges norms and embraces change?
- How aware are we of cognitive biases (like groupthink, anchoring, or confirmation bias) in our decision-making? What steps can we take to reduce their impact?
- How do we balance inclusivity with decisive action? Are there times when building consensus slows us down unnecessarily?
- Is bureaucracy stalling our progress? What specific processes can we simplify or eliminate to accelerate decision-making?

3. LEADING THROUGH UNCERTAINTY

Uncertainty is the new normal, driven by rapid technological disruption, shifting markets, and global volatility. Organizations that thrive embrace agility, foster resilience, and act decisively—even without perfect information.

Discussion Questions:

- How prepared are we to anticipate and adapt to disruptions like AI, digital transformation, or changing workforce patterns?
- What actions can we take to enhance our agility and respond faster to market shifts and customer needs?
- Are we effectively leveraging data and advanced analytics to guide decisions? Where can we improve?

- How can we build a culture of experimentation that allows teams to take calculated risks and learn from failure?
- What role should leadership play in guiding teams through uncertainty? How can leaders inspire confidence and provide clarity when the path forward isn't clear?

4. ACTION OVER PERFECTION

Waiting for perfect information is a losing move. Fast, informed decisions drive progress. Imperfect action beats perfect hesitation.

Discussion Questions:

- Do we encourage decision-making based on *enough* information, or do we delay while chasing perfection?
- How can we empower leaders and teams to make timely decisions with confidence?
- Where in our organization are we hesitating when we should be acting? What's holding us back?

KNOWLEDGE MAP
THE COST OF INDECISION

- **Missed Opportunities:** Innovations are delayed, and competitors pull ahead.
- **Reduced Efficiency:** Bottlenecks form, time is wasted, and costs rise.
- **Lower Morale:** Teams lose patience and motivation.
- **Erosion of Trust:** Leaders lose credibility, and alignment weakens.
- **Impaired Strategy and Growth:** Progress stalls, and resources go unused.
- **Poor Last-Minute Decisions:** Delays force rushed, flawed choices.
- **Damage to Reputation:** Brands lose relevance and market trust.

KEY DRIVERS OF GROWING UNCERTAINTY

- **Technological Disruption:** Rapid advancements in AI, cloud computing, and software.
- **Workforce Shifts:** Hybrid work, gig economies, and changing employee priorities.
- **Hyperconnectivity:** Global ripple effects from local events and decisions.
- **Regulatory Disruption:** Evolving rules create moving compliance targets.
- **Expectation Escalation:** Customers demand faster, better solutions.
- **Data Explosion:** Too much information clouds clarity and complicates decisions.

TRANSFORMATION AS A CATALYST FOR DECISIVENESS

- **Digital Transformation:** Reimagining operations to stay competitive.
- **Hybrid Work:** Navigating productivity and collaboration in a distributed model.
- **Business Agility:** Responding quickly to market shifts and customer needs.
- **AI Integration:** Enhancing decisions, efficiency, and strategic insights.

FIVE SYMPTOMS OF INDECISION

1. **Chaos:** Complexity and uncertainty overwhelm clarity and action.
2. **The Status Quo:** Leaders cling to what worked yesterday instead of embracing change.
3. **Hidden Biases:** Hidden biases like groupthink and anchoring distort judgment.

4. **The Consensus Trap:** Endless alignment efforts delay bold decisions.

5. **Excessive Bureaucracy:** Red tape slows progress and stifles innovation.

STRATEGIES FOR DECISIVE ACTION

- Move fast and embrace imperfection: Focus on moving forward when you have good signal but not perfect data.
- Recognize and mitigate biases: Challenge assumptions to improve decision quality.
- Balance input and action: Consensus matters, but progress must win.
- Simplify systems: Streamline processes and approvals to prioritize speed.
- Plan for uncertainty: Equip teams to adapt, learn, and act decisively in changing environments.

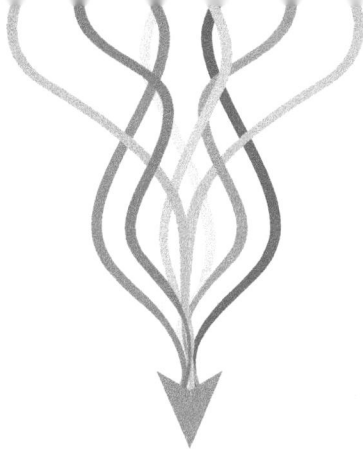

CHAPTER 2

HOW ALIGNED IS YOUR ORGANIZATION?

"Efficiency is concerned with doing things right. Effectiveness is doing the right things."

—PETER DRUCKER

Picture a rowing team in perfect sync—each stroke driving them forward with effortless speed. That's alignment. Now, imagine all the oars on a boat pulling in different directions. The boat wobbles. Progress halts. Frustration rises. One method fuels momentum, the other chaos.

Alignment is more than a concept—it's **a competitive advantage**. When strategy, goals, and purpose converge, organizations move with confidence. Decisions become easier. Actions are faster. People know where they're going and why it matters.

Aligned organizations don't waste time. They don't stall in endless deliberations. They execute. With unity of purpose, teams operate in harmony. Ideas connect. Actions align. The result? Higher engagement, stronger trust, and measurable performance.

One study found that when employees understand and believe in their company's direction, the odds of outperforming competitors' margins double.[21] **Double.** Alignment, then, isn't just about clarity. It's about results.

But alignment does more than enhance performance. It supercharges **decisiveness.**

DECISIVE ACTION STARTS WITH ALIGNMENT

Alignment drives decision-making at every level. When teams understand the company's goals, they act without bottlenecks or second-guessing. Leaders trust their teams. Teams trust their instincts. The result? **Faster, more confident decisions.**

Aligned organizations empower purposeful experimentation. Innovation thrives when every experiment ties back to overarching objectives. Learning accelerates. Progress becomes meaningful and measurable. Without alignment, experimentation turns into **chaos—effort is scattershot, with no clear impact.**

Consider ING Bank's 2015 transformation. They restructured into small, self-managing teams called "squads" grouped into "tribes." Each squad focuses on specific customer needs, enabling faster decisions and accelerated product development. The result? **Greater agility and customer satisfaction**—direct outcomes of aligning team autonomy with corporate strategy.[22]

---

21 Aaron De Smet et al., "The Hidden Value of Organizational Health—and How to Capture It," *McKinsey Quarterly*, April 1, 2014, https://www.mckinsey.com/capabilities/people-and-organizational-performance/our-insights/the-hidden-value-of-organizational-health-and-how-to-capture-it.

22 "Squads, Sprints, and Stand-Ups," ING, November 23, 2017, https://www.ing.com/Newsroom/News/Squads-sprints-and-stand-ups.htm.

MISALIGNMENT: THE ENEMY OF PROGRESS

Misalignment is a silent killer. It breeds confusion and conflict. Teams pull in different directions. Energy is wasted. Loyalty dwindles. Turf wars erupt. Progress stalls.

The symptoms of misalignment are clear:

- **Confusion:** No one knows what their priorities are.
- **Weak Execution:** Decisions falter, and initiatives lose momentum.
- **Rising Turnover:** Frustration drives top performers out the door.
- **Resistance and Mistrust:** Teams lose confidence in leadership's direction.

Aligned organizations thrive on clarity. They cut through complexity, simplify decisions, and turn chaos into cohesion. Leaders communicate a unified vision. Teams focus their energy. Execution accelerates.

The difference is stark: **Clarity fuels action. Misalignment stalls progress.**

ALIGNMENT IS A CHOICE—AND A DISCIPLINE

Alignment doesn't happen by accident. In large organizations, where complexity reigns, achieving alignment requires effort and intention. It's not a one-time initiative—it's an ongoing process that demands consistent focus and discipline.

Alignment starts at the top. **Leaders must set the tone.** They must model clarity, accountability, and communication, ensuring every level of the organization reflects these values.

The payoff is clear:

- **Decisions align with vision and strategy.** Outcomes improve, and teams execute with confidence.
- **Waste declines.** Resources are focused where they matter most.

- **Teams move faster and act smarter.** Alignment creates momentum, even in uncertain or high-stakes situations.

When you boil it all down, one thing stands out: alignment. It separates the decisive from the divided, the agile from the adrift, and the leaders from the laggards.

The question isn't whether alignment matters—it's whether your organization has it.

So ask yourself: **How aligned is your organization?** And more importantly, **what will you do about it?**

EVEN GIANTS STUMBLE

Even the most powerful organizations can fail when alignment breaks down. **When vision, leadership, and operations don't move in sync, the results are predictable:** wasted resources, shattered trust, and reputational damage.

Take Apple.

Apple invested **$10 billion** and a decade into its autonomous-vehicle project. The vision was bold, but **misalignment killed it.** Conflicting priorities, shifting strategies, and endless restarts created chaos. The cost? **Billions wasted. Hundreds of jobs lost. A decade of effort gone.**[23]

Or Boeing.

Boeing's rush to beat Airbus came at a devastating price. Safety was sacrificed for speed, leading to **two fatal crashes and 346 lives lost.** The aftermath? **Billions in lawsuits,** shattered trust, and a brand once synonymous with safety reduced to crisis.[24] **Misalign-**

---

23 Brian X. Chen and Tripp Mickle, "Behind Apple's Doomed Car Project: False Starts and Wrong Turns," *New York Times,* February 28, 2024, https://www.nytimes.com/2024/02/28/technology/behind-the-apple-car-dead.html.

24 Bill George, "Why Boeing's Problems with the 737 MAX Began More Than 25 Years Ago," Harvard Business School Working Knowledge, January 24, 2024, https://hbswk.hbs.edu/item/why-boeings-problems-with-737-max-began-more-than-25-years-ago.

ment between ambition and values turned competition into catastrophe.

Or Facebook.

Facebook's reliance on user data fueled growth—at the cost of ignoring mounting calls for privacy. The **Cambridge Analytica scandal** eroded trust, triggered global backlash, and cost Facebook **billions in fines and lawsuits.** The toll? **A damaged reputation,** loss of user confidence, and years of recovery.[25] **Misalignment between business strategy and user expectations proved a costly mistake.**

WHEN ALIGNMENT WORKS

In contrast, consider Microsoft's remarkable pivot to cloud computing under **Satya Nadella's leadership.** Faced with declining relevance, Microsoft realigned its strategy, culture, and execution:

- **Clear Strategy:** Nadella defined a unifying vision: "To empower every person and every organization on the planet to achieve more."[26] Microsoft's Azure product became central to every roadmap.
- **Cultural Alignment:** Internal silos were dismantled, encouraging collaboration over competition.
- **Execution Aligned to Strategy:** Teams were empowered, progress was measured, and funding was provided for cloud projects, as long as they aligned with the company's goals.

The result? Microsoft's cloud business grew exponentially, reaching **$102 billion in annual revenue in 2024,** and the com-

---

25 Iga Kozlowska, "Facebook and Data Privacy in the Age of Cambridge Analytica," Henry M. Jackson School of International Studies, University of Washington, April 30, 2018, https://jsis.washington.edu/news/facebook-data-privacy-age-cambridge-analytica/.

26 Todd Bishop, "Exclusive: Satya Nadella Reveals Microsoft's New Mission Statement, Sees 'Tough Choices' Ahead," GeekWire, June 25, 2015, https://www.geekwire.com/2015/exclusive-satya-nadella-reveals-microsofts-new-mission-statement-sees-more-tough-choices-ahead/.

pany's market cap soared.[27] Azure now leads the cloud computing market alongside Amazon Web Services (AWS) and Google Cloud.[28]

The Lesson: When alignment is achieved, organizations don't just adapt—they lead. And when it breaks, even giants stumble.

BUILDING THE BRIDGE FROM STRATEGY TO EXECUTION

Alignment doesn't happen through intention alone. **Strategy-to-execution mapping** is the bridge that transforms lofty goals into **tangible results.** It connects vision to action—**step by step, task by task**—ensuring alignment drives measurable outcomes.

The process flows like this:

1. **Strategy Formulation:** Define the vision. Set clear, high-level goals.
2. **Communication:** Make everyone aware of why the goals were set.
3. **Goal Cascading:** Break goals into measurable, actionable targets.
4. **Initiative Identification:** Pinpoint projects or programs that will achieve those targets.
5. **Resource Allocation:** Assign the people, teams, time, and budget needed to execute the targets.
6. **Iterative Planning:** Outline steps, milestones, and priorities. Identify what outcomes would cause the team to reevaluate the plan.
7. **Execution:** Take action, work in small bursts, and measure results.

---

27 Mark Haranas, "AWS vs. Microsoft vs. Google Cloud Earnings Q4 2024 Face-Off," *CRN*, February 10, 2025, 2, https://www.crn.com/news/cloud/2025/aws-vs-microsoft-vs-google-cloud-earnings-q4-2024-face-off?page=2.

28 Haranas, "AWS vs. Microsoft vs. Google," 4, https://www.crn.com/news/cloud/2025/aws-vs-microsoft-vs-google-cloud-earnings-q4-2024-face-off?page=4.

8. **Monitoring:** Track progress, measure performance, and identify adjustments.
9. **Continuous Improvement:** Learn, refine, and optimize as the organization evolves.

When done right, this process **bridges the gap between strategy and reality:**

- **Teams Stay Aligned:** Every project connects back to the organization's overarching goals.
- **Focus Sharpens:** Energy and resources are prioritized to where they will have the most impact.
- **The Organization Adapts:** Teams have the flexibility to adapt their work as new information becomes available.
- **Performance Accelerates:** Progress is tracked, measured, and adjusted continuously. Feedback loops are established.

Without this bridge, strategy remains **abstract and disconnected**—a vision with no clear path forward. In that vacuum, individual agendas fill the void.

A Visual Framework for Enterprise Alignment

It is important to have a visual framework for how your organization will stay aligned. For example, Jonathan Trevor and Barry Varco illustrate enterprise alignment as a tightly managed chain. Their framework may be a good starting point to consider.[29]

---

29 Jonathan Trevor and Barry Varcoe, "How Aligned Is Your Organization?," *Harvard Business Review*, February 7, 2017, https://hbr.org/2017/02/how-aligned-is-your-organization.

STRATEGICALLY-ALIGNED ENTERPRISE

The value chain is only as strong as its weakest link

ENTERPRISE PURPOSE	→	BUSINESS STRATEGY	←→	ORGANIZATIONAL CAPABILITY	←→	RESOURCE ARCHITECTURE	←→	MANAGEMENT SYSTEMS

How well does our business strategy fulfill our enterprise's purpose?	How well does our org capability support delivery of our business strategy?	How well do our resources enable development of our required org capability?	How well do our management systems drive the performance of our valuable resources?

Source: Jonathan Trevor and Barry Varcoe, "How Aligned Is Your Organization?," *Harvard Business Review*, February 7, 2017, https://hbr.org/2017/02/how-aligned-is-your-organization.

The flow is **Purpose → Strategy → Capability → Resources → Performance.**

- **Purpose:** What we do and why we do it.
- **Strategy:** The choices we make to win and fulfill our purpose.
- **Capability:** What we must excel at to deliver on our strategy.
- **Resources:** The people, tools, and systems that enable our capabilities.
- **Performance:** The measurable outcomes that confirm success delivered via management systems.

When this chain holds strong, **alignment flows seamlessly** from vision to execution. Every link reinforces the next, ensuring actions are connected, cohesive, and outcome-driven.

WHAT BLOCKS ALIGNMENT?

Integrating strategy with execution across a diverse workforce is complex and full of friction. **The maze of moving parts, competing priorities, and conflicting opinions** creates formidable challenges. Here are the six biggest obstacles that **undermine alignment** and decision-making:

1. **Missing Context:** Decisions lack clarity. Leaders guess. Teams stumble. Progress halts.
2. **Data Overload:** Noise overwhelms insight. Leaders drown in detail. Focus disappears.
3. **The Growth Conundrum:** Balancing today's needs with tomorrow's goals creates tension. Misalignment follows.
4. **Conflicting Interests and Politics:** Agendas collide. Power struggles pull teams apart. Alignment shatters.
5. **Dependencies:** Teams slow down when one link breaks. Progress ripples backward instead of forward.
6. **Losing Sight of the Why:** Purpose fades. Decisions lose meaning. Motivation and focus collapse.

These obstacles **compound each other**, turning small misalignments into major roadblocks. To overcome them, organizations must understand the **root causes** and take deliberate action to fix them.

Let's break down the six obstacles to see where the cracks form and how they can be repaired.

OBSTACLE 1: MISSING CONTEXT

"In theory, theory and practice are the same. In practice, they are not. Ask any cat herder."

—ANONYMOUS

Context is the invisible thread that connects decisions to reality. It provides the background, circumstances, and influences that shape outcomes. **Without it, decisions lose their footing**—leaders miss critical details, teams misunderstand priorities, and progress stalls.

To bridge these gaps, many organizations rely on "human glue"—individuals who manually connect the dots. Human glue spends time:

- Mapping relationships between strategic goals, decisions, and dependencies.
- Creating custom reports to fill context gaps.
- Piecing together unstructured documents to capture the bigger picture.

The problem? Human glue is not sustainable. It's slow, repetitive, and prone to errors. **These individuals often spend their time fighting friction** instead of focusing on high-value work.

People performing this role often wish for better tools—tools that connect more data points, automate repetitive tasks, and free them to focus on strategic contributions. Instead, they're stuck fighting friction.

The Challenge of Connecting the Dots Across Silos

Connecting data across silos is daunting. It's slow. It's error prone. Leaders crave a clear, comprehensive view—one that highlights customer priorities and aligns decision-making. But that view is elusive. Instead, they get a patchwork: improvised, inconsistent, and outdated.

What happens next?

- **Missed Opportunities:** Insights arrive too late to act.
- **Lost Knowledge:** Data presentations are one-offs, with no impact on future analyses.
- **Lack of Trust:** Leaders doubt the data. Teams question its value.
- **Broken Memory:** Without organizational memory, trends disappear. Insights evaporate.

The result? Decisions falter. Alignment suffers. Progress slows.

So, how can organizations modernize their approach to reduce their reliance on human glue for planning and execution?

Here's the good news: there's a massive opportunity to transform how strategic data is managed. By reducing manual effort and automating connections across their digital infrastructure, companies can:

- Provide faster, more precise data for decision-making.
- Reduce errors caused by human intervention.
- Build trust in the insights that drive strategy.
- Free teams to focus on strategic, high-value work.

The need is clear: replace manual patchwork with connected systems—and turn friction into flow. Context is the foundation for clarity and progress in today's complex world. It's essential. And organizations that get it right will move faster, decide smarter, and align better than those that don't.

OBSTACLE 2: DATA OVERLOAD

"A wealth of information creates a poverty of attention."

—Herbert Simon

In today's digital age, **data pours in from every direction.** Yet, the more data we collect, the harder it becomes to focus on what matters. **Noise overwhelms insight.** Leaders drown in detail. Teams lose direction. Progress stalls.

Does this sound familiar: Teams search for insights where it's easiest to look rather than where the answers actually lie?

- **Convenient data** gets prioritized over **useful data.**
- Leaders act on incomplete or irrelevant information, creating false confidence.

That is known as the **"Streetlight Effect."**

The result? Teams spend energy solving the wrong problems while opportunities slip away. Even with AI, the challenge remains: Without clear priorities, insights get lost in the noise.

This challenge is amplified by information overload, and the data flood comes at a measurable cost:[30]

- **Seventy-six percent of US workers** say information overload increases daily stress.
- **Thirty-five percent report** it negatively impacts their work performance.
- **Forty-one percent waste at least one hour a day** searching for information they need.

Even worse, **data silos** turn the flood into disconnected haystacks:[31]

- Insights remain fragmented and incomplete.
- Leaders miss the bigger picture.
- Decisions become reactive, not strategic.

AI offers a solution by sifting through vast amounts of data to uncover patterns and insights. But **AI isn't magic:**[32]

- **Garbage In, Garbage Out:** If inputs are noisy or unstructured, outputs will lack clarity.
- **Siloed systems** limit AI's effectiveness, preventing it from connecting dots across teams.

To turn data into actionable insights, leaders must:

---

30 Jaime Hampton, "Report: 80% of Global Workers Experience Information Overload," BigDATAwire, August 18, 2022, https://www.datanami.com/2022/08/18/report-80-of-global-workers-experience-information-overload/.

31 Scott Robinson et al., "What Are Data Silos and What Problems Do They Cause?," TechTarget, last modified July 2024, https://www.techtarget.com/searchdatamanagement/definition/data-silo.

32 Muhi S. Majzoub, "Data Dilemmas: Say Goodbye to Silos and Hello to Unrivaled AI Insights," *Forbes*, March 26, 2024, https://www.forbes.com/councils/forbestechcouncil/2024/03/26/data-dilemmas-say-goodbye-to-silos-and-hello-to-unrivaled-ai-insights/.

- **Reduce Noise:** Focus on high-value data that drives decisions.
- **Break Down Silos:** Connect systems so data flows seamlessly across the organization.
- **Clarify the Signal:** Build tools that transform raw data into clear, prioritized insights.

Collecting more data doesn't give you the competitive edge; clarity does. Organizations that master clarity can:

- **Quickly uncover critical insights** to drive smarter decisions.
- **Prioritize actions** that truly drive outcomes.
- **Align teams** by ensuring everyone works from the same source of information.

The takeaway? Data isn't the problem. The problem is focus. Organizations that overcome data overload will **see further, act faster,** and **lead smarter.**

OBSTACLE 3: THE GROWTH CONUNDRUM

"We can't be in survival mode. We have to be in growth mode."
—Jeff Bezos

How do you balance **today's needs** with **tomorrow's opportunities?** This is one of the toughest challenges leaders face. Get it wrong, and you risk one of two outcomes:

- **Stagnation:** Clinging too tightly to current operations while innovation stalls.
- **Overextension:** Chasing growth without a solid foundation, weakening the core business.

This balancing act—between **running the business** and **changing the business**—is the growth conundrum.

One tool to combat the growth conundrum is the Three Horizons Framework. This approach provides a simple way to think about balancing short- and long-term priorities:[33]

1. **Horizon 1: Optimize Today**
   A. Focus on maximizing **existing operations** and revenue streams.
   B. **The Risk:** Overprioritizing the present can stifle future innovation and leave companies vulnerable to disruption.
2. **Horizon 2: Explore Tomorrow**
   A. Invest in **emerging opportunities** with clear growth potential.
   B. **The Challenge:** Medium-term initiatives often compete with Horizon 1 priorities for resources and attention, creating internal friction.
3. **Horizon 3: Shape the Future**
   A. Pursue **transformative innovations** that can redefine the organization's future.
   B. **The Reality:** Long-term bets struggle for attention amid the demands of day-to-day operations. Without leadership support, they risk being deprioritized.

Balancing these horizons requires discipline and alignment. Three ways to improve your results using the Three Horizons Framework are:

1. **Strategic Clarity:** Leaders must set clear priorities that balance immediate performance with long-term growth.
2. **Resource Allocation:** Align people, budgets, and time deliberately across all three horizons.

---

33 Steve Blank, "McKinsey's Three Horizons Model Defined Innovation for Years: Here's Why It No Longer Applies," *Harvard Business Review*, February 1, 2019, https://hbr.org/2019/02/mckinseys-three-horizons-model-defined-innovation-for-years-heres-why-it-no-longer-applies.

3. **Cultural Balance:** Build a culture that values **operational excellence** in Horizon 1 while fostering the experimentation needed to drive Horizons 2 and 3. Also consider that Horizon 3 may not require years to develop as it often did in the past.

Be Sure to Adapt as You Go

Today's pace of change is relentless. The framework isn't static. Some opportunities will **accelerate faster** than expected, while others will need more time. Horizon 3, in particular, demands proactive leadership to protect and champion bold ideas.

The goal is clear: **optimize for today, explore tomorrow, and innovate for the future.** Companies that strike this balance don't just survive change—they shape it.

OBSTACLE 4: CONFLICTING INTERESTS AND POLITICS

"In preparing for battle I have always found that plans are useless, but planning is indispensable."

—DWIGHT D. EISENHOWER

In large organizations, decision-making often feels like navigating a battlefield. **Stakeholders clash,** agendas compete, and **priorities diverge.** Instead of alignment, you get friction:

- **Power Struggles:** Teams protect their turf, slowing collaboration.
- **Competing Goals:** Sales prioritizes revenue. Operations focuses on efficiency. Innovation teams push risk and experimentation.
- **Resource Conflicts:** Limited budgets and talent intensify the fight for resources, pulling focus away from collective success.

The result? **Slow decisions, fragmented efforts,** and a culture of frustration.

Politics has a significant impact on your ability to execute. Politics doesn't just create tension—it cripples progress. When competing interests go unchecked:

- **Misaligned Incentives:** Teams optimize for their own success, not the company's.
- **Lack of Accountability:** Blurred roles and responsibilities delay decisions.
- **Hesitation:** Teams second-guess choices instead of acting with confidence.

So how can your organization turn conflict into collaboration? Addressing politics requires more than good intentions—it demands systemic solutions that foster alignment. A good start includes:

1. **Shared Goals:** Anchor decision-making to the organization's **top-level priorities.** Leaders must reinforce what success looks like **company-wide,** not just locally.
2. **Balanced Incentives:** Design incentives that align individual and departmental goals with the organization's vision. Reward collaboration, not siloed wins.
3. **Transparency:** Increase **visibility** across teams and priorities. Break down silos so stakeholders see how their work connects to the bigger picture.
4. **Clear Accountability:** Define roles and ownership explicitly. Clarity eliminates confusion and ensures **progress moves forward.**
5. **Empowered Decision-Making:** Build a culture of trust where employees are empowered to make decisions **within their scope.** Provide the context and tools they need to act confidently.

Leadership Must Set the Tone

Leaders need to play a pivotal role in fostering collaboration over competition. When they model transparency, alignment, and trust, it sends a clear message that **politics won't stand in the way of progress.**

The goal? Replace friction with focus. Organizations that **tackle politics head-on** don't just make decisions—they make them faster, smarter, and together.

OBSTACLE 5: DEPENDENCIES

"Improving daily work is even more important than doing daily work."
—GENE KIM

Dependencies are the silent killer of agility. Teams, systems, and processes are more interconnected than ever. While small, empowered teams accelerate decisions, **the web of interdependencies** they create can slow execution to a crawl.

Dependencies undermine the very attributes organizations need to be successful: **speed and flexibility.** Here's how:

- **Delayed Decisions:** Teams can't move forward until they secure inputs, approvals, or resources from others.
- **Blockages Ripple Out:** A delay in one area triggers setbacks across projects, stalling momentum.
- **Rigid Processes:** As complexity grows, pivoting in response to change becomes harder.

Dependencies aren't inherently bad—they're a natural byproduct of growth and specialization. The problem arises when they're **unmanaged** or invisible.

- **Team-to-Team Reliance:** One team's progress depends on another's deliverables. If timelines misalign, the entire project suffers.
- **Systemic Interdependencies:** Technology stacks are deeply intertwined. A change in one system often requires coordinated updates across others.
- **Prioritization Conflicts:** Teams have competing priorities, leading to misaligned schedules and missed deadlines.

In large organizations, these interconnections become a **complex web**, where even small disruptions have cascading effects. The results? **Missed deadlines, frustrated teams,** and **stalled innovation.**

So How Do You Master Dependencies?

Dependencies will never disappear, but they **can be managed.** High-performing organizations take these steps:

1. **Map and Visualize Dependencies:** Identify dependencies early across teams, projects, and systems. Tools like **dependency mapping** and visual workflows reveal critical connections, allowing teams to plan accordingly.
2. **Prioritize Decoupling:** Reduce unnecessary interdependencies. Simplify processes and build systems that allow teams to move independently wherever possible. Find recurring dependency patterns. Then, optimize team ontologies to decouple them.
3. **Align Timelines and Goals:** Use shared planning tools to synchronize schedules, priorities, and outcomes across teams. Regular cross-functional reviews keep everyone on the same page.
4. **Focus on Resilience:** Design processes and systems to **minimize disruption** when a dependency fails. Build buffers,

create fallback plans, and identify bottlenecks before they break momentum.

5. **Adopt Modular Architectures:** For technology stacks, modular systems reduce reliance on monolithic structures. Teams can update components independently, improving speed and flexibility.

The Goal Is to Reduce Friction and Improve Flow

Dependencies are inevitable, but they don't have to be **obstacles.** The key is making them **visible, manageable, and resilient.** When organizations take a proactive approach to dependencies:

- Teams move with confidence, not hesitation.
- Delays are reduced, and blocks are minimized.
- Execution accelerates, even in complex environments.

In a fast-changing world, organizations that master dependencies gain the ultimate advantage: **momentum.**

OBSTACLE 6: LOSING SIGHT OF THE WHY

"People don't buy what you do; they buy why you do it."
—SIMON SINEK

In every organization, decisions are made at every level—some big, some small. But when teams don't understand **why** decisions are made, purpose fades and alignment breaks down. The result? Confusion, wasted effort, and a decline in trust.

How often do those executing a decision or goal truly understand why it was made or set?

In large organizations, the "why"—**the intent behind a decision**—can vanish as the decision travels through layers of hierarchy and spans of control. Why?

1. **Too Many Layers:** Messages distort as they move through leadership levels, like a game of telephone.
2. **Competing Goals:** Teams prioritize their local objectives over organizational strategy.
3. **Lack of Communication:** Decisions are shared without context, leaving teams in the dark about intent.

The result? Teams lose sight of what matters most. They execute tasks but miss the bigger picture. Leaders are left wondering why progress feels disjointed.

When teams understand the "why" behind decisions, they:

1. **Focus on the Right Work:** Effort aligns with outcomes that move the organization forward.
2. **Make Confident, Decisive Choices:** Teams can act without waiting for top-down direction.
3. **Feel Motivated and Committed:** Purpose fosters engagement and accountability.

In contrast, when intent is missing, decisions feel arbitrary, risk-taking stalls, and teams disengage. Progress turns into **motion without meaning.**

So you may be wondering how you can reconnect your teams to the why.

Organizations that keep the "why" front and center create alignment at every level. Here's how:

1. **Communicate the Why Consistently:** Leaders must articulate the **intent and purpose** behind decisions—not just the what or how. Repetition matters: Reinforce the message in meetings, strategy sessions, and company updates.
2. **Build Feedback Loops:** Create two-way communication channels to ensure teams understand the "why" and can raise questions. Clarity comes from conversation, not assumption.

3. **Cascade the Why Across Teams:** Link every team's objectives to organizational priorities. Tools like **strategy maps** and **goal-alignment frameworks** make it clear how daily work connects to the bigger picture.

4. **Simplify Layers of Decision-Making:** Reduce unnecessary spans and layers where the "why" can get lost. Empower managers to translate strategic intent effectively to their teams.

5. **Celebrate Decisions Tied to Purpose:** Recognize and reward teams that demonstrate alignment with the organization's goals. Reinforce the connection between actions and outcomes.

Aligning the Why Accelerates Progress

The "why" isn't a nice-to-have—it's a **strategic necessity.** When teams understand the purpose behind decisions, they move with clarity, confidence, and speed.

- Decisions make sense.
- Effort feels meaningful.
- Teams rally behind a shared purpose.

In today's fast-moving world, organizations that communicate and reinforce the "why" don't just align—they inspire. **They turn strategy into action and purpose into performance.**

HOW ALIGNED IS YOUR ORGANIZATION, REALLY?

Alignment isn't a **one-time achievement**—it's a continuous process. As new priorities emerge, markets shift, and teams grow, alignment can fray. The six obstacles we explored don't occur in isolation. They compound, creating friction that slows progress.

To evaluate alignment, leaders must look critically at how strategy flows through their organization. Here are six sets of key questions to help you assess your alignment—and spot gaps:

1. **Missing Content**
   A. How well does your organization connect strategy to execution?
   B. Are your teams clear on the organization's overarching vision—and how their work contributes to it?
   C. **Warning Signs:** Manual processes, fragmented plans, and teams working in silos.

2. **Data Overload**
   A. How effectively do you streamline data into actionable insights?
   B. Can leaders separate **signal from noise** to make confident decisions?
   C. **Warning Signs:** Teams drowning in reports, insights arriving too late, and analysis paralysis.

3. **The Growth Conundrum**
   A. How well do you balance today's performance with tomorrow's opportunities?
   B. Are short-term pressures stifling long-term priorities?
   C. **Warning Signs:** Stagnant innovation, resource conflicts, and reactive decision-making.

4. **Conflicting Interests and Politics**
   A. How well does your organization resolve competing agendas and align diverse objectives?
   B. Do leaders encourage collaboration, or does politics derail progress?
   C. **Warning Signs:** Power struggles, slow decisions, and teams working against each other.

5. **Dependencies**
   A. How effectively do you identify and manage interdependencies?
   B. Are teams empowered to move independently where possible?
   C. **Warning Signs:** Bottlenecks, delays rippling across projects, and overly complex workflows.

6. Losing Sight of the Why
   A. How consistently does your organization communicate **the intent** behind decisions?
   B. Do teams understand why their work matters—and how it aligns with the big picture?
   C. **Warning Signs:** Teams questioning priorities, misaligned efforts, and disengagement.

FIXING ALIGNMENT GAPS

Alignment gaps don't fix themselves—they require deliberate action. To close gaps, start with these steps:

1. **Audit Your Strategy-to-Execution Flow:** Map how decisions move through your organization. Where does strategy stall? Where do silos emerge?
2. **Identify the Biggest Pain Points:** Use the six sets of questions to pinpoint your most pressing alignment challenges. Prioritize fixing the areas that cause the most friction.
3. **Engage Your Teams:** Alignment isn't a top-down exercise. Collect feedback from teams at every level to identify blind spots and foster ownership.
4. **Measure and Adjust Continuously:** Alignment is dynamic. Use performance indicators, regular reviews, and feedback loops to ensure strategy, execution, and purpose remain connected.

ALIGNMENT IS A COMPETITIVE ADVANTAGE

In a world of rapid change, alignment is what separates organizations that lead from those that lag. The companies that thrive are the ones that:

- **Stay ruthlessly focused** on their vision and priorities.
- **Adapt with speed** as markets shift.

- **Empower their teams** with the clarity and context they need to act decisively.

Alignment isn't static—it's a discipline. Organizations that embrace it don't just survive change—they shape the future.

SUMMARY

Alignment isn't a buzzword—it's the backbone of high-performing organizations. Aligned teams move with purpose. They act with clarity. They build trust and drive results. But misalignment? It breeds chaos. Decisions stall. Priorities blur. Progress slows.

This chapter uncovered the six obstacles that stand in the way of seamless flow from strategy to execution:

- **Missing Context:** Decisions falter when teams lack the right information.
- **Data Overload:** Too much noise. Too little insight. Information drowns out direction, leaving teams stressed and scattered.
- **The Growth Conundrum:** Balancing today's needs with tomorrow's opportunities creates tension. Focus too much on one, and the other falters.
- **Conflicting Interests and Politics:** Power struggles, competing agendas, and misaligned incentives pull organizations apart.
- **Dependencies:** Teams and systems are tangled. One delay ripples through the organization, stalling momentum.
- **Losing Sight of the Why:** When teams don't understand the intent behind decisions, effort feels wasted, and motivation fades.

Alignment doesn't happen by accident. It's a choice. It's a discipline. Overcome these obstacles, and your organization won't just move faster—it will lead. Because aligned organizations don't hesitate. They don't waste time. They execute. And they thrive.

DECISION POINTS

Consider This Scenario: A leading organization stands at a critical crossroads. It's ready to grow its market presence with a bold new product line. The strategy from the top is clear—but somewhere along the way, the message gets lost. Teams don't know where they are headed or why it matters. Alignment breaks down. Progress stalls.

To make things worse, the data meant to guide the expansion is muddy. Noise drowns out insight. Confusion creeps in. Endless meetings become the norm—talking replaces doing. Frustration builds. And now the organization faces a choice.

WHICH PATH WOULD YOUR ORGANIZATION CHOOSE?
Path 1: Wait and Hope

- Keep scheduling meetings, hoping consensus will eventually emerge.
- Collect more data from multiple sources to chase a clearer direction.
- Delay decisions until all stakeholders are fully aligned.

The Result: Weeks drag on. Progress remains stuck. Frustration deepens.

Path 2: Decide and Move

- Present clear *why* statements to justify the expansion—or to pause it altogether.
- Identify key data insights needed for clarity, and task teams with resolving conflicting inputs.
- Set a firm deadline: Make the call—up or down—based on the information available today.

The Result: Decisions are made. Teams align. Momentum replaces stagnation.

Your Turn: If this were your organization, would you wait and hope with Path 1—or decide and move with Path 2?

Our Take: Alignment doesn't wait for perfection. It demands action.

KEY TAKEAWAYS AND DISCUSSION QUESTIONS
1. ALIGNMENT DRIVES ORGANIZATIONAL EFFECTIVENESS

Highly aligned organizations achieve clarity of purpose, customer focus, and resilience. Alignment unites teams, drives engagement, and turns strategy into execution.

Discussion Questions:

- How do we measure alignment across teams and departments today? What metrics tell us when alignment is strong—or breaking down?
- Are our enterprise values consistently reflected in daily decisions and actions? Where are the gaps, and how can we close them?
- Where do we currently see misalignment in our organization, and what impact does it have on progress toward our goals?
- How can we design structures, processes, and workflows to promote alignment, collaboration, and a shared vision across all levels?
- What steps can we take to continuously improve alignment in a fast-moving, evolving industry?

2. DECISIVE ALIGNMENT REQUIRES COORDINATED CHOICES

Alignment doesn't happen by accident. It's the discipline of ensuring that every decision—at every level—flows from the organization's strategy, vision, and values.

Discussion Questions:

- How do we ensure decisions made across the organization align with our overarching goals and strategic priorities?
- What systems or processes help us identify misalignment early so we can course correct before it impacts results?
- How can we empower employees to make aligned, confident decisions without relying on top-down approvals?
- What role does leadership play in driving alignment? How can leaders communicate the importance of alignment clearly and consistently?
- How can we leverage technology, tools, and data analytics to support better decision-making and alignment throughout the organization?

3. MISALIGNMENT COMES AT A COST

The failures of Apple, Boeing, and Facebook reveal a harsh truth: Misalignment leads to wasted resources, reputational damage, and financial losses.

Discussion Questions:

- What lessons can we draw from Apple, Boeing, and Facebook's failures? How can we apply these insights to avoid similar risks in our organization?
- Are there areas in our organization where misalignment has already caused setbacks? What steps can we take to address and resolve these issues?
- How can we identify early warning signs of misalignment, such as conflicting goals or priorities, and take action before they escalate?
- What strategies can help us build a culture of alignment, accountability, and transparency so all teams work toward shared goals?
- How do we communicate the value of alignment to employees and stakeholders, ensuring everyone understands how their work connects to the organization's success?

KNOWLEDGE MAP

BENEFITS OF HIGHLY ALIGNED ENTERPRISES

- Unity of purpose and a shared vision.
- Stronger engagement and deeper commitment.
- A high-trust culture with strategic coherence.
- Greater agility and readiness for change.

IMPACT OF MISALIGNMENT ON ORGANIZATIONS

- Confusion, wasted effort, and stalled progress.
- Fractured priorities and weakened execution.
- Rising turnover, resistance to change, and lost trust.

SIX OBSTACLES TO ALIGNMENT

1. **Missing Context:** Teams lack the information necessary to make connected decisions.
2. **Data Overload:** Too much noise hides the insights that matter.
3. **The Growth Conundrum:** Balancing today's needs with tomorrow's ambitions.
4. **Conflicting Interests and Politics:** Competing agendas and misaligned incentives create friction.
5. **Dependencies:** Interconnected teams and systems slow execution.
6. **Losing Sight of the Why:** A lack of understood purpose behind decisions leads to misaligned efforts.

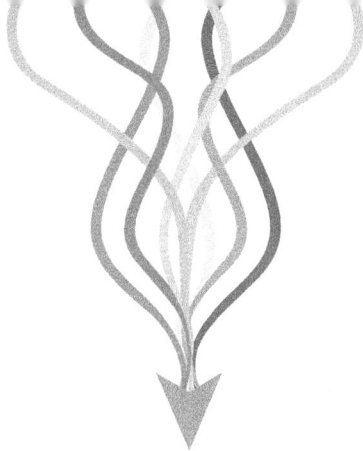

CHAPTER 3

HOW DOES YOUR ORGANIZATION DECIDE?

"Strategy without tactics is the slowest route to victory. Tactics without strategy is the noise before defeat."

—SUN TZU (ADAPTED)

Organizational DNA is your company's invisible blueprint—the core identity that shapes how you work, compete, and grow. Like biological DNA, it carries your values, culture, and ways of operating. As your company expands, that DNA replicates, providing consistency across teams.

Take the Daimler–Chrysler merger. In 1998, German engineering precision (Daimler) met American innovation and speed (Chrysler). The intent? Create a global automotive powerhouse. The challenge? Two organizational DNAs—one meticulous and hierarchical, the other fast-moving and risk-taking—clashed at every level. Employees struggled to adapt, decisions stalled, and collaboration suffered. By 2007, the merger had failed, undone by clashing cultures and misaligned decisions.[34]

The lesson is clear: **When DNAs conflict, decisions suffer.**

Over time, through waves of new hires, shifting strategies, and market disruptions, an organization's DNA adapts. Behaviors evolve. Norms shift. Yet the core—what makes your organization *your* organization—remains.

Why does this matter?

Because your organization's DNA shapes its decisions. It influences how quickly your company acts, how your teams collaborate, and how well strategy turns into execution. Ignore it, and you'll wonder why decisions stall or misfire. Understand it, and you'll unlock a tailored approach to decision-making—one that honors your strengths while adapting to the demands of today.

WHAT'S IN YOUR ORGANIZATIONAL DNA?

Your organizational DNA is your company's identity—it defines how you compete, collaborate, and grow. It's built on four essential elements:[35]

- **Incentives:** What motivates behavior and aligns actions with strategy.
- **Structure:** How teams are organized to drive clarity and execution.
- **Knowledge Management:** How information flows, enabling smarter decisions.
- **Decision Rights:** Who decides what—and how accountability is shared.

---

34 Julia Hollmann et al., "The DaimlerChrysler Merger—A Cultural Mismatch?," *Revista de Administração da UFSM* 3, no. 3 (2010): 431–440, https://doi.org/10.5902/198346592506.

35 Amgad Bahaa EL Din Abdel-Raheem and Mohamed Saad, "Organizational Personality as a Moderating Variable of the Relationship Between Organizational DNA and Innovative Performance," *Journal of Business and Management Sciences* 7, no. 3 (2019): 131–139, https://pubs.sciepub.com/jbms/7/3/4/index.html.

ORGANIZATIONAL DNA

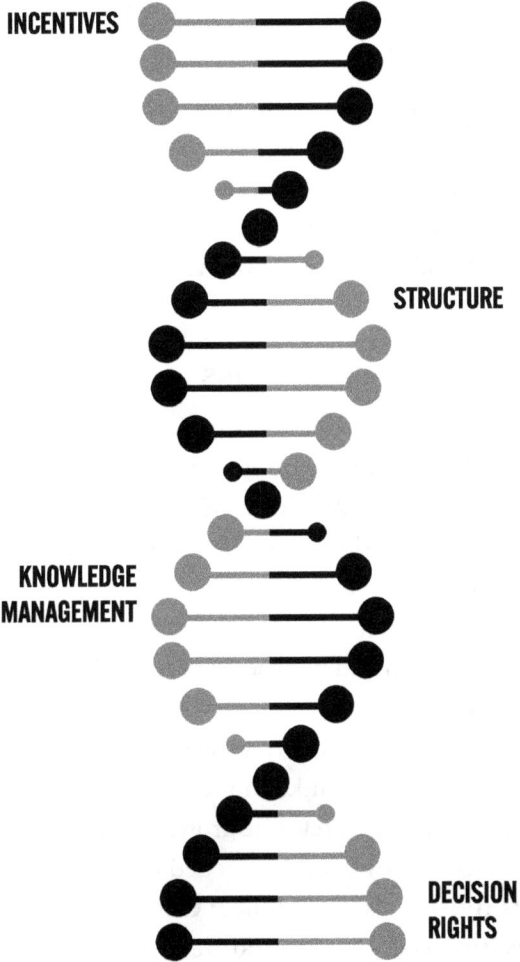

INCENTIVES

STRUCTURE

KNOWLEDGE
MANAGEMENT

DECISION
RIGHTS

Together, these elements shape how decisions are made, strategies are executed, and teams perform.

Your DNA sets the foundation, but **business capabilities** build the future. Your capabilities—your organization's skills, processes, and technologies—are the muscles powered by your DNA. They reveal two things:

- Where you excel today.
- Where you need to grow tomorrow.

When you understand and align your DNA with your capabilities, you amplify strengths, eliminate weaknesses, and unlock smarter, faster decisions that move the business forward.[36]

HOW INCENTIVES SHAPE DECISIONS

Incentives are the silent architects of behavior—they shape decisions, align actions, and fuel momentum. When incentives align with strategy, teams move with clarity and purpose. When they don't, progress breaks down, and short-term gains override long-term priorities.

Here's an example:

A global sales team tied bonuses exclusively to individual performance. The outcome? Targets were hit, but collaboration collapsed. Colleagues became competitors, and customer relationships suffered. In contrast, a competitor linked incentives to team performance, customer satisfaction, and revenue growth. The result? Sales teams collaborated, shared leads, and exceeded targets by 20 percent.

Leaders must strike a balance: Collaboration encourages innovation but risks slowing momentum, while decisiveness fuels speed but can silence key voices.

---

36 Mark Bonchek, "How to Discover Your Company's DNA," *Harvard Business Review*, December 12, 2016, https://hbr.org/2016/12/how-to-discover-your-companys-dna.

Striking a balance is essential. Leaders must align incentives to motivate purposeful action while ensuring decisions happen with both speed and inclusivity.

THE ROLE OF POLITICS

Politics, as we explored earlier, influences alignment. But it is more than just an obstacle—it's deeply embedded in an organization's culture. Politics shapes how decisions are made, how influence is wielded, and how individuals navigate the system.

Politics is an unavoidable part of every organization. When harnessed constructively, it enables advocacy for ideas, pushing for change, and aligning personal ambitions with organizational goals.

However, politics has a **dark side**:

- **Favoritism** erodes trust and undermines merit-based progress.
- **Manipulation** drains enthusiasm and stifles engagement.
- **Influence battles** shift the focus from shared outcomes to personal agendas.

The difference lies in intent:

- **Positive politics** unites teams, aligns decision-making with broader goals, and drives meaningful progress.
- **Negative politics** creates division, resentment, and friction—derailing decisions and slowing momentum.

The goal isn't to eliminate politics but to **align it with shared success**. Leaders play a critical role in fostering a culture of trust and clarity, ensuring political dynamics drive alignment rather than disruption.

CONNECTING EFFORT TO PURPOSE

When people see how their work contributes to the bigger picture, everything changes:

- **Engagement Rises:** Employees feel connected to a shared mission.
- **Motivation Deepens:** The "why" fuels effort and persistence.
- **Decisions Align:** Teams prioritize actions that drive real impact.

It's not just about **financial rewards.** While bonuses and promotions matter, leaders must balance them with intrinsic motivators:

- **Recognition** for contributions and achievements.
- **Growth opportunities** that challenge and develop talent.
- **Work–life balance** that fosters sustainable performance.

The result? Valued employees don't just work harder—they make **better decisions.** By linking effort to purpose, leaders build a culture where teams act with clarity, confidence, and commitment.

CREATING A CULTURE THAT VALUES DECISIVENESS

In high-performing organizations, **culture isn't accidental—it's intentional.** Incentives, leadership styles, and organizational politics don't operate in silos—they interact, amplify, and shape decision-making.

Great leaders **understand the dynamic:**

- **Incentives Drive Behavior:** When aligned with goals, they create purposeful momentum.
- **Leadership Balances Speed with Inclusivity:** Empowering teams without stalling decisions.
- **Trust Turns Politics into Progress:** Aligning ambitions with shared outcomes.

The result? **A culture that motivates, aligns, and enables.**

- Teams act with clarity and purpose.
- Decision-making moves faster and smarter.
- Politics becomes a force for collaboration—not competition.

Leaders who get this right **build more than a culture—they build momentum.**

DESIGNING A STRUCTURE THAT SPEEDS DECISIONS

In today's fast-moving markets, **your structure can make or break decision speed.** Layers of management and tangled approval chains slow momentum, turning decisions into bottlenecks. Feedback zigzags, cross-functional plans stall, and opportunities slip by.

Now, imagine a **leaner, clearer structure:**

- **Fewer management layers** streamlines communication and cuts decision time.
- **Vertical alignment**—from the top floor to the front lines—ensures priorities stay connected.

But speed has its risks. Without crystal-clear **roles and responsibilities,** horizontal decision-making can spiral into chaos:

- Who owns the outcome?
- Who has the final say?

Even flat structures **crumble without clarity.**

The key is balance: **a structure that enables speed** while maintaining accountability. The right design removes friction, aligns teams, and transforms strategy into action—fast.

Every organizational structure has strengths. Every structure also has weaknesses.[37]

TYPES OF ORG STRUCTURES

HIERARCHICAL

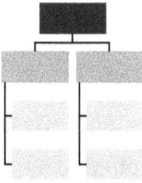

FUNCTIONAL

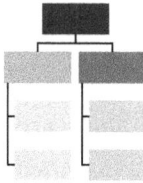

MATRIX

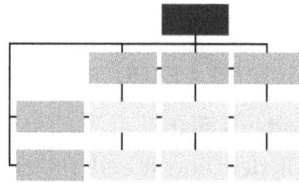

DIVISIONAL

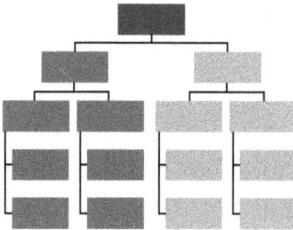

NETWORK

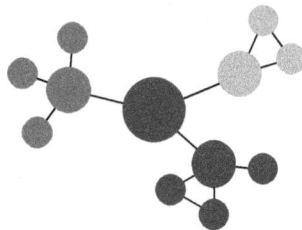

TEAM-BASED

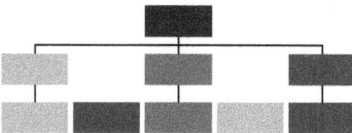

HORIZONTAL / FLAT

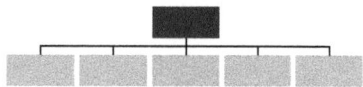

37 "10 Types of Organizational Structures for Businesses," Indeed, last modified January 28, 2025, https://www.indeed.com/career-advice/career-development/types-of-organizational-structures.

- **Traditional Hierarchies** offer clarity. Decisions flow from the top down. But decision-making can be slow. They limit input from the bottom up.
- **Flat Organizations** move fast. Teams collaborate. More voices are heard. But unclear roles can create confusion over who's accountable.
- **Networked Structures** thrive on innovation. Teams form and flex to tackle new challenges. But if job boundaries blur too much, coordination suffers.
- **Hybrid Models** aim for the best of both worlds—structure and speed, adaptability and clarity.

The key? Build a structure that matches your goals and market needs, one that speeds up your most critical decisions without creating chaos.

TURNING STRUCTURE INTO ACTION

Your organizational structure sets the foundation of your company, but operational processes bring it to life. These methodologies and practices determine how teams collaborate, adapt, and decide. The right framework shapes three key areas:

- **Collaboration:** Teams align and share insights seamlessly.
- **Feedback Flow:** Decisions improve through constant iteration and learning.
- **Adaptability:** The organization pivots quickly in response to real-world feedback.

Take **agility**, for example:

- **Customer Centric:** Prioritizes rapid feedback and iterative progress.

- **Real-Time Adjustments:** Teams test, learn, and refine continuously.
- **Results Oriented:** Faster decisions drive innovation and execution.

The right ways of working don't just improve decision speed—they create a **culture of adaptability**. Decisions aren't static. They evolve, fueled by learning, collaboration, and purpose.

THE BUILDING BLOCKS OF DECISION AGILITY

Teams are where decisions come to life. The right team structure empowers speed, focus, and collaboration—turning strategy into execution.

There are three primary types of teams, each with its own strengths and challenges:

- **Dedicated Teams**
    - **Focus:** Each team works on a singular mission or product, creating clear ownership and direction.
    - **Strength:** Decisions flow smoothly because team members share priorities and focus.
    - **Challenge:** Overspecialization can create silos, limiting broader collaboration and innovation.
- **Functional Teams**
    - **Focus:** Teams are organized by expertise (e.g., marketing, engineering, finance), delivering deep knowledge and precision.
    - **Strength:** Decisions are informed by specialized skills and insights.
    - **Challenge:** Functional teams risk tunnel vision, missing the bigger picture or failing to align cross-functionally.
- **Temporary Teams**
    - **Focus:** Diverse skills and perspectives are brought together

temporarily to form a team to tackle a specific project or problem.

- ○ **Strength:** Agility thrives—teams form quickly, solve problems, and disband when the work is done.
- ○ **Challenge:** Coordination can falter when roles, priorities, or workflows lack clarity.

To build decision agility, teams must align with the organization's strategy and goals. The **right balance** of dedicated, functional, and temporary teams ensures:

- **Clear Ownership:** Teams know their responsibilities and decision rights.
- **Cross-Functional Collaboration:** Silos are broken, and insights flow freely across teams.
- **Speed and Focus:** Work remains adaptable without sacrificing strategic alignment.

The right structure aligns strategy, roles, and decision-making. It eliminates ambiguity with:

- **Clear Reporting Lines:** Teams know who owns decisions and who provides input.
- **Accountability:** Ownership is explicit—delays, confusion, and finger-pointing are minimized.
- **Alignment:** Vertical and horizontal coordination ensure decisions serve broader goals.

But structure alone isn't enough. Without effective ways of working, even the best-designed organizations stall. **Adaptive ways of working**—the frameworks, processes, and behaviors teams adopt—bring that structure to life. Together, they create decisive organizations that move with purpose, speed, and adaptability.

A well-designed structure eliminates ambiguity, and adaptive ways of working fuel execution. Together, they ensure teams decide and act with clarity and speed.

ADAPTIVE WAYS OF WORKING

Ways of working define *how* decisions get made and executed. They turn plans into action, ensuring teams can adapt and deliver. Common frameworks include:

- **Agile:** Prioritizes collaboration, iterative progress, and customer feedback. Decisions are data-driven and refined in real time.
- **Lean:** Reduces waste and optimizes resources. Decisions focus on value creation and speed.
- **Design Thinking:** Drives innovation by focusing on empathy, ideation, and experimentation. Decisions are creative and user centered.
- **DevOps:** Breaks down silos between development and operations, enabling faster, more reliable execution.

THE IMPACT

When organizational structure and ways of working align, organizations unlock three critical advantages:

1. **Speed:** Teams execute faster, with fewer delays and bottlenecks.
2. **Adaptability:** Processes remain flexible, empowering teams to pivot as conditions change.
3. **Clarity:** Decision rights, workflows, and accountability are transparent at every level.

BRINGING IT TOGETHER

Effective organizations build a bridge between structure and execution:

- **Structure** provides clarity and removes friction.
- **Ways of working** drive adaptability and action.
- **Teams** operate as the engine—turning plans into results.

Key Takeaway: The right organizational structure, empowered teams, and adaptive ways of working are essential for fostering decision speed, clarity, and adaptability.

KNOWLEDGE IS POWER—WHEN IT MOVES

Decisions thrive on knowledge. When insights move freely, teams align and act with confidence. But when information is siloed or outdated, progress stalls.

Knowledge serves as the bridge between **gut instinct** and **data-driven decisions**. Experienced leaders rely on intuition—signals and patterns sharpened by years of experience. But intuition only thrives when paired with **evidence**: accurate data, timely insights, and expert analysis.

- **Without data,** decisions become guesses.
- **Without intuition,** decisions lose creativity and context.

When knowledge flows seamlessly, organizations achieve the best of both worlds: **evidence-backed, instinct-guided decisions** that drive progress.

Take Amazon, for example. Amazon leverages real-time data to guide decision-making at every level.

- **Customer behavior** drives product recommendations.
- **Logistics data** optimizes supply chains.
- **Sales trends** forecast demand.

From its warehouses to leadership meetings, everyone has access to the insights they need—turning **raw data** into precise, **real-time decisions.**

THE JOURNEY FROM DATA TO KNOWLEDGE

Organizations must transform **raw data** into **actionable knowledge.** This transformation follows a clear progression:

1. **Data:** Raw, uninterpreted facts—sales numbers, customer clicks, and feedback logs.
2. **Information:** Data given context—trends, benchmarks, and reports.
3. **Knowledge:** Insights gained by combining information with experience and analysis—**actionable intelligence that drives decisions.**

This flow is the backbone of effective decision intelligence. Without it, teams get stuck chasing noisy data or missing critical patterns.

BREAKING THROUGH THE NOISE

The challenge? **Data overload** and disconnected systems create noise that overwhelms leaders and teams. To turn knowledge into an advantage, organizations must:

- **Streamline Access:** Ensure teams can quickly access relevant, trusted information.
- **Break Down Silos:** Connect systems, teams, and insights so knowledge flows seamlessly across the organization.
- **Promote Insights over Noise:** Prioritize high-value data that drives action—not just reporting for the sake of reporting.

Organizations that master this flow don't just make decisions—they make progress.

Key Takeaway: Knowledge doesn't just inform decisions—it empowers action. When data becomes knowledge and knowledge drives decisions, teams move faster, smarter, and in alignment.

CLARIFY DECISION RIGHTS TO ELIMINATE CONFUSION

Who gets to decide? It's a simple question, but the answer determines how effectively an organization operates, responds, and thrives. In large organizations, decision rights define:

- Who makes decisions and at what level.
- Who owns the outcomes.
- How accountability flows across teams.

When decision rights are clear, teams act quickly, opportunities are seized, and progress accelerates. When they're unclear, confusion spreads, decisions stall, and friction slows the organization down.

Effective decision rights require three critical components:

1. Ownership: Who is responsible for making the decision?
2. Authority: What level of decision-making power does the individual or team have?
3. Accountability: Who owns the result of the decision—and its success or failure?

With these in place:

- Confusion Fades: Teams know who to turn to and where their responsibility ends.
- Decisions Flow Faster: Bottlenecks disappear, and leaders intervene only when needed.

- **Confidence Builds:** Empowered employees take ownership, trust their judgment, and act with purpose.

CENTRALIZED VERSUS DECENTRALIZED DECISION RIGHTS

Decision rights can follow **two distinct approaches,** each with trade-offs:

1. **Centralized Decision Rights**
    A. **Authority:** Senior leaders retain control of key decisions, ensuring consistency and oversight.
    B. **Strengths:** Decisions are **clear and deliberate**—perfect for high-stakes, strategic choices.
    C. **Risks:** Slow speed, disengaged teams, and a disconnect between leadership and frontline insights.

Example: In highly regulated industries, centralized decisions ensure compliance but may hinder agility.

2. **Decentralized Decision Rights**
    A. **Authority:** Decision-making is distributed closer to the action, empowering teams to act.
    B. **Strengths:** Decisions happen **faster** and are often better informed. Innovation thrives because initiative is encouraged.
    C. **Risks:** Without alignment, teams risk fragmentation, conflicting priorities, or redundant efforts.

Example: Tech companies often decentralize decisions to foster experimentation and speed, but clear alignment on strategy remains critical.

FINDING THE BALANCE

Neither system is perfect. The solution lies in **balance:**

1. **Empower Teams:** Give employees the autonomy to make decisions at the right level.
2. **Align Decisions:** Ensure decisions tie back to organizational strategy, vision, and priorities.
3. **Define Accountability:** Clearly communicate roles, ownership, and responsibilities to eliminate confusion.

Example: A global consumer goods company shifted to a hybrid model for decision rights. Core strategic decisions stayed centralized for clarity and consistency. Operational and frontline decisions were decentralized to accelerate local execution.

The result? Faster decisions, stronger alignment, and higher team engagement.

Key Takeaway: Clear decision rights create a culture of **clarity, accountability,** and **action.**

- **Ownership** fuels progress.
- **Authority** empowers teams.
- **Alignment** ensures everyone moves in the same direction.

In today's fast-paced world, organizations that define decision rights clearly don't just move faster—they **move smarter.**

IDENTIFYING YOUR ORGANIZATION'S TYPE

Understanding organizational types provides a mirror for leaders, revealing strengths and blind spots that impact decision speed, alignment, and execution. Knowing where your organization stands is the first step toward unlocking better decisions and improved outcomes.

Your **organizational DNA** does more than define how you operate—it shapes how you think, act, and decide. Understanding your organization type gives you a **clear lens** through which you can assess your organization's strengths, weaknesses, and decision-making patterns. This clarity reveals where decisions **thrive** and where they **stall**.

Organizations often blend traits from multiple categories, though each organization typically has one type that dominates. Here are the **seven organization types**—along with the decision-making styles they inspire:[38]

1. THE RESILIENT ORGANIZATION

The resilient organization thrives under pressure. It adapts quickly, tackles uncertainty head-on, and transforms challenges into opportunities. **Agility**, **problem-solving**, and **grit** define its culture.

- **Decision Style: Adaptive** and **bold**—ready to pivot when needed.
- **Key Strengths:** Flexibility and speed during change.
- **Risk:** Without focus, constant adaptation can create chaos or directionless experimentation.

2. THE PRECISE ORGANIZATION

The precise organization values **structure, clarity,** and **consistency.** It runs like a well-oiled machine: standardized processes, tight controls, and streamlined decision flows.

- **Decision Style: Systematic** and **reliable**—designed for clarity and uniformity.
- **Key Strengths:** Consistency and repeatability.
- **Risk:** Precision can stifle innovation or slow adaptation to change.

---

38 Gary L. Neilson et al., "The 7 Types of Organizational DNA," *strategy+business* 35 (Summer 2004), https://www.strategy-business.com/article/04210.

3. THE JUST-IN-TIME ORGANIZATION

Resourceful and **lean,** the just-in-time organization thrives on efficiency. It delivers exactly what's needed—**no more, no less**—and responds rapidly to changing demands.

- **Decision Style: Lean, focused, and timely.**
- **Key Strengths:** Efficiency in execution.
- **Risk:** Overemphasis on optimization may leave the organization vulnerable to disruption or long-term neglect of innovation.

4. THE FITS-AND-STARTS ORGANIZATION

The fits-and-starts organization's productivity comes in waves—**high bursts of activity** followed by lulls of uncertainty. Goals shift frequently, priorities compete, and teams work hard but feel disjointed.

- **Decision Style: Reactive** and **uneven**—momentum struggles to build or sustain.
- **Key Strengths:** Capacity for short-term progress.
- **Risk:** Lack of strategic alignment leads to inconsistent execution and low morale.

5. THE OUTGROWN ORGANIZATION

What worked yesterday no longer fits today for the outgrown organization. Systems, processes, and leadership structures feel **outdated**—straining to keep up with growth. Scaling becomes a challenge, innovation stalls, and teams feel constrained.

- **Decision Style: Slow, constrained, and limited** by legacy systems.
- **Key Strengths:** Familiar processes that work—until they don't.

- **Risk:** Inertia and resistance to change slow growth and dampen decision agility.

6. THE OVERMANAGED ORGANIZATION

In the overmanaged organization, layers of **bureaucracy** weigh decisions down. Control is tight, oversight is heavy, and employees are reluctant to take risks. Progress feels slow, stifled, and frustrating.

- **Decision Style: Cautious, controlled,** and **risk averse.**
- **Key Strengths:** Predictability and order in complex environments.
- **Risk:** Overmanagement drains creativity, engagement, and innovation.

7. THE PASSIVE-AGGRESSIVE ORGANIZATION

On the surface, everything looks fine in the passive-aggressive organization. Beneath the surface, problems fester. Communication is indirect, accountability is avoided, and decision-making stalls. Teams appear aligned but often pull in **different directions.**

- **Decision Style: Hesitant** and **unclear**—dominated by avoidance and indecision.
- **Key Strengths:** Politeness and superficial alignment.
- **Risk:** Unresolved conflicts and unclear ownership cripple progress.

WHAT'S YOUR TYPE—AND WHAT'S NEXT?

Knowing your organization type is only the **first step.** The real value lies in what you **do** with that insight.

1. **Play to Your Strengths:** Lean into what works for your organization—whether it's agility, consistency, or efficiency.
2. **Fix the Gaps:** Address weaknesses that hold you back, such as overmanagement, fragmented priorities, or outdated systems.
3. **Realign Decision-Making:** Ensure your decision-making architecture supports your organization's goals, culture, and strengths.

Your type reflects where you are **today**. The actions you take define where you'll go **tomorrow**.

Key Takeaway: Your organizational DNA doesn't have to be a limitation. When you identify your strengths and confront your gaps, you can realign decisions, **unlock momentum**, and build a culture that drives progress.

BUILD A SYSTEM TO IMPROVE DECISIONS

"The way to improve decisions in an organization is to improve the decision making practices in the organization."

—OLIVIER SIBONY

Decisions don't just happen—they're **built**.

Decision architecture is the **operating system** of your organization's DNA. It's the blueprint that defines how decisions are made, who makes them, and what processes guide them.

The problem? Most organizations lack an intentional decision architecture. Instead, decisions happen ad hoc—**reactive, unstructured**, and **inconsistent**. Leaders guess, teams stall, and outcomes suffer.

WHY DECISION ARCHITECTURE MATTERS

Decision architecture organizes and aligns the critical elements of decision-making:

1. **Who decides** and at what level.
2. **What information** and criteria are used.
3. **How alternatives**, risks, and outcomes are evaluated.

Without this clarity, decision-making becomes chaotic. Meetings multiply. Confusion spreads. **Momentum stalls.**

The data on decision-making flows reveals a troubling reality:[39]

- **Sixty-eight percent** of middle managers say their decision-making process is a waste of time.
- **Fifty-seven percent** of C-level executives agree.

Unclear decision-making processes lead to delays, misalignment, and missed opportunities.

The solution? A well-designed decision architecture that eliminates guesswork, accelerates progress, and ensures alignment.

THE FOUR PILLARS OF DECISION ARCHITECTURE

Effective decision-making doesn't happen by chance—it's the result of a strong framework. To navigate complexity and act with confidence, organizations need a decision architecture built on four essential pillars.

1. Clear Decision Roles

Clear roles create clarity and accountability:

- **Who decides:** Identify the decision-makers and their authority levels.

---

39 Iskandar Aminov et al., *Decision Making in the Age of Urgency* (McKinsey & Company, 2019), 5, https://www.mckinsey.com/~/media/mckinsey/business%20functions/people%20and%20organizational%20performance/our%20insights/decision%20making%20in%20the%20age%20of%20urgency/decision-making-in-the-age-of-urgency.pdf?shouldIndex=false.

- **Who owns outcomes:** Ensure accountability is assigned and communicated.
- **Who contributes:** Identify stakeholders who provide input but don't hold final authority.

Example: The RACI (responsible, accountable, consulted, informed) model is a simple way to clarify roles. It ensures decisions don't bottleneck and teams know where responsibility lies.

2. Structured Decision Processes

A consistent, step-by-step decision process eliminates ambiguity and reduces delays. Include these critical steps:

1. **Frame the Decision:** Define the problem, objective, and desired outcome.
2. **Generate Alternatives:** Explore multiple options, avoiding tunnel vision.
3. **Evaluate Trade-Offs:** Assess risks, benefits, and constraints for each option.
4. **Make the Call:** Choose the path forward with clear ownership and communication.
5. **Track and Learn:** Monitor the outcome, assess the impact, and document lessons learned.

Pro Tip: Use decision templates or scorecards to standardize and streamline the process.

3. Designed for Human Behavior

Decision architecture isn't just about processes—it's about **people**. Cognitive biases, group dynamics, and emotions influence every decision. Great systems account for these factors:

- **Manage Biases:** Identify and mitigate common biases like groupthink, overconfidence, and anchoring.
- **Encourage Diversity of Thought:** Bring diverse perspectives into the process to challenge assumptions and uncover blind spots.
- **Set Clear Boundaries:** Establish time limits, rules, and escalation points to avoid analysis paralysis.

Example: Behavioral economics techniques, such as premortems to surface risks or structured frameworks to prioritize alternatives, can significantly improve outcomes.

4. Built-in Measurement and Improvement

Decisions are rarely perfect, but they are always an opportunity to learn:

- **Track Outcomes:** Measure the impact of key decisions against defined goals.
- **Document Insights:** Build a decision repository to capture lessons learned and create institutional memory.
- **Refine the Process:** Continuously improve your decision architecture based on feedback and performance data.

The Goal: Create a system that evolves with your organization—ensuring decisions become faster, smarter, and more aligned over time.

FROM CHAOS TO CLARITY

Intentional decision architecture transforms decision-making:

- **Decisions happen faster** because roles and processes are clear.
- **Teams act confidently** because biases are managed and input is streamlined.

- **Leaders learn continuously,** refining decisions based on real-world outcomes.

The result? **Decisions that drive results.**

Key Takeaway: Decision architecture eliminates guesswork. It aligns people, processes, and priorities to ensure decisions are intentional, informed, and repeatable. Build it, refine it, and let it guide your path forward.

Once your decision architecture is strong, the next step is ensuring it aligns with your organizational DNA—the invisible framework that shapes how decisions flow in your organization.

EVALUATE YOUR ORGANIZATIONAL DNA

Your organizational DNA—your company's identity—drives how you compete, collaborate, and decide. It's built on five essential elements that shape your strengths and strategy:

- **Structure:** How teams are organized and decisions flow.
- **Incentives:** What motivates behavior and drives alignment.
- **Knowledge Management:** How information moves, is shared, and becomes actionable.
- **Decision Rights:** Who decides, who owns, and who acts.
- **Ways of Working:** The habits, processes, and systems that bring plans to life.

Together, these elements shape how your organization thinks, operates, and decides.

YOUR ORGANIZATIONAL DNA SCORECARD

Rate your organization in each category on a scale of 1 to 5:

1 = Very Poor | 2 = Poor | 3 = Moderate | 4 = Good | 5 = Excellent

Structure

- **Speed of Decision-Making:** How quickly can decisions be made and implemented?
- **Role Clarity:** Are roles, responsibilities, and authority clearly defined?
- **Cross-Functional Alignment:** How well do teams collaborate across functions?
- **Flexibility:** Can the organizational structure adapt to changing priorities and market shifts?
- **Escalation Efficiency:** Are unnecessary bottlenecks slowing decisions?

Incentives

- **Alignment with Goals:** How well do incentives align with organizational strategy and outcomes?
- **Decision Empowerment:** Do incentives encourage autonomy and confident decision-making?
- **Risk Tolerance:** Are employees motivated to take smart, calculated risks?
- **Team Collaboration:** Do rewards promote teamwork or create unhealthy competition?
- **Long-Term Versus Short-Term Focus:** Do incentives balance short-term results with long-term success?

Knowledge Management

- **Accessibility:** Can employees easily find and access the information they need?
- **Relevance:** Is knowledge current, accurate, and actionable?
- **Cross-Team Flow:** Does knowledge flow seamlessly across silos and teams?
- **Insights into Action:** How effectively is information turned into decisions?

- **Knowledge Retention:** Are lessons learned documented and reused to improve future decisions?

Decision Rights

- **Clarity:** Is it clear who has the authority to make key decisions?
- **Ownership:** Are decision-makers accountable for their outcomes?
- **Decentralization:** How effectively are decisions pushed closer to where the work happens?
- **Alignment:** Do decisions align with the organization's vision and strategy?
- **Speed:** Are decisions timely, avoiding unnecessary delays?

Ways of Working

- **Collaboration:** Do teams have clear processes for working together effectively?
- **Adaptability:** Can teams adjust quickly when priorities shift?
- **Feedback Loops:** How often is progress reviewed and improvements made?
- **Execution Discipline:** Do daily habits ensure consistent delivery of results?
- **Innovation Readiness:** Are teams empowered to experiment and iterate?

SCORE INTERPRETATION

Once you've rated your organization across all five elements, analyze your results:

- **Strengths:** Celebrate areas where you scored a 4 or 5. These are your core advantages—lean into them to drive alignment and momentum.

- **Gaps:** Focus on areas where you scored a 1 or 2. These weaknesses create friction and slow progress. Prioritize fixing them.
- **Opportunities:** Look for areas where you scored a 3—find where there's room to optimize processes, sharpen execution, and improve alignment.

YOUR NEXT STEP: TAKE ACTION

Improving your organizational DNA starts with intentional steps:

1. **Start Small:** Tackle the biggest gaps first. Small wins build momentum.
2. **Engage Teams:** Use feedback from across the organization to identify blind spots.
3. **Measure Progress:** Track how changes improve speed, clarity, and alignment.
4. **Refine Continuously:** Your DNA evolves with your strategy— make improvement a habit.

The Bottom Line: When you strengthen your operational DNA, decision-making improves, teams align, decisions flow, and results accelerate.

EVALUATE YOUR ORGANIZATION TYPE

Every organization has a dominant type—an identity that influences how decisions are made, teams operate, and strategies come to life. Understanding your type provides a lens through which you can assess where decisions thrive, where they stall, and what changes are needed to align decision-making with your goals.

We previously covered the seven organization types. Reflect on your organization's traits, and choose the type that fits best. If your organization blends characteristics, you can also identify a secondary type. Here's a quick summary:

1. The Resilient Organization
   A. Thrives under pressure, adapts quickly, and sees challenges as opportunities.
   B. **Strengths:** Agility and bold decision-making in uncertain environments.
   C. **Weaknesses:** Can lack structure, leading to inconsistency.
2. The Precise Organization
   A. Runs like a machine—structured, efficient, and focused on consistency.
   B. **Strengths:** Streamlined processes and reliable decision-making.
   C. **Weaknesses:** Risk-averse tendencies can stifle innovation.
3. The Just-in-Time Organization
   A. Lean and resourceful, delivering results exactly when needed.
   B. **Strengths:** Efficiency and ability to optimize resources.
   C. **Weaknesses:** Can struggle with long-term planning and scaling efforts.
4. The Fits-and-Starts Organization
   A. Productivity surges in bursts but lacks sustained momentum and focus.
   B. **Strengths:** Moments of breakthrough and creativity.
   C. **Weaknesses:** Inconsistent execution and unclear priorities.
5. The Outgrown Organization
   A. Systems, processes, and structures no longer fit the scale of operations.
   B. **Strengths:** Potential for transformation when weaknesses are addressed.
   C. **Weaknesses:** Slow decision-making and operational bottlenecks.
6. The Overmanaged Organization
   A. Bureaucracy slows progress, with excessive oversight stifling creativity.
   B. **Strengths:** Clear authority and risk control.

C. **Weaknesses:** Delayed decisions, disengaged employees, and reduced innovation.

7. **The Passive-Aggressive Organization**
   A. Appears aligned externally but avoids conflict and responsibility internally.
   B. **Strengths:** Teams often collaborate superficially.
   C. **Weaknesses:** Misalignment, unresolved tensions, and stalled decisions.

IDENTIFY YOUR ORGANIZATION TYPE

Ask yourself:

- Which type best reflects our current state?
- Do we exhibit traits from multiple types? If so, which is dominant?
- How does our type influence decision-making, collaboration, and execution?

Primary Organization Type: _____

Secondary Organization Type (if applicable): _____

EVALUATE YOUR DECISION ARCHITECTURE

How strong is your organization's decision-making foundation?

The following **benchmark**—adapted from Dr. David Ullman's work on decision architecture—offers a clear, actionable way to assess your current practices.[40] Whether evaluating the organization as a whole or a single silo, use this tool to identify strengths and uncover opportunities for improvement.

Instructions: Score each statement on a scale of **0 to 5**:

---

40 David G. Ullman, *Making Robust Decisions: Decision Management for Technical, Business, and Service Teams* (Trafford, 2006).

- 0 = Never
- 1 = Rarely
- 2 = Occasionally
- 3 = Often
- 4 = Frequently
- 5 = Always

_____ There is an attitude that decision-making is an important part of all processes.

_____ For each decision to be made, the stakeholders and ownership are clear.

_____ The objectives of decision-making activities are clearly known.

_____ Multiple alternatives are generated for each decision.

_____ Information and analysis used to evaluate alternatives clearly support the process.

_____ An appropriate decision-making method is used for each decision.

_____ Risk consideration is a core part of the decision-making process.

_____ The decision-making process is adept at managing uncertainty and ambiguity.

_____ It is clear when a decision has been made.

_____ Decisions are recorded, reviewed, and reused.

_____ There is decision buy-in.

After completing the benchmark, review your scores and identify the areas with the lowest ratings. Focus on these as opportunities for improvement. Develop an action plan to strengthen your decision-making practices, starting with the highest-priority gaps. Use this as a foundation to build a more decisive and effective organization.

NEXT STEPS

Decisions shape everything: your strategy, culture, and ability to compete. By understanding your organization's DNA, decision rights, and decision architecture, you've taken a critical first step: clarity.

But clarity alone isn't enough. Action is what drives change. Act now:

- Align incentives.
- Streamline structure.
- Unblock knowledge flow.
- Clarify decision rights.

Better decisions are engineered—and now's the time to build them.

Evaluate. Align. Act. Build decision systems that are fast, intentional, and aligned. The best organizations don't just keep up—they lead.

SUMMARY

Every organization has a decision engine—its processes, habits, and systems for choosing a path forward. Understanding how well this engine runs is the first step toward making decisions that are faster, smarter, and more aligned.

At the heart of it all is **organizational DNA**—the invisible blueprint that shapes how your company works, competes, and grows. It's made up of structure, incentives, knowledge management, decision rights, and ways of working. Together, these elements define how decisions flow—or where they stall.

Organizational **structure** determines the pace of decisions. Traditional hierarchies bring clarity but can slow progress. Flat or networked models speed things up but risk chaos without clear roles and responsibilities. The answer lies in balance—designing a structure that matches your goals and keeps decisions moving.

Incentives are the silent architects of behavior. Get them right, and teams move with purpose. Get them wrong, and progress fragments. Leadership style, rewards, and culture must align to create momentum without stifling innovation.

Knowledge is power—but only when it flows. From raw data to actionable knowledge, organizations must ensure information is accessible, current, and trusted. When knowledge moves freely, decisions are informed, patterns emerge, and teams act with confidence.

Clear **decision rights** eliminate confusion. Who decides? Who owns the outcome? Balancing control and agility requires clear roles and accountability. The best organizations strike a balance, empowering teams while maintaining strategic alignment.

Finally, **ways of working** bring your structure to life. Agile, lean, and collaborative frameworks accelerate decisions, turning plans into action and insights into innovation. Teams—dedicated, functional, or temporary—are the building blocks of decision agility.

Every organization has a type: resilient, precise, lean, or overmanaged, among others. Knowing your type reveals where decisions thrive and where they falter. Your organizational DNA determines how you decide—but it doesn't define your future.

The call to action is clear: **Evaluate your decision-making architecture.** Find the gaps. Fix the flaws. Build systems that are intentional, agile, and aligned with your strategy.

Better decisions aren't an accident. They're engineered. And when you master decision-making, you don't just keep up—you lead.

DECISION POINTS

Consider This Scenario: Imagine an organization at a standstill. The CEO is visionary. The leadership team is passionate. But product development? Scattered. The CEO is hands-on, involved in everything—from minor tweaks to major strategy. What worked for a smaller team now causes delays. New products are stuck.

The problem runs deeper: there's no unified product strategy. Only the CEO and a handful of top executives understand the overall plan. Product managers are left guessing. Their proposals misalign. Confusion builds. Chaos spreads. Without a scalable decision-making system, the company risks losing momentum—and falling behind competitors.

WHICH PATH WOULD YOUR ORGANIZATION CHOOSE?
Path 1: Centralize and Clarify

- Schedule a series of meetings between the CEO and product teams to clarify the strategic vision and align everyone's work.
- Require product managers to submit detailed reports to the CEO and top leadership, centralizing decisions at the top.
- Form a committee to tackle decision-making roadblocks as they arise.

The Result: Decisions remain bottlenecked. Meetings multiply. Delays persist. Progress stagnates.

Path 2: Decentralize and Align

- Commit the CEO to defining and sharing a clear, detailed product strategy that matches the company's long-term goals.

- Implement a decision-making framework that defines roles and responsibilities, empowering teams to act faster.
- Publicly document how product leader's choices impact the company's key objectives, using metrics tied to key results.

The Result: Clarity replaces confusion. Teams align around shared goals. Decisions flow faster. Products move from plan to launch with purpose and speed.

Your Turn: If this were your organization, would you cling to old habits with Path 1—or empower your teams with clarity and trust to execute faster with Path 2?

Our Take: Growth demands systems that scale. Decisive leadership fuels momentum.

KEY TAKEAWAYS AND DISCUSSION QUESTIONS
1. ORGANIZATIONAL DNA SHAPES DECISION-MAKING

Your organizational DNA—structure, incentives, knowledge management, decision rights, and ways of working—dictates how decisions are made, how teams collaborate, and how quickly strategy turns into action. By understanding and leveraging your DNA, you can amplify strengths and address weaknesses to make your company more decisive.

Questions to Reflect On:

- How well do we understand the role our organizational DNA plays in shaping our decision-making processes?
- What specific strengths in our DNA (e.g., clear structure, effective incentives) can we lean on to improve decisiveness?
- Which elements of our DNA hinder decision-making (e.g., misaligned incentives, lack of clarity in decision rights), and how can we address them?
- How has our organizational DNA evolved over time, and does it still align with our goals and market needs?

- What steps can we take to intentionally shape our DNA to enable faster, smarter decisions?

2. INCENTIVES AND CULTURE DRIVE DECISION EFFECTIVENESS

Incentives are the "silent architects" of behavior, shaping decision-making and employee engagement. When aligned with strategy and culture, they drive purposeful action. Leadership styles, organizational structure, and incentives must work together to create clarity, balance collaboration, and fuel momentum.

Questions to Reflect On:

- How well do our current incentives (financial and nonfinancial) align with strategic goals and drive the right behaviors?
- Does our leadership style strike the right balance between collaboration and decisive action?
- How does our organizational culture—formal or informal— affect the speed and quality of decisions?
- Are there structural barriers (e.g., bureaucracy or unclear roles) that slow decision-making, and how can we address them?
- How can we better communicate strategy, incentives, and roles to ensure alignment across all levels of the organization?

3. CLEAR KNOWLEDGE MANAGEMENT AND DECISION RIGHTS ENABLE AGILITY

Agility relies on trusted, accessible knowledge and clear decision rights. When employees know who decides what and have access to the right information, decisions become informed, timely, and aligned with organizational goals.

Questions to Reflect On:

- How effectively are we capturing, sharing, and using knowledge to drive decision-making?

- Are our decision rights clearly defined, empowering employees while ensuring alignment with strategy?
- How can we ensure knowledge flows freely across teams and levels?
- What processes or systems can we implement to ensure decision-making remains agile and responsive to change?
- How do we balance empowerment with alignment, so decision-makers act quickly without creating fragmentation?

4. DECISION ARCHITECTURE IS THE FOUNDATION FOR BETTER DECISIONS

Intentional decision architecture removes guesswork and builds consistency. Organizations that intentionally design their decision-making processes move faster, achieve clarity, and align their actions with strategy.

Questions to Reflect On:

- How well-defined is our current decision architecture? Are roles, processes, and goals clear at all levels?
- How can we better integrate behavioral insights to identify and mitigate decision biases (e.g., groupthink or anchoring)?
- Do our decision processes prioritize speed while maintaining quality and alignment with strategy?
- How effectively do we track, evaluate, and learn from past decisions to improve future ones?
- What steps can we take to align our decision architecture with our organizational DNA and long-term objectives?

KNOWLEDGE MAP
ORGANIZATIONAL DNA SHAPES DECISION-MAKING

- **Structure:** How teams are organized to balance speed, clarity, and accountability.

- **Incentives:** The rewards and motivators that guide behavior and drive outcomes.
- **Knowledge Management:** How information flows, is shared, and becomes actionable.
- **Decision Rights:** Who makes decisions, how authority is distributed, and how accountability is shared.
- **Ways of Working:** The methods, procedures, and behaviors teams use to turn strategy into action.

ORGANIZATION TYPES AND THEIR DECISION STYLES

- **The Resilient Organization:** Thrives under pressure, adapts quickly, and tackles uncertainty head-on.
- **The Precise Organization:** Structured, systematic, and focused on clear, consistent decisions.
- **The Just-in-Time Organization:** Lean, efficient, and designed for timely, resource-optimized decisions.
- **The Fits-and-Starts Organization:** Bursts of productivity followed by lulls of inconsistency and unclear priorities.
- **The Outgrown Organization:** Struggles with outdated systems, unable to scale or innovate effectively.
- **The Overmanaged Organization:** Bureaucratic and tightly controlled, slowing progress and stifling creativity.
- **The Passive-Aggressive Organization:** Avoids direct responsibility, leading to indecision, unresolved issues, and misalignment.

DECISION ARCHITECTURE

- **Purpose:** Design a clear, repeatable process for how decisions get made.
- **Key Elements:**
  - Who is involved and why.
  - Where information comes from.
  - How goals, risks, and alternatives are evaluated.

- **Behavioral Focus:** Mitigate biases, improve group dynamics, and ensure alignment with strategy.

THE FLOW FROM DATA TO KNOWLEDGE

- **Data:** Raw, uninterpreted facts (e.g., sales numbers).
- **Information:** Data given context and meaning (e.g., sales trends by region).
- **Knowledge:** Insights from combining information with experience, analysis, and strategy to inform decisions.

DECISION ARCHITECTURE QUESTIONS

- Is decision-making treated as a critical process?
- Are decision ownership and stakeholder roles clear?
- Are goals, risks, and alternatives evaluated for each decision?
- Are decisions consistent, tracked, and reviewed for improvement?

CLARITY, ACTION, AND ALIGNMENT

- Understand your organizational DNA.
- Align structure, incentives, and decision rights with strategy.
- Break silos so knowledge flows and empowers decisions.
- Build decision systems that are intentional, agile, and results-driven.

PART 2

ARCHITECT A MORE DECISIVE FUTURE

Understanding the state of decision-making in your organization is just the beginning. Now, it's time to act.

The path to a decisive organization isn't paved with wishful thinking—it's built with intention. By aligning incentives, clarifying decision rights, and redesigning structures, you can transform scattered decision-making into a system that's fast, focused, and effective.

In this section, I'll show you how to architect a decision-making framework that works for your organization. You'll learn how to design structures that reduce friction, leverage knowledge that drives action, and empower teams to move with clarity and speed.

Because decisive organizations don't wait for the future—they build it.

CHAPTER 4

WIRE FOR CONTEXT

"The goal is to turn data into information and information into insight."

—CARLY FIORINA

Disruption is constant.

Data is everywhere.

But context? It's missing.

Without it, leaders struggle, decisions stall, and opportunities fade.

In today's world, context isn't optional—it's your lifeline.

Context is situational clarity—the background and conditions shaping every decision. Without it, teams guess instead of acting with certainty.

Why does context matter? Let's look at an example.

Imagine a large company considering a new enterprise resource planning (ERP) system. Is it the right move? It depends on context.

- What are the existing systems' strengths and weaknesses?
- Is the workforce ready for the change?

- What operational disruptions might occur?
- Are market conditions favorable?
- Do competitors have similar technologies?
- Does the budget allow for the investment? Will the return on investment (ROI) justify it?

The answers vary for every organization and situation, but they determine when and how the decision should be made.

Lacking situational clarity leads to fragmented strategies, missed opportunities, and slowed momentum. Without context, decisions become guesswork, leaving teams unaligned and critical opportunities untapped.

Here's the truth: In organizations where context is siloed, scattered, or incomplete, decision-makers are forced to rely on instinct rather than insight. The result? Teams move blindly, strategies disconnect, and opportunities vanish.

Missing context blinds decisions, fractures strategies, and hinders team adaptability.

How do you fix this? **You wire for context.**

You create systems that ensure the right information reaches the right people at the right time, making every decision informed, relevant, and aligned.

WHAT IT MEANS TO WIRE FOR CONTEXT

Wiring for context isn't about gathering more data—it's about connecting the dots:

- Harmonizing relevant data from across the business to build a complete, real-time picture.
- Integrating that picture into decision-making at every level so teams see not just the what but the why behind choices.
- Sharing the assumptions, principles, and beliefs that guide decisions to ensure alignment from strategy to execution.

A context-driven organization doesn't just react—it anticipates. Teams don't operate in silos; they operate with clarity. Decisions aren't guesses; they're grounded in understanding.

When context flows freely, every choice becomes a confident step forward.

This clarity doesn't just guide decisions—it shapes perspectives. From executives to functional leaders, situational clarity enables everyone to see the bigger picture and act in alignment.

ALIGNING PERSPECTIVES THROUGH CONTEXT

Context is the lens through which leaders see their world—and it shapes the way they think, decide, and act.

From the executive suite to product teams to functional leaders, every decision-maker relies on context to navigate complexity. Why? Because situational clarity helps leaders anticipate trends, spot opportunities, and tackle challenges with clarity.

EXECUTIVE PERSPECTIVES

The job of an executive is to steer the big picture. For executives, context provides the strategic landscape:

- Market dynamics, industry trends, and economic conditions.
- Risks emerging on the horizon.
- Resources that must be allocated for maximum impact.

Armed with this context, executives align strategy with reality, driving the organization forward with confidence.

PRODUCT OWNER PERSPECTIVES

The job of product owners is to innovate for market impact. Product and service owners rely on situational clarity to innovate effectively:

- What are customers asking for?
- What are competitors offering?
- Where do market gaps and opportunities lie?

With this knowledge, product owners build solutions that resonate, anticipate trends, and differentiate offerings that win.

FUNCTIONAL LEADER PERSPECTIVES

The job of functional leaders is to align domains for success. Functional leaders—operations, finance, marketing, HR—use context to guide their strategies:

- How can we adapt processes to shifting demands?
- How do our campaigns align with broader goals?
- What constraints and opportunities exist in our domain?

When context flows at every level, scattered perspectives become aligned action. Leaders act with confidence, strategy sharpens, and execution accelerates. But turning raw data into actionable insight is where context becomes a true competitive advantage.

TURNING DATA INTO INSIGHTS THAT MATTER

Context turns raw data into insights that guide strategy and sharpen decision-making. But insights don't just appear—they're refined.

Raw **data** becomes structured information. **Information** layered with experience becomes knowledge. And **knowledge**, refined through analysis and intuition, becomes **insights**—breakthroughs that fuel strategy, innovation, and growth.

When leaders refine context, they amplify their strategic impact.

BUILDING PERSPECTIVES FROM CONTEXT

CONTEXTUAL KNOWLEDGE   STRATEGIC NEEDS

INFORMATION

KNOWLEDGE

INSIGHTS

PERSPECTIVES

OBJECTIVES

STRATEGIC GOALS

VISION

| Organized data in context | Combines information with understanding and experience | Actionable knowledge that clarifies what to do | A leader's distinct viewpoint shaped by experiences, values, context, and strategic needs | Goals aimed at immediate needs or challenges | Goals designed to move toward its longer-term vision | Organization's overarching ambitions and direction |

Other leaders' perspectives

Context feeds each decision and over time informs strategic planning

In general, data reveals the what, information shows the how, knowledge explains the why, and insight answers, "What's next?"

Take the example of refining vision into short-term goals. Data processed in context empowers every leader to contribute informed views, build better strategies, and execute more effectively.

But insights are only valuable if they reach the right people in the right way. This is where effective communication ensures context drives alignment and action.

COMMUNICATING FOR ALIGNMENT

Leadership perspectives must be communicated effectively to inspire alignment and action. A few ways to communicate perspectives while driving alignment are:

1. STRUCTURED DOCUMENTS

- **Six-pagers** distill complex ideas into focused narratives.
- **One-pagers** deliver concise, high-impact takeaways.

The goal? Clarity on the page. These formats bring focus, ensuring key insights reach the right people with precision.

2. GROUP PRESENTATIONS

- **Town halls** foster dialogue, transparency, and alignment.
- **Visual aids**—charts, slides, graphs—make ideas relatable.

The goal? Bringing vision to life. Dynamic presentations connect leaders with teams, turning strategy into shared purpose.

3. INDIVIDUAL COMMUNICATIONS

- One-on-one meetings build trust and alignment.
- Mentoring sessions share wisdom and connect roles to strategy.
- Informal discussions create space for open dialogue and connection.

The goal? Trust built one conversation at a time.

So, what do we do with all these communications over time? Leadership insights often get scattered—lost in emails, drives, and tools. The result? Confusion, inefficiency, and misalignment.

The solution is to centralize perspectives. Build systems where leadership insights are organized, accessible, and actionable. Not all context is created equal. Organizing it into clear categories focuses teams on what matters most, ensuring no critical signals are missed.

THE FIVE CATEGORIES OF CONTEXT

To improve how teams use context, organize it into five clear categories:

- **Competitive Context:** Align decisions with market goals and positioning.
- **Customer Context:** Understand behaviors, needs, and expectations.
- **Technological Context:** Identify tools that drive innovation and optimization.

- **Environmental Context:** Navigate external forces—regulations, trends, and disruptions.
- **Organizational Context:** Align strategy, teams, and resources for impact.

You might wonder if organizing this information is worth the effort. Spoiler alert: yes, it is. A well-wired organization uses these contexts as its compass—anticipating changes, aligning teams, and sharpening decisions.

Context is the glue that holds strategy together. It connects leaders, teams, and decisions.

But when it's scattered? You get chaos.

When it's refined? You get progress.

Organizing context is step one, but gaps still exist. What about blind spots—those fragments of understanding that slow decisions? Fixing them is another way to level up your decisiveness.

FIXING BLIND SPOTS THAT HINDER PROGRESS

So how do you fix the blind spots that stall decisions? Focus on three essential tools:

1. **Knowledge Centralization:** Build a single source of truth.
2. **Shared Ontology:** Use a unified language for data and processes.
3. **Strategic Capture:** Track decisions, goals, and insights in one place.

Together, these tools can help you capture and connect context relationally—turning scattered facts into actionable knowledge.

MINI USE CASE: THE POWER OF KNOWLEDGE CENTRALIZATION

The benefits of knowledge centralization are both clear and measurable, as the following list illustrates. While I've summarized the outcomes here for brevity, the referenced sources provide detailed examples from real-world organizations. These results demonstrate how centralizing knowledge reduces inefficiencies, accelerates decision-making, and strengthens alignment. Through knowledge centralization, organizations have achieved:

- Discontinued unsuccessful products nearly twice as fast as their more decentralized peers.[41]
- Executed projects and decision-making 20 to 30 percent faster.[42]
- Enhanced collaboration and alignment across global teams.[43]
- Millions saved through reduced duplication, improved efficiency, and accelerated innovation.[44]

By centralizing knowledge, these organizations eliminated silos, empowered teams with timely insights, and unlocked significant business value. With a centralized knowledge system and ontology, businesses can create a relational map of their operations—guiding decisions, uncovering opportunities, and driving progress.

These examples highlight how wiring for context—through clarity and connected knowledge—can transform the way global teams collaborate, decide, and execute.

CONNECTING THE DOTS

Imagine every piece of context—decisions, goals, insights, outcomes—mapped and connected relationally. It's a network, not a pile of files. It shows patterns. It reveals gaps. It guides teams to act.

---

41 John Joseph and Ronald Kingebiel, "Centralized Decision Making Helps Kill Bad Products," *Harvard Business Review*, October 18, 2016, https://hbr.org/2016/10/centralized-decision-making-helps-kill-bad-products.

42 Joseph and Kingebiel, "Centralized Decision Making."

43 "Case Studies: Successful Knowledge Management Implementations," Knowledge Base Script, September 16, 2023, https://www.knowledgebase-script.com/successful-km-case-studies.

44 Cisco, *Cisco IT Case Study: How Cisco Accelerated Product Development Using Quad* (Cisco Systems, 2011), https://www.cisco.com/c/dam/en_us/about/ciscoitatwork/downloads/ciscoitatwork/pdf/Accelerating_Product_Development_Using_Quad.pdf.

This is what relational mapping does:

- Captures the interconnected nature of your business.
- Filters complexity, leaving only what matters.
- Transforms overwhelming data into actionable clarity.

But you don't get there overnight. Wiring for context is an **incremental process**. Each blind spot you fix makes context sharper. Each connection you map makes decisions better.

To make it real, use tools like data lakes, advanced analytics, AI, and machine learning. These technologies can organize, analyze, and surface insights at scale. But they'll only work if the foundation is solid:

- Centralized knowledge.
- A shared ontology.
- Captured decisions, goals, and insights.
- Relational context mapping.

When context is clear, the organization moves faster. Leaders see further. Teams understand better. Decisions become smarter.

WIRED FOR CONTEXT

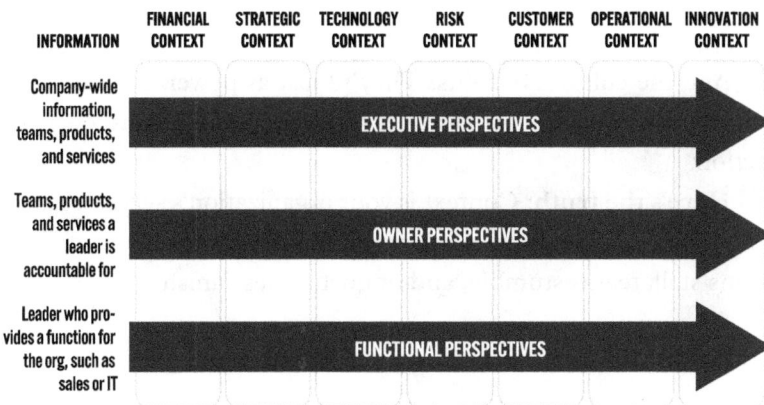

INFORMATION	FINANCIAL CONTEXT	STRATEGIC CONTEXT	TECHNOLOGY CONTEXT	RISK CONTEXT	CUSTOMER CONTEXT	OPERATIONAL CONTEXT	INNOVATION CONTEXT
Company-wide information, teams, products, and services	EXECUTIVE PERSPECTIVES						
Teams, products, and services a leader is accountable for	OWNER PERSPECTIVES						
Leader who provides a function for the org, such as sales or IT	FUNCTIONAL PERSPECTIVES						

The result of wiring for context isn't just better decisions—it's a smarter, faster, and more resilient organization. The rewards go beyond strategy to transforming culture, collaboration, and execution.

THE PATH AHEAD

Wiring for context isn't a one-time effort—it's a continuous commitment. It's about building systems where knowledge flows, insights connect, and decisions align seamlessly with strategy. When context becomes accessible, findable, up to date, and actionable, everything changes:

- **Collaboration Improves:** Teams align faster, work smarter, and share a common understanding.
- **Insights Are Discovered Faster:** Breakthroughs emerge when information flows freely across the organization.
- **Organizational Memory Grows:** Lessons from past decisions are captured, building a culture of learning and avoiding repeated mistakes.
- **Decisions Get Better and Faster:** Leaders act with confidence, backed by the full picture.
- **Knowledge Transfers Seamlessly:** Context lives on, even as employees leave or new ones join.

And the cultural benefits? They're just as powerful. Teams see their impact, confusion disappears, and leaders inspire decisive action.

Here's the truth: Context is your organization's secret weapon, ensuring every decision is informed and aligned. Without it, decisions stall, teams stumble, and opportunities vanish.

- Use **knowledge centralization** to eliminate silos and enable real-time access to critical context.
- Build a **shared ontology** to connect people, processes, and resources within a common framework.
- **Capture decisions, goals, and insights** to build a living record that enhances alignment and learning.
- **Relationally map context** to reveal patterns, gaps, and opportunities that drive progress.

Act now. Eliminate blind spots, wire for context, and lead with clarity and confidence.

SUMMARY

In today's disruptive world, **context is everything**. It's the background information, relationships, and conditions that turn noise into insight, guesswork into confidence, and decisions into progress. Without it, leaders stumble, teams guess, and opportunities vanish.

Wiring for context builds systems where knowledge flows seamlessly to the right people at the right time so decisions are informed, aligned, and fast.

Context isn't just data—it's the perspective leaders need to see clearly, innovate, and adapt. From **competitive and customer insights** to **technological and environmental awareness**, every layer of context sharpens strategy, execution, and results.

But blind spots remain—scattered information, outdated knowledge, fragmented systems. Fixing them requires action:

- **Centralize knowledge** to eliminate silos.
- **Build a shared ontology** so everyone speaks the same language.
- **Capture decisions, goals, insights, and outcomes** to create a living history of strategic choices.

- **Map context relationally** to connect the dots and reveal what matters most.

The reward? Context becomes a superpower. Teams collaborate better. Insights surface faster. Decisions are made confidently, backed by shared understanding. Organizational memory grows, learning accelerates, and leadership becomes decisive.

In a well-wired organization, confusion disappears, culture thrives, and progress is inevitable. Wire for context now—eliminate confusion, align teams, and lead decisively into a smarter, faster future.

DECISION POINTS

Consider This Scenario: A large organization is at a crossroads. Critical decisions are stalling because context is fragmented—important insights are scattered across emails, shared drives, and teams. Its leaders see the impact: missed opportunities, slow decisions, and growing frustration.

The leadership team knows they need a better system—one that centralizes knowledge, eliminates blind spots, and enables context to flow seamlessly. But how bold should they be?

WHICH PATH WOULD YOUR ORGANIZATION CHOOSE?
Path 1: Start Small and Test

- Approve a pilot project to centralize context within a few key departments.
- Test new tools and processes on a small scale.
- Measure improvements in decision speed, collaboration, and insight discovery.
- Gather feedback, refine the approach, and assess feasibility for a full rollout.

The **Result:** Risk is minimized, and quick wins build confidence. But progress is slow, and challenges beyond the pilot remain hidden.

Path 2: Commit and Scale

- Go all in on launching a full-scale initiative to wire the entire organization for context.
- Conduct a thorough audit of systems and identify gaps.
- Prioritize high-impact departments for rapid implementation and early wins.
- Allocate resources for training, change management, and technology adoption.
- Build a unified framework where context is centralized, accessible, and actionable.

The **Result:** Momentum builds across the organization as silos disappear and decision-making accelerates. Up-front investment and careful coordination are required to avoid disruption.

Your Turn: If this were your organization, would you cautiously test the waters with Path 1—or act decisively to scale context across the business with Path 2?

Our Take: Centralizing context is about speed, clarity, and alignment. Whether you test or scale, the key is to start—because the cost of waiting is confusion, missed opportunities, and stalled progress.

KEY TAKEAWAYS AND DISCUSSION QUESTIONS
1. WIRING FOR CONTEXT ENABLES SMARTER, FASTER DECISIONS

Context is the background that shapes every decision. When organizations harmonize and refine context, decisions become timely, informed, and aligned with strategy. Without it, teams rely on guesswork, momentum slows, and opportunities vanish.

Questions to Reflect On:

- How does fragmented or incomplete context impact our current decision-making processes?
- What steps can we take to ensure teams at all levels have access to relevant, real-time context?
- How effectively does our organization connect data, knowledge, and insights to drive decision-making?
- What processes or tools can improve how context flows across our organization?

2. LEADERSHIP RELIES ON CONTEXT TO ALIGN STRATEGY AND ACTION

Context shapes leadership perspectives—executives, product owners, and functional leaders rely on it to anticipate trends, identify opportunities, and tackle challenges. When leadership operates with shared context, scattered efforts turn into unified momentum.

Questions to Reflect On:

- Do our leaders have access to the right context to make confident, forward-looking decisions?
- How effectively are leadership perspectives communicated across teams and departments?
- What systems or formats (e.g., structured documents, group presentations) could improve the flow of leadership context?
- How can leadership encourage better collaboration by aligning teams around shared context?

3. REFINING DATA INTO INSIGHTS TRANSFORMS STRATEGY

The journey from data to insight—data → information → knowledge → insights—turns noise into action. When leaders refine context effectively, they unlock strategic clarity, uncover opportunities, and anticipate risks.

Questions to Reflect On:

- How well are we translating raw data into actionable insights that drive strategy?
- What tools or processes do we need to refine data into knowledge and insights more efficiently?
- How can we ensure insights are captured, shared, and acted upon across the organization?
- Are there gaps in our ability to analyze data in real time to guide decision-making?

4. BLIND SPOTS EMERGE WHEN CONTEXT IS FRAGMENTED OR OUTDATED

Contextual blind spots—scattered knowledge, outdated data, and hidden insights—slow decisions and stall progress. Mitigating these blind spots requires centralization, structure, and a commitment to relational mapping.

Questions to Reflect On:

- Where are the biggest blind spots in how we manage and share organizational context?
- How can centralizing knowledge improve visibility, reduce friction, and drive alignment?
- Are we capturing both explicit and implicit decisions to understand the "why" behind our actions?
- How can technology (e.g., AI, advanced analytics) help us surface gaps and connect critical context faster?

5. WIRING FOR CONTEXT FUELS COMPETITIVE EDGE AND STRENGTHENS CULTURE

When context flows seamlessly, teams align, decisions accelerate, and progress becomes inevitable. The benefits of wiring for context extend to culture: Teams understand their impact, confusion disappears, and leadership becomes decisive.

Questions to Reflect On:

- How does improving context management strengthen our competitive position?
- What tangible benefits (e.g., faster decisions, clearer alignment) would a wired-for-context organization create for our teams?
- How can we build a culture where context is valued, shared, and actively used to guide decisions?
- What steps can we take to turn context into a superpower that drives innovation and agility?

KNOWLEDGE MAP
DATA REFINED INTO INSIGHTS THAT SHAPE DECISIONS

- **Data:** Raw facts and observations.
- **Information:** Structured, organized data that reveals trends and patterns.
- **Knowledge:** Information layered with experience and expertise.
- **Insights:** Actionable discoveries that drive strategy, innovation, and growth.

TYPES OF CONTEXT

- **Competitive Context:** Aligns decision-making with market trends, competitor moves, and long-term goals.
- **Customer Context:** Captures evolving behaviors, preferences, and needs to deliver better experiences.

- **Technological Context:** Tracks emerging tech to boost innovation, optimization, and readiness for disruption.
- **Environmental Context:** Accounts for regulatory, societal, and economic forces shaping external decisions.
- **Organizational Context:** Aligns internal culture, resources, and processes with strategy and execution.

CONTEXTUAL BLIND SPOTS

- Scattered, siloed knowledge.
- Outdated or incomplete data.
- Implicit decisions left undocumented.
- Context buried in disparate tools and platforms.

MITIGATING BLIND SPOTS

- **Knowledge Centralization:** Build a single source of truth for organizational context.
- **Shared Ontology:** Create a unified framework that connects people, processes, and resources.
- **Strategic Capture:** Document explicit and implicit decisions, goals, insights, and outcomes.
- **Relational Mapping:** Map interconnected context to surface patterns, gaps, and opportunities.

BETTER CONTEXT BECOMES A SUPERPOWER THAT

- Improves **cross-functional collaboration** and alignment.
- Accelerates **insight discovery** for strategic advantage.
- Builds **organizational memory** to retain knowledge.
- Enhances **learning and decision-making** speed.
- Enables rapid **knowledge transfer** to reduce the impact of turnover.
- Strengthens **culture**, making teams confident, informed, and aligned.

CHAPTER 5

WIRE FOR FLOW

"In any moment of decision, the best thing you can do is the right thing, the next best thing is the wrong thing, and the worst thing you can do is nothing."

—THEODORE ROOSEVELT

When organizations embrace decisive measures, they unlock extraordinary value. A recent **Accenture study** found that S&P 500 firms focused on transformation, and breakthrough speed could increase earnings before interest, taxes, depreciation, and amortization (EBITDA) from 3.8 percent to 6.9 percent and boost revenue compound annual growth rate (CAGR) by from 2.7 percent to 3 percent within three years.[45] Compounded over time, these gains foster innovation, create resilience amid uncertainty, and drive a lasting competitive edge.

But what separates the "winners" from the rest? Winners consis-

---

45   Christian Campagna et al., *CFO Now: Breakthrough Speed for Breakout Value* (Accenture, 2021), 5, https://insuranceblog.accenture.com/wp-content/uploads/2021/02/CFO-Now-Research-2021-Accenture.pdf.

tently make **fast, high-quality decisions**—and the payoff is clear. Their teams are twice as likely to report superior financial returns from recent big decisions.[46] How do they get there?

- They make decisions at the **right level** of the organization.
- They focus on **enterprise-level value** rather than isolated gains.
- They ensure **aligned buy-in** across the company.

The losers? They pay a heavy toll: missed opportunities, lost momentum, and frustration. And that's before accounting for the **hidden costs**: stalled innovation, eroded employee satisfaction, and the damage caused by misalignment.

In Chapter 4, we explored how "**wiring for context**" lays the groundwork for better decision-making. Context ensures leaders and teams have the right information at the right time to make informed choices. But context alone isn't enough.

To transform that understanding into momentum, organizations must **wire for flow**—creating systems that not only connect the dots but ensure decisions move swiftly, align teams, and drive action. If wiring for context helps you see the playing field, wiring for flow enables you to move decisively and win the game.

If context is the price of entry, flow is how your organization turns that context into action and unlocks its full value.

So, how can organizations wire themselves for better flow? Let's begin with two real-world examples:

HITACHI

Hitachi, a 114-year-old industrial giant, transformed itself by prioritizing digital capabilities and value flow. Historically known

---

46 Iskandar Aminov et al., *Decision Making in the Age of Urgency* (McKinsey & Company, 2019), 2, https://www.mckinsey.com/~/media/mckinsey/business%20functions/people%20and%20organizational%20performance/our%20insights/decision%20making%20in%20the%20age%20of%20urgency/decision-making-in-the-age-of-urgency.pdf?shouldIndex=false.

for its diverse portfolio, the company streamlined operations by reducing subsidiaries and doubling down on AI-driven industrial solutions. This shift enabled Hitachi to provide real-time insights and decision-making tools across energy, mobility, and digital infrastructure.

By leveraging its Lumada digital platform, Hitachi integrated AI, IoT, and data analytics to optimize industrial processes.[47] The results were undeniable—its market value tripled from 2022 to 2024, surpassing $100 billion.[48] This success wasn't just about technology; it was about aligning the entire organization around a decisive, digital-first mindset.

FREEPORT-MCMORAN

This global mining company blended **AI-driven insights** with the institutional knowledge of its veteran engineers to improve decision speed and quality. When copper prices dropped, Freeport reevaluated an existing expansion plan. Instead of proceeding with the original high-cost strategy, it pivoted to a more cost-effective, AI-powered approach—delivering better results faster.[49]

Both cases prove that **a digital mindset and real-time insights drive decisive action and better results.** These are keys to wiring an organization for flow. The examples of both companies underscore the truth that **superior decision flow needs three things:** technology, empowerment, and clear decision frameworks. These

---

47 Ricardo Goulart, "Hitachi's Digital Makeover: A Success Story of Global Growth and Streamlined Strategy," Global Financial Market Review, December 17, 2024, https://www.gfmreview.com/technology/hitachi-s-digital-makeover-a-success-story-of-global-growth-and-streamlined-strategy.

48 Harry Dempsey and David Keohane, "'Monetising Data': How Hitachi Has Soared with Bets on AI Future," *Financial Times*, December 16, 2024, https://www.ft.com/content/56eb8539-ed4d-45ce-bcc2-6774354091d2?accessToken=zwAGLm5JtqX4kc9W64U57U1FztO8wmdoNUCRog. MEUCIA4zmoWX-1X7NNmqMoFbT837XVTVBB2aWjTkkoome8A8AiEApYFBTsNU83UVXlPAlG66 RTFYYbvWCGj9zzmopTPbDRM&sharetype=gift&token=33a6afdc-22d7-4972-a4a0-b6b7d68e403b.

49 "How Six Companies Are Using Technology and Data to Transform Themselves," McKinsey Digital, August 12, 2020, https://www.mckinsey.com/capabilities/mckinsey-digital/our-insights/how-six-companies-are-using-technology-and-data-to-transform-themselves.

factors let organizations respond quickly, align easily, and disrupt their industries with confidence.

To build a truly decisive organization, you need more than just speed—you need a clear system for making decisions. That system is your decision architecture.

WHAT IS YOUR DECISION ARCHITECTURE?

As discussed in Chapter 3, decision architecture is the system of processes, structures, and practices organizations use, consciously or not, to make decisions. It's the framework that determines how choices are made, communicated, and aligned with strategy.

Successful leaders make countless decisions daily, balancing speed with accuracy. Yet indecision frustrates even the best leaders, **especially in large organizations where ambiguity clouds the process.**

How can leaders tasked with making decisions remain so frustrated by organizational indecision? The problem lies in the murky process that surrounds decision-making in most companies. Spend a day at any organization, and you'll hear inconsistent or incomplete answers to questions like:

- How are strategic decisions made and communicated?
- Where are past decisions and their rationales stored?
- How do we measure the success of our goals and know when to revisit or reverse decisions?
- What is our decision velocity, and is it improving?
- How are decisions aligned to strategy, and how does each role contribute?

In many cases, the answer will be, "I don't know."

This ambiguity reveals a weak or undefined decision architecture—a gap that slows organizations down and stifles alignment. Building a robust decision architecture ensures these questions have clear, consistent answers. It enables faster decisions, greater accountability, and alignment across the organization.

Decision architecture isn't just theory—it's the practical blueprint that ensures these questions have consistent, actionable answers.

While defining decision architecture creates the foundation, the real challenge lies in putting it into practice—especially when decisions get bogged down by complexity and uncertainty.

WHY IS DECISIVENESS SO ELUSIVE?

Decisiveness is hard. It means acting amid uncertainty. Growth multiplies complexity—teams splinter, priorities compete, alignment strains. Leaders face a paradox: **move fast while keeping everyone aligned.**

It's a delicate balance.

Indecisive leaders often hesitate because they are waiting for perfect clarity. But perfect clarity never comes. Decisiveness thrives on imperfection. Jeff Bezos's **70 Percent Rule** says it all: act with 70 percent of the information. Waiting for 90 percent? You're too slow.[50]

This is a common problem for many organizations. Among Fortune 500 companies, indecision costs an average of **530,000 lost days**, equating to **$250 million in wasted labor**, each year.[51]

Decisive leaders also empower teams. They create trust. They push authority down so decisions happen at the right level, aligned to top-level goals. The result? Faster, smarter choices—and a culture that thrives on ownership.

Decisive organizations do more than empower leaders—they empower *employees*. They trust their teams to make decisions, as long as those decisions align with top-level goals. The payoff is

50 Don Reisinger, "All Companies Should Live by the Jeff Bezos 70 Percent Rule," Inc., June 27, 2020, https://www.inc.com/don-reisinger/all-companies-should-live-by-jeff-bezos-70-percent-rule.html.

51 Aminov et al., *Age of Urgency*, 5.

immense. Empowered employees are more engaged, dedicated, and loyal. Organizations with empowered leaders are **four times more likely** to make good decisions. They achieve far greater financial success than their industry peers.[52]

Without an adaptive decision framework, organizations risk being **paralyzed by process—or lost in chaos.** Too much process creates bottlenecks and slows decisions, too little creates chaos and misalignment. The key is finding an adaptive decision-making framework that keeps the business aligned without sacrificing agility.

Corporate decision-making is about more than just choosing a course of action—it's about answering the **how, why, and when** of every decision.

Challenges arise when organizations lack consistency:

- Are decision-making methods clearly defined and followed?
- How are decisions documented, assessed, and communicated?
- Are outcomes aligned with strategy and objectives?

Consistently asking—and answering—these questions strengthens the organization's decision architecture. Solid answers reveal clarity, alignment, and an ability to learn and adapt.

Ultimately, great organizations don't just make decisions—they make decisions **well.** They balance process and action. They ensure every choice is intentional, clear, and aligned with the organization's goals.

Where does your organization land? Are decisions clear, consistent, and aligned—or stuck in ambiguity?

Even with a clear strategy, uncertainty can paralyze decision-making. The organizations that succeed are those that embrace uncertainty and turn it into opportunity.

---

52 Aaron De Smet et al., "For Smarter Decisions, Empower Your Employees," McKinsey Insights, September 9, 2020, https://www.mckinsey.com/capabilities/people-and-organizational-performance/our-insights/for-smarter-decisions-empower-your-employees.

BEING DECISIVE UNDER UNCERTAINTY

Uncertainty is constant.

  It challenges leaders.

  It tests organizations.

  And it demands decisiveness.

  But here's the problem:[53]

- Fifty-three percent of leaders fear failure.
- Forty-three percent discourage debate.
- Seventy-six percent limit independent decisions.

When uncertainty abounds, progress stalls. Innovation slows. Leaders hesitate.

Uncertainty isn't the enemy. The real danger is inaction.

These numbers reveal a dangerous pattern. Fear of failure leads to hesitation. A culture of consensus drowns out bold ideas. Uncertainty becomes a roadblock.

However, for organizations that embrace uncertainty, the data tells a different story. Treating uncertainty as an opportunity allows them to outperform their peers consistently.

McKinsey's research on the 2008 global financial crisis found that while many faltered, top-performing companies pulled ahead—outpacing their peers by **over 150 percent** by 2017. Their secret? Acting decisively when others hesitated.[54]

Satya Nadella, Microsoft's CEO, acts at **80 percent confidence**—knowing that waiting for perfection means falling behind.[55]

---

53 Alison Blair et al., *PwC's 26th Annual Global CEO Survey: Winning Today's Race While Running Tomorrow's* (PricewaterhouseCoopers, 2023), 17, https://www.pwc.com/gx/en/ceo-survey/2023/main/download/26th_CEO_Survey_PDF_v1.pdf.

54 Fritz Nauck et al., "The Resilience Imperative: Succeeding in Uncertain Times," McKinsey Insights, May 17, 2021, https://www.mckinsey.com/capabilities/risk-and-resilience/our-insights/the-resilience-imperative-succeeding-in-uncertain-times.

55 Terence Mauri, "Want to Be a Great Leader? Follow Satya Nadella's 3 Clever Rules Every Day," Inc., August 16, 2019, https://www.inc.com/terence-mauri/want-to-be-a-great-leader-follow-satya-nadellas-3-clever-rules-every-day.html.

Under his leadership, decisive moves paired with long-term vision have transformed Microsoft into a leader in a volatile world.

The organizations that succeed under uncertainty follow a clear, repeatable process. So, how do decisive organizations operate under uncertainty? A clear pattern emerges:

1. **Interpret the Signals:** Leaders gather key indicators—customer behaviors, market trends, internal metrics, economic shifts. These signals are data points, whispers from the market telling them where to look next.
2. **Form Hypotheses:** Teams take those signals and form educated guesses—assumptions about what's changing and where opportunities lie. What could we do? What should we try?
3. **Build Conviction:** With hypotheses in hand, teams test, validate, and analyze. Data sharpens the picture. Experience adds judgment. Conviction grows. When the team believes in the path forward, action follows.
4. **Take Decisive Action:** The moment of truth. Teams implement the decision quickly and confidently. No overthinking. No endless debate. They know the trigger points that will cause a pause or pivot.
5. **Communicate Effectively:** Once a decision is made, it must flow through the organization like electricity. Leaders explain the what, the why, and the how. Teams align. Execution begins.

This cycle—**signal → hypothesis → conviction → action → communication**—creates momentum. Repeated often enough, it becomes muscle memory. Organizations learn faster. Decisions get sharper. Confidence replaces hesitation.

This is where technology accelerates the process. Tools like **context graphs**, which we'll explore in later chapters, amplify decision-making power. They map context, expose patterns, and enable data-driven choices at scale.

But tools aren't enough. Technology can speed decisions, but mindset transforms them. To thrive under uncertainty, organizations must shift how they think—seeing disruption not as a threat but as an opportunity to act faster, smarter, and stronger.

Uncertainty will always exist. But decisive organizations know how to conquer it.

They interpret signals, build conviction, take action, and communicate with precision. Over time, this cycle becomes the foundation of a culture that doesn't fear the unknown. It learns from it. It thrives in it.

Operating decisively under uncertainty requires not only bold action but also a well-defined process for how decisions are made, communicated, and evaluated. This brings us to the importance of deciding how to decide.

DECIDING HOW TO DECIDE

Why does decision-making so often feel chaotic?

The meetings drag on. The conflicts repeat. Teams push in opposite directions. Progress slows to a crawl, and frustration fills the void. Sound familiar? It's not because people don't care. It's not because leaders lack skill. It's because the organization hasn't decided *how* to decide.

When you clearly define how decisions are made, everything changes.

Deciding how to decide brings clarity to chaos. It reduces ambiguity. It minimizes conflict. Everyone knows the process, their role in it, and how decisions align with the bigger picture. The result? Better decisions. Faster outcomes. Trust and accountability that ripple through the organization.

Here's what a strong decision-making process delivers:

1. Clarity: Who decides, how, and why? Everyone knows. No more guessing.

2. **Consistency:** The same process every time across teams and departments.
3. **Accountability:** Clear ownership. Clear outcomes. Decisions don't disappear into the void.
4. **Learning:** You don't just decide—you improve. Every choice informs the next one.
5. **Agility:** When change happens—and it always does—you adapt without breaking stride.

So, how do you get there? How do you streamline decision-making across your organization?

It begins with a clear, well-communicated **decision architecture: the systems, processes, and practices that guide how decisions are made.**

Imagine your organization at a crossroads. How does it approach strategic decisions today?

Which of these scenarios hits closest to home?

SCENARIO 1

- Endless, energy-draining meetings that lead nowhere.
- Department silos that hoard information and block collaboration.
- Conflicts that simmer, never resolved, never learned from.
- Slow, rigid processes that buckle under change.
- Disconnection between individual goals and the company mission.

Or...

SCENARIO 2

- Goals align—individuals and teams pull in the same direction.
- Agile decision-making adjusts quickly to new data.

- Change becomes opportunity. Innovation thrives.
- Conflicts resolve proactively, leaving lessons instead of scars.
- Collaboration crosses departments seamlessly, unlocking shared problem-solving.

Most organizations live somewhere in between. **They dream of agility but struggle with rigidity.** They crave alignment but live with confusion.[56]

And yet, the solution is within reach: a mature **decision architecture.**

When you invest in designing how decisions are made, two powerful things happen:

1. The quality of decisions improves. Better choices. Better strategy. Better results.
2. The buy-in for those decisions grows. People understand the process. They trust it. They own the outcomes.

This is more than process optimization. It's a cultural transformation. Strong decision architecture aligns strategy, fosters collaboration, and accelerates innovation. It turns decision-making from a bottleneck into a catalyst—empowering teams to act faster, smarter, and together.

Ask yourself, are you still stuck in the chaos of the status quo, or are you ready to define how you decide?

Because when you decide how to decide, you don't just fix decision-making. You unlock your organization's full potential.

When decision-making becomes a strength, strategy transforms into a driving force for success.

With a structured decision process in place, it's essential to

56   David G. Ullman, *Making Robust Decisions: Decision Management for Technical, Business, and Service Teams* (Trafford, 2006), 21–22.

understand what separates a good decision from a bad one beyond just the outcome.

A MINI USE CASE: MASTERING DECISIVENESS AT SCALE

Amazon didn't become a global powerhouse by accident.

- **1999:** Launched Marketplace, enabling third-party sellers to expand offerings.
- **2005:** Introduced Prime—two-day shipping that redefined e-commerce.
- **2006:** Streamlined logistics with Fulfillment by Amazon, helping sellers scale.
- **2006:** Reshaped cloud computing with AWS, unlocking billions in revenue.
- **2007:** Disrupted publishing with Kindle, delivering instant access to books.
- **2008:** Reduced waste with Frustration-Free Packaging, enhancing the user experience.
- **2011:** Expanded its ecosystem with Kindle Fire—an affordable, accessible tablet.
- **2012:** Transformed warehouse operations by integrating robotics.
- **2014:** Pioneered voice-controlled AI with Amazon Echo and Alexa for smart homes.
- **2015:** Created Prime Day—a global shopping event to rival Black Friday.
- **2016:** Redefined physical retail with Amazon Go cashier-less stores.
- **2017:** Expanded into online and offline grocery shopping with Amazon Fresh and Whole Foods.
- **2019:** Raised delivery expectations with one-day shipping for Prime members.
- **2020:** Entered telehealth with Amazon Care, expanding into virtual healthcare.

- **2021:** Launched Amazon Astro—home robotics for monitoring and mobility.
- **2023:** Delivered core AI tools with AWS Bedrock, driving the next era of innovation.

At every turn, Amazon acted decisively—fueled by clear decision-making principles:

1. **Decision Types:** Type 1 decisions are high-stakes and irreversible, requiring careful thought. Type 2 decisions are low-stakes and reversible, so make them quickly—momentum matters.[57]
2. **Seventy Percent Rule:** Move when you have 70 percent of the data. Waiting for 90 percent is too slow.[58]
3. **Disagree and Commit:** Debate hard, decide, and commit fully.[59]

Amazon's success teaches us a crucial truth: **decisiveness at scale isn't luck.** It's a disciplined approach that balances speed, clarity, and execution with an intense customer obsession. By relentlessly prioritizing customer needs and maintaining agility, Amazon disrupted retail, cloud computing, publishing, and beyond—all while continuing to scale.[60]

WHAT MAKES A DECISION GOOD?

Good decisions don't always lead to good outcomes. Bad decisions don't always end in disaster.

---

57   Jeffrey P. Bezos, "2015 Letter to Shareholders," exhibit 99.1, US Securities and Exchange Commission, 2015, https://www.sec.gov/Archives/edgar/data/1018724/000119312516530910/d168744dex991.htm.

58   Jeffrey P. Bezos, "2016 Letter to Shareholders," Amazon News, April 17, 2017, https://www.aboutamazon.com/news/company-news/2016-letter-to-shareholders.

59   Bezos, "2016 Letter."

60   Jeffrey P. Bezos, "2018 Letter to Shareholders," Amazon News, April 11, 2019, https://www.aboutamazon.com/news/company-news/2018-letter-to-shareholders.

And yet, we often judge decisions only by their results. When a choice leads to success, we celebrate it. When it fails, we blame it. But outcomes are tricky. Timing, luck, and external forces—things we can't control—often have the final say.

Brian Armstrong, CEO of Coinbase, challenges the common thinking. To him, a good decision is about process, not just results. It's about weighing options, assessing risks, and acting with conviction.

The truth is this: A good decision is made thoughtfully, informed by context, analysis, and judgment. A bad decision? That's a shot in the dark, a choice driven by guesswork instead of reasoning.

Look at it like this:

WHAT DOES A GOOD DECISION LOOK LIKE?

GOOD DECISION-MAKING	BAD DECISION-MAKING
People seek the truth	People seek to be right
Decision-makers chosen in advance	No clear decision-maker, or decided too late
Appropriate number of decision-makers given the risk	Too few or too many decision-makers
All input providers feel heard; buy-in is achieved.	Some feel their point of view was not considered; there is grumbling, resentment, and second guessing
Even those who disagree commit to work toward the decision (disagree and commit)	Those who disagree don't contribute to the decision
Minimizes the effect of unconscious bias	Suffers from unconscious bias
Fully connected information sharing	Partial or unidirectional information sharing
Made quickly with few meetings	Made slowly with too many meetings
Lightweight process	Too much process
A record of the decision and each participant's input is kept for later review and learning	People's memories fade (and history is revised) as time passes

Credit: Brian Armstrong

Source: Brian Armstrong, "How We Make Decisions at Coinbase," Medium, May 8, 2018, https://barmstrong.medium.com/how-we-make-decisions-at-coinbase-cd6c630322e9.

Armstrong reminds us that outcomes are uncertain. No leader can guarantee success. But what we *can* control is the quality of the decision-making process:[61]

- Did we gather the right information?
- Did we consider the consequences?
- Did we act with clarity and confidence?

A decision made this way—rigorous, thoughtful, and well-executed—is a good decision. Even if the result doesn't go our way.

Because in a world of uncertainty, you can't chase perfect outcomes. But you can build a system that produces good decisions consistently. Over time, that's what drives success.

Understanding what makes a decision "good" is one piece of the puzzle. A good decision process doesn't chase certainty—it drives confidence. Combined with a clear decision flow, it ensures teams make consistently strong decisions.

DESIGNING A PATH TO DECISIVENESS

Crafting a **decision architecture** is the key to unlocking organizational success. Without it, decisions stall, conflicts rise, and progress halts.

Deciding how to decide transforms chaos into clarity, aligning teams and accelerating results. But what does it mean to "decide how to decide"?

It means make the implicit explicit. Create clear processes that guide decision-making—who's accountable, what steps to follow, and how outcomes are evaluated. A strong decision architecture doesn't just make better decisions—it makes decisions faster, more consistently, and with broader buy-in.

---

61 Brian Armstrong, "How We Make Decisions at Coinbase," Medium, May 8, 2018, https://barmstrong. medium.com/how-we-make-decisions-at-coinbase-cd6c630322e9.

To streamline decision-making, break it into **five phases** with **two recurring disciplines**. This provides a practical framework that boosts visibility, flow, and execution.

UNLOCKING DECISION FLOW

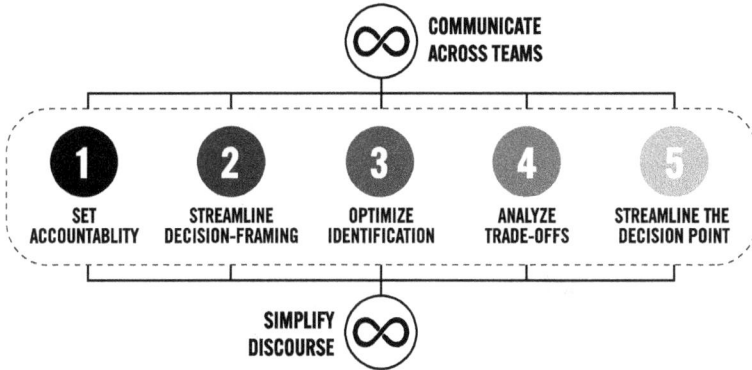

Think of it as building a toolbox. Each phase has tools that bring unique strengths to the table. Some tools address accountability; others sharpen analysis or test assumptions. No single tool works for every decision, but blending techniques creates a flexible, robust process.

An agile mindset amplifies this flow. Agile decision-making values iteration, experimentation, and speed. Teams test, learn, and pivot. They adapt in real time rather than clinging to rigid plans. Agility fosters collaboration and transparency, aligns decisions with customer needs, and drives innovation.

Let's explore how to unlock decision flow.

Every decision needs a **who**—who owns it, who acts, and who informs the process. Without clear roles, accountability fades and decisions stall.

Useful tools to set accountability:

1. **RAPID Framework** (Bain & Co): Clearly defines who recommends, agrees, performs, provides input, and makes the decision.[62]
2. **DACI Model:** Assigns a driver, an approver, contributors, and those who need to be informed to clarify roles and eliminate confusion.[63]

DACI in Action: When Dropbox embarked on a major redesign of its user interface, it used the DACI model to streamline accountability. The **driver** pushed the project forward. The **approver** finalized decisions. **Contributors** shared expertise, and the **informed** stayed in the loop. This clarity eliminated confusion, minimized delays, and delivered a seamless redesign faster than anticipated.[64]

The Impact: Accountability transforms ambiguity into action. Roles are clear, silos disappear, and progress accelerates. Teams trust the process and each other.

---

62 "RAPID® Decision Making," Bain & Company, October 2023, https://www.bain.com/insights/rapid-decision-making/.

63 Sam Ingalls, "DACI Decision-Making Framework: Everything You Need to Know," PMcom, October 4, 2024, https://project-management.com/daci-model/.

64 Dropbox, "Dropbox Goes Virtual First," *Work in Progress* (blog), October 13, 2020, https://blog.dropbox.com/topics/company/dropbox-goes-virtual-first.

Phase 2. Streamline Decision Framing

Good decisions begin with the right frame—a clear problem definition, strategic alignment, and a structured look at options. Poor framing leads to poor choices.

DECISION-FRAMING

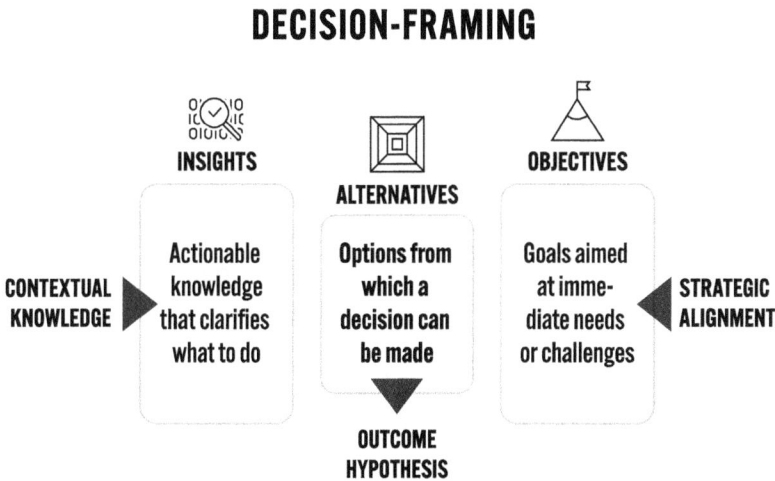

CONTEXTUAL KNOWLEDGE ▶	INSIGHTS / Actionable knowledge that clarifies what to do	ALTERNATIVES / Options from which a decision can be made	OBJECTIVES / Goals aimed at immediate needs or challenges	◀ STRATEGIC ALIGNMENT

OUTCOME HYPOTHESIS

Useful tools to streamline decision framing:

1. **The Rumsfeld Matrix:** Categorizes knowns and unknowns to prioritize risks and focus on what matters.[65]
2. **Mini Delphi Method:** Uses iterative, anonymous group input to forecast solutions and future trends.[66]

---

65 Andrea Mantovani, "Known Knowns, Known Unknowns, Unknown Unknowns & Leadership," Medium, April 28, 2020, https://medium.com/@andreamantovani/known-knowns-known-unknowns-unknown-unknowns-leadership-367f346b0953.

66 Monday.com, "What Is the Delphi Method—Pros, Cons, and Examples," *Monday Blog*, October 27, 2024, https://monday.com/blog/project-management/delphi-technique/.

3. **Outcome Trees:** Maps potential outcomes and consequences, helping teams visualize paths forward and pitfalls to avoid.[67]

Mini Delphi Method in Action: Microsoft used the Mini Delphi Method to predict emerging technology trends. By gathering input from internal and external experts anonymously, it avoided groupthink, refined its assumptions, and forecasted trends that fueled its innovation strategy. This process positioned Microsoft ahead of most competitors in cloud computing and AI.[68]

The Impact

Thoughtful framing ensures teams tackle the right problems and align on the right solutions. Bias is reduced, options are explored, and decisions align with strategy.

Phase 3. Optimize Identification

In complex decisions, new options often emerge when we step back, rethink, or test assumptions.

Useful tools to optimize identification:

1. **Vanishing Options Test:** Forces teams to think creatively by imagining their current options no longer exist.[69]
2. **Eisenhower Matrix:** Prioritizes tasks and decisions by distinguishing between urgency and long-term importance.[70]

---

67 "How to Make a Decision Tree Diagram," Lucidchart, accessed April 21, 2024, https://www.lucidchart.com/pages/how-to-make-a-decision-tree-diagram.

68 William Jones et al., "'For Telling' the Present: Using the Delphi Method to Understand Personal Information Management Practices," *CHI 2015: Proceedings of the 33rd Annual CHI Conference on Human Factors in Computing Systems* (2015): 3513–3522, https://doi.org/10.1145/2702123.2702523.

69 Mikkel Sciegienny, "Vanishing Options Test," Medium, November 12, 2020, https://medium.com/@sciegienny/vanishing-options-test-d0f3ad8399c7.

70 "The Eisenhower Matrix: How to Prioritize Your To-Do List," Asana, January 29, 2025, https://asana.com/resources/eisenhower-matrix.

3. **Stacey Matrix:** Categorizes decisions as simple, complicated, complex, or chaotic, guiding how to approach them.[71]

STACEY MATRIX

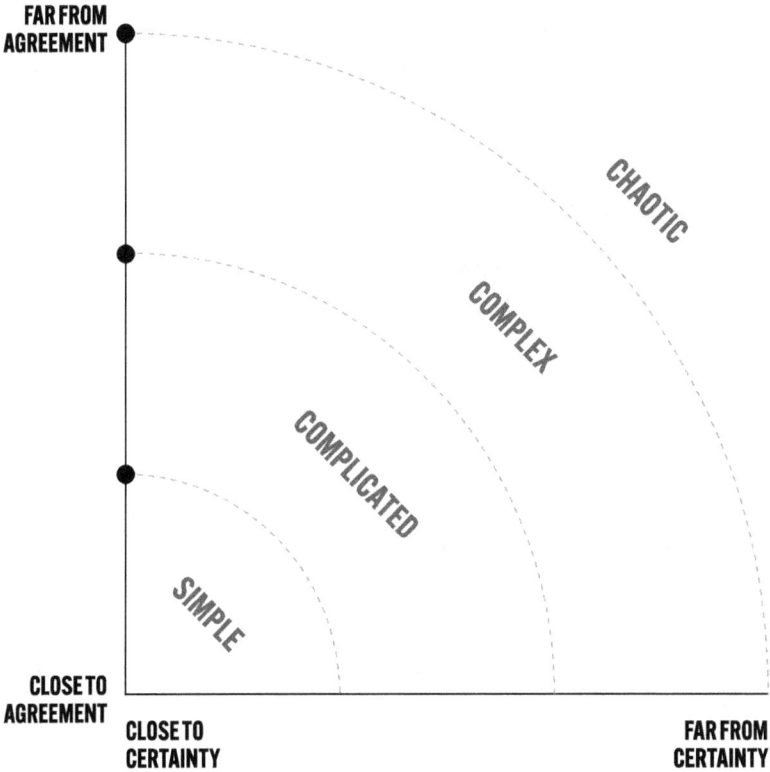

Eisenhower Matrix in Action: Trello, a project management tool, applies the Eisenhower Matrix to help teams prioritize work. Tasks are sorted into "urgent" and "important" categories, ensuring

---

71 "Stacey Matrix," Praxis Framework, accessed April 21, 2024, https://www.praxisframework.org/en/library/stacey-matrix.

critical decisions receive attention while low-priority items are delegated or delayed. This prioritization helps teams focus on strategic goals without getting bogged down by less important tasks.

The Impact

Teams generate fresh ideas, prioritize effectively, and manage complexity with confidence. Better options lead to smarter, faster choices.

Phase 4. Analyze Trade-Offs

Every decision comes with trade-offs. When you choose one path, you let go of another. Understanding this is essential.

Useful tools to analyze trade-offs:

1. **Wargaming:** Simulates future scenarios to identify risks and stress-test strategies.[72]
2. **Trip Wires:** Establishes triggers for revisiting or reassessing decisions based on changing conditions.[73]
3. **"Even over" Statements:** Makes trade-offs explicit, e.g., "Customer satisfaction even over short-term profitability."[74]
4. **Value Engineering:** Treats decisions like bets, pivoting or persevering based on measurable outcomes.[75]

72 Harry Thomsett, "Wargaming Is More Than a Rehearsal," *Harvard Business Review*, October 26, 2010, https://hbr.org/2010/10/wargaming-more-than-a-rehearsa.

73 Chip Heath and Dan Heath, *Decisive: How to Make Better Choices in Life and Work* (Currency, 2013), 218–238.

74 Jurriaan Kamer, "Even/Over Statements: The Prioritization Tool That Brings Your Strategy to Life," *The Ready* (blog), Medium, January 11, 2021, https://medium.com/the-ready/even-overs-the-prioritization-tool-that-brings-your-strategy-to-life-e4f28f2949ac.

75 Barry O'Reilly, "Value Engineering for Outcome-Based Bets," *Explore Insights* (blog), January 22, 2019, https://barryoreilly.com/explore/blog/value-engineering-for-outcome-based-bets/.

Wargaming in Action: Shell used wargaming to prepare for oil-price fluctuations. By simulating potential market scenarios, it anticipated future disruptions and created contingency plans. When oil prices spiked, Shell was ready—outpacing competitors who failed to plan for uncertainty.[76]

The Impact

Clarifying trade-offs sharpens focus, reduces risk, and makes priorities explicit. Teams can pivot quickly when assumptions change.

Phase 5. Streamline the Decision Point

Every decision needs a moment. A point where clarity, speed, and alignment turn talk into action. This is the decision point. Without it, progress halts and momentum fades.

But decisions aren't born in silence. They emerge from discussion. From divergence. From agreement. The process begins with robust conversations—teams exploring perspectives, weighing trade-offs, and debating possibilities. Divergence follows, where differing viewpoints stretch the boundaries of thinking. It's messy but necessary. Only through divergence can the strongest ideas rise to the surface. And then comes the shift: alignment. Agreement crystallizes. Teams unify around a clear path forward.

---

76 Paul J. H. Schoemaker and Cornelius A. J. M. van der Heijden, "Strategic Planning at Royal Dutch/Shell," *Strategic Change* 2, no. 3 (May/June 1993): 157–171, https://doi.org/10.1002/jsc.4240020307.

DECISION-MAKING

PERSPECTIVES	DECISION FRAME
Leader perspectives on choices available to achieve a goal	1. Discussion: Brainstorming and Exploration 2. Divergence: Productive Debate Is Encouraged 3. Agreement: Decision Selection with Commitment to Action

The transition from divergence to agreement depends on one thing: defining the problem. Do this well, and discussions stay grounded. Do it poorly, and even the most productive debates wander. As William Markle wrote, quoting an unnamed Yale professor, "If I had only one hour to solve a problem, I would spend up to two-thirds of that hour in attempting to define what the problem is."[77] Those forty minutes are the foundation. They sharpen focus. They guide teams through the chaos of divergence toward clarity.

Defining the problem starts with three principles: precision, relevance, and scope. **Precision** keeps the focus sharp, eliminating ambiguity. **Relevance** ties the discussion to the outcomes that matter most. **Scope** ensures the problem is broad enough to capture the big picture yet narrow enough to act. Together, these principles keep the conversation productive, divergence meaningful, and agreement impactful.

A clearly defined problem is a compass. It keeps teams aligned, discussions focused, and the decision point clear. Leaders who master this process don't just make decisions—they navigate through discussion, divergence, and agreement to ensure every

---

77 William H. Markle, "The Manufacturing Manager's Skills," in *The Manufacturing Man and His Job*, ed. Robert E. Finley and Henry R. Ziobro (American Management Association, 1966), 18.

decision drives real progress. They lead with purpose. And they deliver results.

Useful tools to streamline the decision point:

1. **OODA Loop:** Rapidly cycles through observe, orient, decide, and act to adapt to changing conditions.[78]
2. **Decision Types:** Classifies decisions as Type 1 (irreversible, high-stakes) or Type 2 (reversible, low-stakes). This helps determine how much rigor is needed for different types of decisions.
3. **Speed Tests:** Assesses urgency, balancing decision quality with the need for speed.
4. **Multichoice Matrix:** Scores options against key criteria for a transparent, structured evaluation.[79]

Decision Types in Action: At Amazon, Jeff Bezos differentiates between Type 1 decisions (irreversible, high-stakes) and Type 2 decisions (reversible, low-stakes). Major decisions, like launching a new product, require careful deliberation, while tweaks to a marketing campaign are delegated for speed. By differentiating decision types, Amazon improves decision velocity and maintains agility at scale.[80]

The Impact

Clarifying decision points turns discussion into action. With tools like these, teams move from debating options to confidently choosing a path—and executing it.

---

78 Brett Crowley, "The OODA Loop," The Decision Lab, accessed April 21, 2024, https://thedecisionlab.com/reference-guide/computer-science/the-ooda-loop.

79 Simon Bell, "Decision Matrix Analysis: Making a Decision by Weighing Up Different Factors," Mindtools, accessed April 21, 2024, https://www.mindtools.com/aksic2i/decision-matrix-analysis.

80 Jeff Haden, "Amazon Founder Jeff Bezos: This Is How Successful People Make Such Smart Decisions," Inc., December 3, 2018, https://www.inc.com/jeff-haden/amazon-founder-jeff-bezos-this-is-how-successful-people-make-such-smart-decisions.html.

These tools don't just clarify decision roles—they ensure the right decision is made at the right time with the right level of rigor.

Strong decision flow transforms chaos into clarity. It starts with accountability, sharpens through framing, expands with better options, clarifies trade-offs, and concludes with decisive action.

These tools aren't just simple process enhancers—when thoughtfully combined across these five phases, they drive real results.

Dropbox aligned teams. Microsoft forecasted trends. Trello prioritized what mattered. Shell anticipated uncertainty. Amazon scaled and improved decision velocity.

When organizations decide how to decide, they don't just make better decisions—they make them faster and with greater confidence, alignment, and impact.

Even the best decision-making process can falter without one critical element: communication. **Clear communication bridges the gap between decisions and execution,** ensuring plans turn into action. Let's explore how to effectively communicate decisions to drive alignment and results.

DRIVING ALIGNMENT THROUGH COMMUNICATION

Decisions need champions, not skeptics. To build champions, communication around decisions must answer three critical questions:

- Why are we making this decision?
- What happened after the decision?
- What did we learn?

Leaders must clearly explain the **what, why,** and **how** behind every decision. This ensures teams align, see the bigger picture, and understand how their actions contribute to organizational goals.

POST-DECISION COMMUNICATION

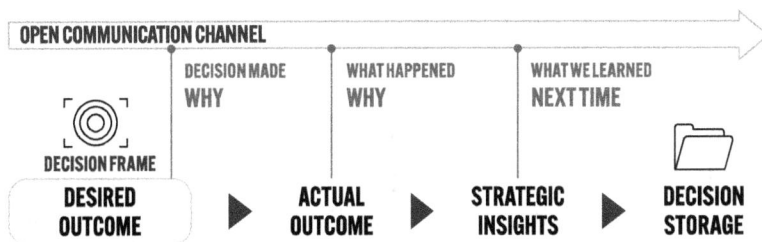

OPEN COMMUNICATION CHANNEL

| DECISION MADE | WHAT HAPPENED | WHAT WE LEARNED |
| WHY | WHY | NEXT TIME |

DECISION FRAME

DESIRED OUTCOME ▶ ACTUAL OUTCOME ▶ STRATEGIC INSIGHTS ▶ DECISION STORAGE

The result of good communication? Decisions don't just happen—they flow seamlessly into execution. **Transparency builds trust. Clarity drives ownership.** Alignment transforms isolated choices into shared momentum.

This flow of communication turns decisions into collective action, reinforcing purpose and eliminating confusion.

STREAMLINE DISCOURSE FOR BETTER RESULTS

Discourse is where decisions take shape. It's where perspectives are shared, assumptions are challenged, and consensus emerges. Done well, it leads to clarity and action. Done poorly, it leads to noise and confusion.

So, how do we simplify discourse to make it productive, focused, and outcome-driven?

We use tools—tools that structure the conversation, surface the hidden risks, and give every voice a seat at the table.

THE TOOLS

1. Premortem Analysis

The premortem flips the script. Instead of asking, "What could go wrong?," teams assume it already has. They imagine the decision has failed spectacularly and then work backward to identify why.[81]

This approach creates a safe space for dissenters—those who see weaknesses but hesitate to speak up. The premortem turns caution into contribution. It surfaces risks before they become realities.

Premortem in Action: NASA famously uses premortem techniques to evaluate mission plans. By imagining failures before liftoff, its teams find risks. They refine solutions and improve mission success rates.[82]

2. Nominal Group Collaboration

Traditional brainstorming? It's noisy, messy, and often dominated by the loudest voice in the room. Nominal group collaboration changes that.

Here's how it works:[83]

- Each team member generates ideas independently.
- The ideas are shared, discussed, and clarified.
- Finally, the group ranks the ideas to prioritize the best solutions.

The result? Everyone contributes. Ideas are judged on merit, not volume. Decisions reflect the collective wisdom of the team.

Nominal Group Collaboration in Action: Toyota used a

---

81 Gary Klein, "Performing a Project Premortem," *Harvard Business Review*, September 2007, https://hbr.org/2007/09/performing-a-project-premortem.

82 Julie White, "The Test Like You Fly (TLYF) Process—Creating Operationally Realistic Tests and Finding Mission Critical Faults Before It's Too Late," *PPI SyEN* 94 (October 30, 2020): 36–37, https://www.ppi-int.com/wp-content/uploads/2020/10/PPI-SyEN-94.pdf.

83 "Nominal Group Collaboration," The Uncertainty Project, accessed April 21, 2024, https://www.theuncertaintyproject.org/tools/nominal-group-collaboration.

method of collaboration to prioritize initiatives in its global growth strategy. It ensured equal input from team members across regions. In doing so, it found innovative opportunities that unstructured discussions would have overlooked.

Simplified discourse changes everything:

- Risks are exposed early, not late.
- The quiet voices are heard alongside the loud ones.
- Ideas sharpen. Consensus strengthens. Decisions improve.

Good discourse doesn't waste time—it saves it. It moves teams from scattered opinions to aligned action, from uncertainty to clarity.

When teams learn to simplify discourse, decision-making becomes what it should be: a process of discovery, alignment, and progress. By simplifying discourse, teams not only improve decisions but also strengthen alignment and trust—key ingredients for flow.

WIRING FOR DECISION FLOW: THE PAYOFF

Wiring for flow pays huge dividends. It strengthens organizational effectiveness, clarity, and success. Clear processes for decision-making ensure the right people are involved. They help make decisions efficiently and maintain accountability. By reducing ambiguity, being transparent, and promoting collaboration, organizations can eliminate bottlenecks. They can align with strategic goals and adapt quickly to change. The result? Informed choices, improved agility, and the confidence to achieve goals with purpose and clarity.

But tools alone won't make your organization decisive. The real shift comes from committing to a culture of clarity, accountability, and action. Decisive organizations clarify **how** to make decisions. They ensure every choice aligns with strategic goals. They also frame decisions with the bigger picture in mind. Mechanisms to disagree, commit, and move forward quickly become essential—because indecision is often the biggest risk of all.

TAKING ACTION

Now is the time to transform your organization's decision flow. Take the first step:

- Audit your decision-making process. Are roles clear, and is the process agile?
- Commit to building a decision architecture that balances speed, clarity, and accountability.
- Invest in tools and practices that foster alignment and empower teams to act decisively.

The future belongs to organizations that don't wait for certainty—they create it. Start today, and wire your organization for unstoppable flow.

SUMMARY

Winners move faster.

They make decisions that are bold, clear, and aligned while others hesitate. In a world of complexity and uncertainty, the ability to act decisively—moving information, people, and strategy seamlessly—is what separates the best from the rest.

To achieve this, organizations must **wire for flow.** Flow turns knowledge into action and decisions into progress. It ensures decisions are made at the right level by the right people with the speed to match opportunity.

It begins with **decision architecture**—a clear, practical system for how decisions are made, communicated, and executed. Wired-for-flow organizations eliminate ambiguity, dismantle bottlenecks, and strengthen alignment. When decisions flow, teams respond faster, act smarter, and adapt with confidence.

Being decisive isn't just about action—it's a process:

- **Interpret the Signals:** Spot trends, anticipate changes, and uncover opportunities.
- **Form Hypotheses:** Test assumptions and make sense of the data.
- **Build Conviction:** Validate options and commit to a path.
- **Take Decisive Action:** Move quickly, decisively, and without overthinking.
- **Communicate Effectively:** Ensure decisions flow across teams with clarity and purpose.

Tools like decision flows, structured frameworks, and wargaming bring order to decisions while keeping teams agile. Techniques such as premortems, trade-off matrices, and realignment checkpoints ensure decisions remain deliberate, adaptable, and fast.

But tools alone aren't enough—**culture affects flow**. Trust, transparency, and accountability transform decision-making into momentum. Leaders must decide how to decide. Teams must prioritize clarity over chaos. Alignment must drive every step.

The reward?

- Decisions don't stall—they accelerate.
- Teams don't splinter—they align.
- Opportunities don't slip away—they are seized with confidence.

In a world that won't wait, **wired-for-flow organizations** lead the way. They act with speed, adapt with agility, and move with purpose.

Start now. Build the systems, embrace the tools, and commit to decisive action. The future belongs to those who flow.

DECISION POINTS

Consider This Scenario: The strategic programs team faces growing friction in decision velocity—a critical priority for driving the next growth phase. What was once an efficient operation has become a bottleneck, weighed down by escalating dependencies, shifting targets, and scattered priorities.

Decision-related communication is spread across multiple platforms, creating confusion, misalignment, and lost progress. Meetings that should drive decisions spiral into tangents, extending timelines and creating analysis paralysis. Leaders recognize the need to untangle dependencies, restore clarity, and accelerate decision flow to keep the organization on track for sustained momentum.

WHICH PATH WOULD YOUR ORGANIZATION CHOOSE?
Path 1: Patch the Gaps

- Address decisions reactively: Tackle issues as they surface and escalate roadblocks when critical decisions stall.
- Introduce an interim communication channel to centralize decision-related updates for better tracking.
- Reinforce meeting discipline: Set tighter time limits and agendas to keep discussions on track and decisions moving.

The Result: Short-term visibility is gained and immediate friction reduced. However, the underlying problems—ambiguity, dependency chaos, and scattered ownership—persist, limiting long-term progress.

Path 2: Build a Sustainable System

- Define roles, responsibilities, and processes to clarify ownership, streamline accountability, and prioritize decisions efficiently.
- Deploy tools to capture decisions, showing who made them, why

they were made, and the trade-offs considered. Build visibility into outcomes to enable learning and alignment.
- Implement a unified communication strategy for decisions— ensuring clarity, consistency, and alignment across teams.
- Map interdependencies across teams and decisions to resolve bottlenecks before they emerge.

The Result: Decision flow becomes a repeatable strength. Teams gain clarity, dependencies untangle, and decisions happen with speed, focus, and accountability. Meetings drive outcomes, not confusion, and momentum builds consistently across the organization.

Your Turn: If this were your organization, would you settle for quick fixes with Path 1—or build the systems and frameworks for lasting decision flow with Path 2?

Our Take: Quick wins offer relief, but true growth demands systems that align people, decisions, and priorities. Path 2 unlocks clarity, accelerates decisions, and positions the organization to act faster, smarter, and with confidence.

KEY TAKEAWAYS AND DISCUSSION QUESTIONS
1. HIGH-QUALITY DECISION FLOW DRIVES RESULTS

Organizations that wire for flow consistently make fast, high-quality decisions. These decisions align with enterprise goals, reduce friction, and propel competitive advantage. The winners move quickly, while hesitation creates hidden costs—stalled innovation, misalignment, and frustration.

Questions to Reflect On:

- Where are the biggest bottlenecks slowing our organization's decision flow today?
- Are our decisions being made at the right level of the organization, with the right level of rigor?

- How can we better align decision-making with enterprise-wide value rather than isolated goals?
- What are the hidden costs of slow or ineffective decisions in our organization?

2. NAVIGATING UNCERTAINTY REQUIRES DECISIVE ACTION

Decisive organizations thrive under uncertainty. They interpret signals, form hypotheses, test assumptions, act confidently, and communicate with precision. A repeatable process for embracing uncertainty—like the **signal → hypothesis → conviction → action → communication** cycle—turns disruption into opportunity.

Questions to Reflect On:

- How well does our organization interpret signals from the business environment to anticipate opportunities and risks?
- Do we have a structured process for making decisions when uncertainty is high?
- How can we encourage a culture that embraces "70 percent confidence" for speed without sacrificing accountability?
- What practices or tools can help us validate assumptions and build conviction quickly?

3. DECISION ARCHITECTURE CREATES ALIGNMENT AND ACCOUNTABILITY

A well-designed decision architecture clarifies roles, responsibilities, and processes—turning decision-making into a repeatable strength. By "deciding how to decide," organizations eliminate ambiguity, reduce bottlenecks, and ensure decisions happen quickly, consistently, and with clear ownership.

Questions to Reflect On:

- Does our current decision-making process clarify who is accountable, who contributes, and who approves?
- What tools or frameworks (e.g., RAPID, DACI) can help clarify roles and streamline accountability?
- How can we document and communicate decisions effectively to ensure transparency and alignment across teams?
- What recurring obstacles or misalignments can a clearer decision architecture help us resolve?

4. TOOLS AND FRAMEWORKS ACCELERATE DECISION FLOW

Decision flow improves with structured tools across five phases:

- **Accountability:** The RAPID framework clarifies decision roles.
- **Framing:** Outcome trees visualize consequences and options.
- **Identification:** The Vanishing Options Test spurs creativity.
- **Trade-Offs:** Wargaming simulates risks and strengthens strategies.
- **Execution:** OODA loops drive rapid, confident action.

Questions to Reflect On:

- Which phases of our decision flow (e.g., accountability, framing, trade-offs) present the greatest challenges today?
- How can tools like the Eisenhower Matrix, premortem analysis, or wargaming improve our decision process?
- Are we classifying decisions effectively (e.g., Type 1 versus Type 2) to balance speed and rigor?
- How can we integrate tools into daily operations to build a repeatable, agile decision flow?

5. COMMUNICATION AND DISCOURSE
TURN DECISIONS INTO ACTION

Strong decisions fail without strong communication. Effective decision flow requires teams to communicate the **what**, **why**, and **how** clearly while simplifying discourse to resolve risks, align perspectives, and maintain focus.

Questions to Reflect On:

- How can we improve communication so decisions are understood, trusted, and executed efficiently?
- Are we fostering productive discourse that aligns teams and reduces noise during decision-making?
- What tools (e.g., premortems, nominal group collaboration) can help surface hidden risks and give every voice a chance to contribute?
- How can leadership ensure decisions are communicated consistently across teams and levels?

KNOWLEDGE MAP
WIRING FOR FLOW UNLOCKS DECISIVE ACTION

- Flow transforms context into momentum, enabling fast, aligned decision-making.
- A clear **decision architecture** provides the framework for accountability, consistency, and speed.
- Organizations that wire for flow make better decisions, act confidently, and maintain alignment—turning uncertainty into opportunity.

THE FIVE PHASES OF DECISION FLOW

I. **Set Accountability**
   A. Define who recommends, agrees, performs, provides input, and makes decisions (e.g., RAPID or DACI framework).

B. Clarity on roles eliminates ambiguity and accelerates progress.

2. **Streamline Decision Framing**
   A. Frame the problem clearly, align it with strategy, and explore options.
   B. Tools like the Rumsfeld Matrix, outcome trees, and the Mini Delphi Method reduce bias and sharpen focus.

3. **Optimize Identification**
   A. Generate new ideas, prioritize effectively, and rethink assumptions.
   B. Tools like the Vanishing Options Test, Eisenhower Matrix, and Stacey Matrix guide teams through complexity.

4. **Analyze Trade-Offs**
   A. Clarify the trade-offs inherent in every decision and prepare for change.
   B. Techniques like wargaming, trip wires, and "even over" statements sharpen focus and reduce risk.

5. **Streamline the Decision Point**
   A. Move from discussion to decisive action with clarity and speed.
   B. Tools like OODA loops, decision types (Type 1 and Type 2), and speed tests focus teams on execution.

SIMPLIFY DISCOURSE TO IMPROVE DECISIONS AND ACCELERATE ALIGNMENT

Effective decision flow depends on clear, transparent communication. Leaders must explain the why, what, and how behind every decision to align teams, build trust, and drive execution. By simplifying discourse and fostering productive conversations, organizations surface hidden risks, resolve conflicts, and ensure decisions are understood and acted upon with clarity and purpose.

- **Clarity:** Decision roles, processes, and trade-offs are explicit and visible.
- **Confidence:** Teams act decisively and pivot quickly when conditions change.
- **Alignment:** Decisions connect seamlessly to strategy, driving unified action.
- **Agility:** The organization adapts rapidly to uncertainty and complexity.

When flow is wired into an organization, decisions sharpen, momentum builds, and progress becomes inevitable.

CHAPTER 6

WIRE FOR ACTION

"Effort and courage are not enough without purpose and direction."

—JOHN F. KENNEDY

Strategy without execution is a dream. Execution without strategy is chaos. To thrive, organizations must align the two seamlessly.

Misalignment costs organizations more than wasted effort. It harms performance, innovation, and long-term success. Companies that cannot align strategy with action often fall behind. However, those with strong alignment outperform their peers.

Ongoing research highlights just how pervasive this challenge is:

- **Sixty-one percent** of executives report a disconnect between strategy and execution, often due to misaligned functions, resulting in wasted resources.[84]

---

84 The Economist, *Why Good Strategies Fail: Lessons for the C-Suite* (The Economist Intelligence Unit, 2013), 6, https://www.pmi.org/-/media/pmi/documents/public/pdf/learning/thought-leadership/why-good-strategies-fail-report.pdf.

- **Thirty-three percent** of leaders identify silos and conflicting departmental objectives as a significant source of organizational inefficiency.[85]
- **Thirty-seven percent** of executives struggle to effectively communicate strategic priorities across all levels of their organizations.[86]
- **Thirty percent** of CDAOs said their top challenge is the inability to measure data, analytics and AI impact on business outcomes.[87]
- **Seventy-four percent** of executives admit their strategies are not well translated into concrete actions.
- **Seventy-nine percent** of executives worry their firms lack resources to implement strategy.

The numbers paint a clear picture: Translating strategic vision into actionable plans remains one of the most significant challenges leaders face.

Why? Alignment is more than setting objectives. It's about driving execution through consistent decisions, priorities, and resource allocation. Execution demands deep coordination and a willingness to recalibrate systems so they align with strategic goals.

Yet, execution is rarely straightforward. Misalignment creeps in when:

1. Departments operate on competing priorities.

---

85 Patrick Simon et al., *The State of Organizations: 2023* (McKinsey & Company, 2023), 12–13, https://www.mckinsey.com/~/media/mckinsey/business%20functions/people%20and%20organizational%20performance/our%20insights/the%20state%20of%20organizations%202023/the-state-of-organizations-2023.pdf.

86 KPMG, "2023 CEO Outlook," October 2023, available at https://kpmg.com/xx/en/home/insights/2023/10/ceo-outlook-2023.html.

87 Press Release, "Majority of CDAOs Do Not Have Defined Business Impact Metrics for Use Cases," Gartner, February 20, 2025, https://www.gartner.com/en/newsroom/press-releases/2025-02-20-gartner-survey-finds-one-third-of-cdaos-cite-measuring-data-analytics-and-ai-impact-as-top-challenge?utm_term=1741688642&utm_campaign=SM_GB_YOY_GTR_SOC_SF1_SM-PR-GTS-IT&utm_source=linkedin,threads,twitter&utm_medium=social&utm_content=Gartner+for+IT,Gartner_inc,gartner_inc.

2. Resources are stretched too thin to deliver on commitments.
3. Leadership struggles to communicate goals effectively across levels of the organization.

To bridge the gap between strategy and execution, organizations must wire for action. This means creating systems that turn vision into action. Teams must understand priorities, optimize resources, and focus on measurable progress.

Vision sets the path, but execution requires coordination. Silos often slow progress, but they don't have to. **The answer isn't to break silos—it's to make them work smarter.**

BALANCE FREEDOM AND FOCUS TO ACCELERATE TEAMS

The journey from strategy to execution demands focus, alignment, and the ability to adapt in real time. Many organizations fall into a familiar trap: They either impose too much structure, which stifles creativity and slows decisions, or too little, which leads to confusion, misaligned efforts, and wasted resources.

The answer isn't to dismantle silos or impose rigid rules—it's to strike the right balance between freedom and focus.

FROM SILOS TO ACCELERATORS

Silos get a bad reputation, but they're not the enemy. When designed with transparency and discipline, silos allow teams to work independently, move quickly, and innovate while staying aligned with the big picture.

What we need is **transparent silos** that turn barriers into accelerators by answering a few essential questions:

- **Why are we doing this?** Clarify the purpose, goals, and strategic intent behind the work.

- **Is it working?** Share results openly to build trust and measure success.
- **What are the trade-offs?** Make the choices and alternatives visible to align priorities.
- **What have we learned?** Capture both successes and failures to improve future decisions.

This transparency gives teams the freedom to move independently while ensuring their work stays connected to organizational goals.

FINDING THE SWEET SPOT

Freedom without alignment is chaos. Alignment without freedom is bureaucracy. Leaders must find the sweet spot—a balance where teams have the autonomy to innovate and the clarity to stay focused on strategic priorities. **This is where leaders walk a fine line.**

Here's how great leaders strike that balance:

1. **Trust and Openness:** Leaders share context and provide clarity. Teams feel ownership and share critical information without friction.
2. **Alignment with Flexibility:** Shared goals set the direction, but teams have the freedom to decide how to get there.
3. **Minimalist Structure:** Rules exist, but only the ones that matter. Guardrails provide focus without creating unnecessary friction.

Imagine a well-run IT organization. Software teams experiment with tools, ideas, and code. They're free to innovate and adjust quickly. But this freedom doesn't exist in isolation—it's guided by shared goals, clear priorities, and regular communication. Technology and business teams row together. The result? Creativity flourishes, momentum builds, and teams adapt confidently.

When teams operate with freedom and focus:

- Innovation thrives because teams aren't micromanaged.
- Decisions happen faster because teams have clarity on their priorities.
- Progress is fueled because silos collaborate rather than compete.

The magic happens when autonomy fuels progress—not confusion. Leaders who build trust, provide clarity, and simplify alignment enable teams to move quickly and think big while ensuring every effort pushes the organization forward.

Balance isn't about choosing between freedom and alignment. **It's about creating a system where both exist** so teams can accelerate progress without losing sight of the destination. And in doing so, they build an organization **where every step, every choice, every action moves the company forward.**

Once silos are aligned and balance is achieved, the real challenge begins: translating strategy into execution. Success hinges on building a bridge that connects big ideas with real-world results.

IMPROVE THE BRIDGE BETWEEN STRATEGY AND EXECUTION

Alignment is the bridge where big ideas become real-world results. But building this bridge demands balance—where autonomy empowers innovation and alignment ensures every effort drives the organization forward.

When alignment hits the sweet spot, it accelerates strategy into real results—connecting vision, action, and measurable outcomes. Teams move faster, decisions happen with confidence, and progress becomes unstoppable.

The numbers tell the story: **only 29 percent of strategists believe their organizations adapt quickly to disruption.**[88] Why? Vague objectives. Flawed processes. Leaders who are disengaged.

---

88 Jackie Wiles, "What Functional Leaders Should Know About Scenario Planning," Gartner, July 12, 2024, https://www.gartner.com/smarterwithgartner/what-functional-leaders-should-know-about-scenario-planning?source=BLD-200123&utm_medium=social&utm_source=bambu&utm_campaign=SM_GB_YOY_GTR_SOC_BU1_SM-BA-SWG-ART-CF.

Alignment—connecting strategy to execution—is where organizations win or lose.

Strategy sets the vision—defining the where and the why.

Execution delivers the results. It answers the what, the how, and the when.

But between strategy and execution lies the bridge—and that bridge is where alignment happens.

When organizations get it right, the benefits are clear:

- **Rapid response** to market shifts.
- **Enhanced operational efficiency** for smoother workflows.
- **Higher engagement and accountability** across teams.
- **Increased productivity** that drives measurable results.
- **Greater customer satisfaction** through consistent value.

Alignment isn't just about setting goals—it's about ensuring every part of the organization pulls in the same direction. To achieve this, leaders must evaluate alignment from multiple perspectives—financial, operational, and strategic—so decisions are informed, connected, and actionable.

USING ALIGNMENT FRAMES

Alignment frames act as a compass, guiding leaders to evaluate decisions across critical dimensions. Key frames include:

- **Financial:** Are resources allocated to top priorities?
  - Example: Redirecting budget from underperforming initiatives to high-growth areas ensures the organization focuses on the most impactful opportunities.
- **Technology:** Does our infrastructure support strategy?
  - Example: Investing in cloud tools to streamline cross-team collaboration accelerates execution and improves efficiency.
- **Governance:** Are decisions aligned with goals?

- Example: Standardizing approval processes reduces bottlenecks, enabling faster decision-making across departments.
- **Risk Management:** Are we balancing risks against strategic opportunities?
  - Example: Conducting regular risk assessments ensures mitigation plans align with long-term objectives.
- **Innovation:** Are we prioritizing ideas that drive long-term growth?
  - Example: Funding experimental projects in emerging technologies positions the company ahead of market trends.
- **Customer-centric:** Do plans meet evolving customer needs and expectations?
  - Example: Creating customer feedback loops ensures product development aligns with user demands.
- **Supply Chain:** Are operations efficient and aligned with cost and delivery goals?
  - Example: Optimizing supplier relationships reduces costs and improves delivery timelines.
- **Competitive:** Are we staying ahead of market trends and competitor moves?
  - Example: Monitoring industry shifts and proactively adapting strategies keep the organization competitive.
- **Talent Management:** Are we developing the right skills to support strategic goals?
  - Example: Implementing targeted training programs ensures the workforce is prepared for future challenges.
- **Capability:** Do we have the right systems, processes, and expertise in place?
  - Example: Building scalable processes supports both current and future growth initiatives.
- **Operational:** Are cross-team dependencies managed for efficiency and flow?
  - Example: Mapping dependencies and resolving overlaps streamline collaboration and eliminate delays.

By systematically addressing these frames, leaders ensure alignment across every facet of the organization, turning strategy into actionable and measurable progress.

TRANSLATING VISION INTO ACTION

Alignment frames provide the foundation, but planning is where the rubber meets the road. Organizations must move from broad strategy into specific, actionable steps that teams can deliver.

UNLOCKING STRATEGIC ADVANTAGE

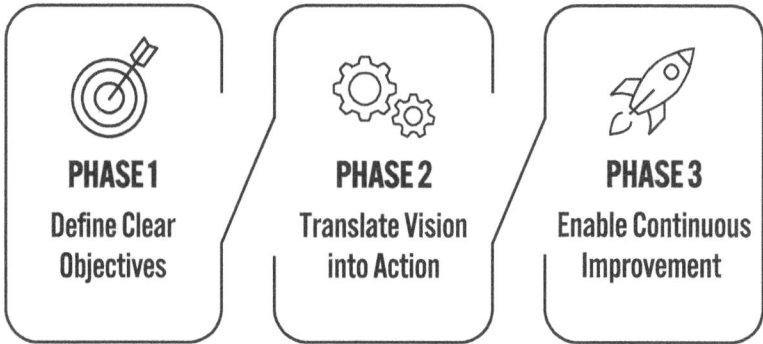

PHASE 1
Define Clear
Objectives

PHASE 2
Translate Vision
into Action

PHASE 3
Enable Continuous
Improvement

This journey unfolds in three broad phases:

- **Phase 1. Define Clear Objectives:** Turn vision into measurable goals.
- **Phase 2. Translate Vision into Action:** Focus execution through cadence and feedback.
- **Phase 3. Enable Continuous Improvement:** Build momentum with measured improvement loops integrated into your operating rhythm.

Alignment is the engine. Strategy fuels it. Execution drives it. Together, they transform complexity into progress, uncertainty into opportunity, and vision into results. That's where the magic happens.

Organizations that master the flow from strategy to execution don't just keep pace—they pull ahead. They move faster, adapt smarter, and create lasting value. Now, let's dive deeper into each phase.

PHASE 1: DEFINE CLEAR OBJECTIVES

Every great journey begins with a vision—one that defines why the organization exists, where it is headed, and how it plans to get there. A clear, compelling vision provides direction, aligns teams, and serves as the foundation for decision-making.

However, in large organizations, aligning teams to the vision is a challenge. Communication fragments, updates lose impact, misalignment creeps in, and progress slows.

To fix this, leaders must overcommunicate the vision and make its purpose explicit at every level:

- **Tell the Story:** Reinforce the why behind the work at every meeting, town hall, and update.
- **Make It Visible:** Tie performance metrics directly to strategic objectives so teams see the connection.
- **Keep It Fresh:** Vision isn't static. Adapt it as market conditions shift or leadership changes.
- **Build Buy-In:** Involve employees in shaping and refining the vision. People commit more when they feel ownership.

A clear vision alone isn't enough. Vision needs **specific, deliberate choices** to translate into action. Winning strategies require focus—making hard choices about where to play and how to win.

A. G. Lafley and Roger Martin's book *Playing to Win* offers a powerful framework:[89]

- What are our aspirations?
- Where will we play?
- How will we win?
- What capabilities do we need?
- What systems must support us?

Similarly, **Richard Rumelt** highlights in *Good Strategy/Bad Strategy* that **good strategy isn't a wish list.** A good strategy identifies real problems, prioritizes critical issues, and focuses resources on clear, coherent actions.[90]

The lesson? Vision becomes action when leaders make bold, focused choices—and avoid the trap of vague or wishful thinking.

Turn Vision into Objectives

Once bold choices are made, organizations need clear, measurable objectives to translate strategy into execution.

A popular method is OKRs. **OKRs provide a proven framework for turning strategy into actionable steps.** Used by companies like **Google,** OKRs align aspirational goals (objectives) with specific, measurable outcomes.[91] OKRs comprise:

1. **Objectives:** What are we aiming to achieve?
2. **Key Results:** How will we measure progress?

---

89 A. G. Lafley and Roger L. Martin, *Playing to Win: How Strategy Really Works* (Harvard Business Review Press, 2013), 14–15.

90 Richard Rumelt, *Good Strategy/Bad Strategy: The Difference and Why It Matters* (Crown Business, 2011), 2.

91 John Doerr, *Measure What Matters: How Google, Bono, and the Gates Foundation Rock the World with OKRs* (Portfolio/Penguin, 2018), 7.

The result? Teams move with purpose, clarity, and focus—tracking results that tie directly to the vision.[92]

Balance Strategic Time Horizons

Alignment also requires balancing priorities across short-term needs and long-term innovations. A popular method is investing across three horizons:[93]

- **Horizon 1:** This horizon addresses the core business. It focuses on protecting current revenue streams, optimizing operations, and defending market share.
- **Horizon 2:** This horizon targets emerging opportunities. It invests in growth areas that have the potential to fuel tomorrow's success by nurturing new markets, products, and ideas.
- **Horizon 3:** This horizon is about long-term bets. It encourages taking risks on innovation and research and development (R&D), with a focus on breakthroughs that could redefine the future.

The challenge? Balancing all three without neglecting any.

Phase 1 Recap

- **Clarify the Vision:** Inspire teams with a clear "why" that drives focus.
- **Make Bold Choices:** Define where to play, how to win, and where to focus resources.
- **Translate Vision into Objectives:** Turn strategy into measurable, actionable goals with OKRs or another goal framework.

---

92 Bryan Schuldt, "27 Companies That Use OKRs and Success Stories," *ODT* (blog), Tability, March 19, 2024, https://www.tability.io/odt/articles/companies-that-use-okrs-and-success-stories.

93 Steve Blank, "McKinsey's Three Horizons Model Defined Innovation for Years: Here's Why It No Longer Applies," *Harvard Business Review*, February 1, 2019, https://hbr.org/2019/02/mckinseys-three-horizons-model-defined-innovation-for-years-heres-why-it-no-longer-applies.

- **Balance Horizons:** Deliver today, invest in tomorrow, and bet on the future.

When organizations get this right, they grow sustainably. Teams deliver immediate results while building the foundation for future success—ensuring the vision is achieved across time horizons.

With a clear vision and defined objectives in place, the next step is to translate these into actionable steps. Execution requires more than plans—it demands agility, alignment, and a relentless focus on progress.

PHASE 2: TRANSLATE VISION INTO ACTION

A clear vision is just the starting point. Success lies in converting that vision into strategic goals and actionable objectives—steps that guide teams to execute with precision. Every member of the organization must understand not only the big picture but how their work connects to it. When vision becomes action, teams gain focus, alignment, and the agility to adapt.

Design a Process to Refine Your Strategy

Execution thrives on agility—where teams read the signals, uncover opportunities, and adapt swiftly as new information unfolds. It's less about rigidity and more about staying light on your feet. Here are four steps to get you moving:

1. **Explore Futures:** Develop a long-term vision using future-scenario simulations.
2. **Explore Directions:** Assess risks and prioritize investments over a six- to twelve-month period. Evaluate lever combinations and timing.
3. **Explore Opportunities:** Determine success criteria and design work chunks for the next quarter based on investments.

4. **Explore Work:** Develop hypotheses from initiatives to meet success criteria—plan for upcoming sprints or months to validate bets.

STRATEGIC REFINEMENT

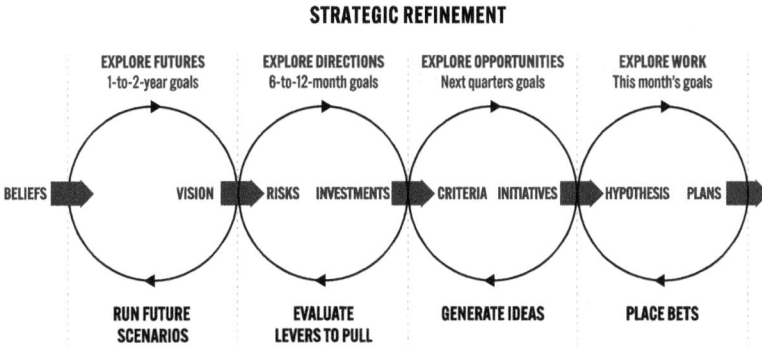

EXPLORE FUTURES	EXPLORE DIRECTIONS	EXPLORE OPPORTUNITIES	EXPLORE WORK
1-to-2-year goals	6-to-12-month goals	Next quarters goals	This month's goals

BELIEFS → VISION → RISKS INVESTMENTS → CRITERIA INITIATIVES → HYPOTHESIS PLANS →

| RUN FUTURE SCENARIOS | EVALUATE LEVERS TO PULL | GENERATE IDEAS | PLACE BETS |

The result? Teams remain attuned to real-time conditions, enabling sharper decisions, tighter alignment, and sustained momentum—turning strategy into action and plans into progress.

Navigate the Dependency Maze

Modern organizations are complex, interconnected systems. Teams depend on other teams. Services depend on technology. Goals depend on shared resources.

Dependencies complicate planning and execution. An example is when engineering teams are building interconnected parts that only work when interfaced together. When overlooked, dependencies slow progress, increase friction, and limit agility.

To navigate the **dependency maze:**

1. **Map the Dependencies:** Identify where teams, systems, and processes intersect.
2. **Adopt Agile Practices:** Plan in smaller, iterative steps to reduce risk and improve adaptability.

3. **Use Tools for Visibility:** Real-time dependency-tracking software helps teams anticipate impacts and manage change.

Mapping dependencies isn't just about solving today's problems. It reveals opportunities to redesign workflows, improve collaboration, and increase efficiency. Over time, this visibility becomes a strategic advantage—making the organization faster, smarter, and more resilient.

Balance Trade-Offs

Trade-offs are inevitable. Do we prioritize growth or efficiency? Speed or quality? Today's revenue or tomorrow's innovation?

Strategic portfolio management helps resolve these trade-offs. It evaluates priorities based on:

- **Alignment** with strategic goals.
- **Resource availability** (budget, people, time).
- **Potential impact** on overall performance.

Trade-off analysis provides clarity:

- What risks are we taking?
- What resources are needed?
- What are the costs of one path versus another?

The result? Leaders make informed choices, teams align, and the organization moves forward cohesively.

Establish a Cadence for Effective Interlock

The path from strategy to execution requires synchronized movement across teams—without sacrificing autonomy. Enter **interlock:**

a regular cadence for alignment that balances independence with organizational unity.

Interlock ensures clarity, coordination, and smooth handoffs:

- **Goals** are set.
- **Progress** is shared.
- **Dependencies** are managed.

A simple quarterly interlock might look like this:

QUARTERLY INTERLOCK

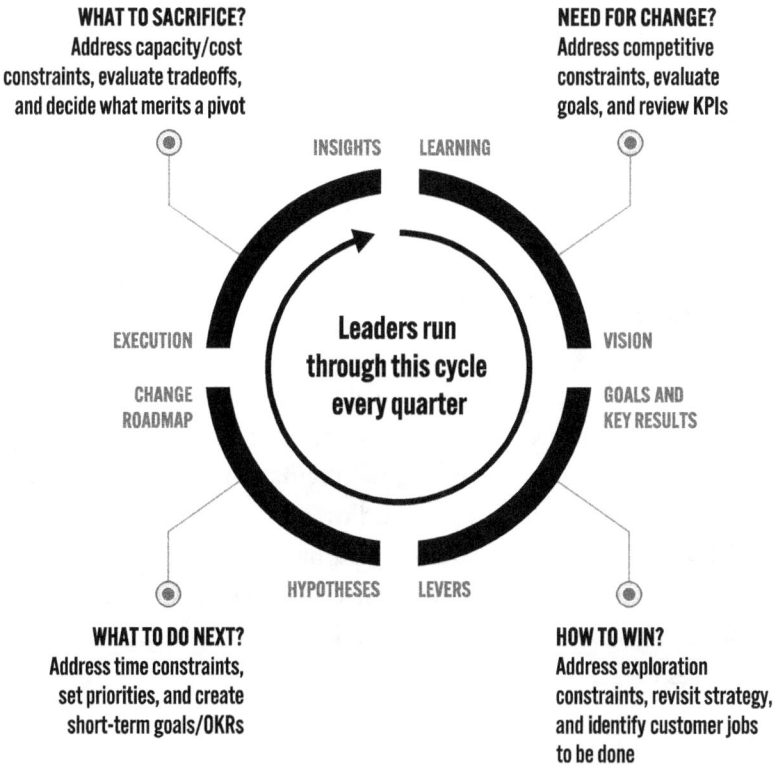

WHAT TO SACRIFICE?
Address capacity/cost constraints, evaluate tradeoffs, and decide what merits a pivot

NEED FOR CHANGE?
Address competitive constraints, evaluate goals, and review KPIs

INSIGHTS   LEARNING

EXECUTION

Leaders run through this cycle every quarter

VISION

CHANGE ROADMAP

GOALS AND KEY RESULTS

HYPOTHESES   LEVERS

WHAT TO DO NEXT?
Address time constraints, set priorities, and create short-term goals/OKRs

HOW TO WIN?
Address exploration constraints, revisit strategy, and identify customer jobs to be done

Focus on **alignment, not friction.** It's not about overloading teams with process—it's about streamlining communication so everyone knows:

- Where we're headed.
- How we're progressing.
- What needs to adjust.

The result? Teams stay aligned without losing their freedom to execute.

Phase 2 Recap

- **Act on Insights:** Continuously adapt priorities and plans based on real-time signals.
- **Simplify Dependencies:** Map workflows, reduce friction, and unlock faster progress.
- **Prioritize Trade-Offs:** Make informed choices to align decisions with strategic goals.
- **Stay Agile:** Use interlock rhythms to balance structure with flexibility.

Teams that master Phase 2 excel at turning plans into measurable progress—without losing sight of the bigger vision. With vision translated into clear goals, aligned teams, and actionable plans, execution doesn't just happen—it flows.

Now that things are working, you have to keep them working. Continuous improvement isn't a nice-to-have—**it's the engine of sustained progress.** When every cycle refines the next, the reward becomes clear: progress that compounds.

PHASE 3: ENABLE CONTINUOUS IMPROVEMENT

Continuous improvement is the lifeblood of high-performing organizations. It seems obvious—who doesn't want to get better? But in practice, it's deceptively hard. Why?

By the time strategy moves into execution, teams are fully absorbed in delivering results. The focus shifts to implementation, deadlines, and performance. Interlock sessions wrap up, and the plans are in motion. The problem? The opportunity to **reflect**, **refine**, and **improve** is often lost in the urgency of execution.

The result is a cycle of reactivity. Teams race to deliver without pausing to identify what's working, what isn't, and where the process can improve. Opportunities for innovation, efficiency, and better execution slip through the cracks.

To break this cycle, continuous improvement must be **deliberate** and **lightweight**. It doesn't need to slow teams down. Instead, it should enhance their ability to adapt, optimize, and accelerate outcomes.

Build a Culture of Improvement

The secret to continuous improvement is **discipline**—small, consistent actions that create big results over time. Here's how to make it part of your flow:

1. **Reflect Regularly:** Build lightweight mechanisms to review what worked, what didn't, and what can be improved. This isn't about heavy postmortems—it's about focused, actionable feedback loops.
2. **Prioritize Opportunities:** Identify the improvements that will have the biggest impact. Fixing every problem isn't realistic. Focus on what will improve flow, alignment, and outcomes.
3. **Learn and Apply:** Turn insights into action. Use lessons from one cycle to make the next cycle better—faster decisions, smoother execution, and fewer bottlenecks.

Picture this: A team finishes a quarterly execution cycle. Instead of diving straight into the next phase, they pause for a **thirty-minute reflection session to share:**

1. **What worked?** Teams share successes and highlight practices worth repeating.
2. **What didn't work?** Teams identify challenges, blockers, and inefficiencies that slowed progress.
3. **What should we do differently?** Teams prioritize one to two key improvements to test in the next cycle.

This simple, focused process keeps improvement lightweight and actionable. It builds momentum without interrupting execution.

Embed Continuous Improvement from End to End

To ensure continuous improvement becomes part of your organization's DNA:

1. **Make Feedback Cyclical:** Integrate lightweight feedback loops at the end of every interlock and execution phase. Continuous improvement isn't a one-time activity—it's ongoing.
2. **Capture Knowledge:** Document key insights from each cycle. Use this "living knowledge" to inform future strategies, align teams, and prevent repeat mistakes.
3. **Simplify Tools:** Use simple templates or digital tools to capture what works and what needs adjustment. Keep it easy, fast, and accessible for teams.

Continuous improvement isn't about perfection. It's about momentum. Every small tweak makes the flow from strategy to execution stronger:

- Teams accelerate because they've eliminated blockers.

- Decisions improve because insights are applied to each new cycle.
- Alignment deepens because everyone learns together and adapts as one.

When organizations commit to continuous improvement, success isn't accidental—it's inevitable.

Phase 3 Recap

- **Reflect Fast:** Use quick, focused feedback loops to capture insights.
- **Prioritize Impact:** Target the highest-value opportunities for improvement.
- **Embed Learning:** Apply lessons to drive growth, efficiency, and continuous momentum.

By refining each cycle, you transform good execution into unstoppable momentum—an organization that keeps getting better.

Momentum fuels progress. Continuous improvement transforms small wins into sustainable impact, accelerating execution, decisions, and alignment.

The result? A cycle of **execution and reflection** that propels the organization forward—faster, smarter, and better every time.

PUTTING IT ALL TOGETHER

When you're wired for action, strategy flows into execution, progress compounds, and every team moves with clarity and confidence.

Navigating execution isn't about perfection—it's about progress. This chapter offers a flexible framework to help you align strategy with action, not a rigid prescription. Think of it as the skeleton for organizational coherence: strong enough to provide structure, flexible enough to adapt to your culture.

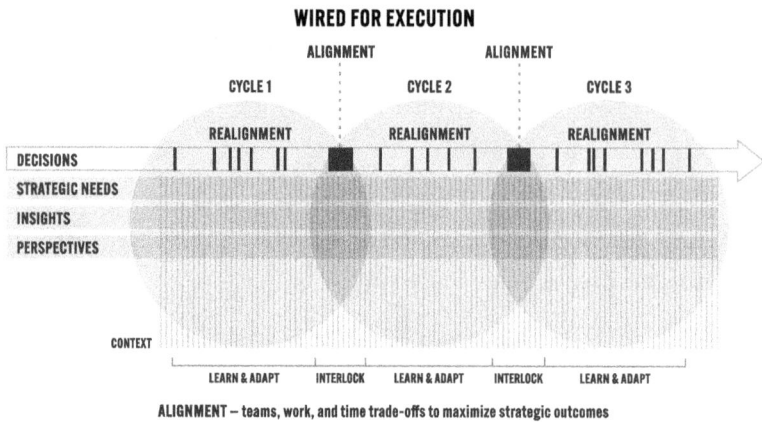

WIRED FOR EXECUTION

ALIGNMENT — teams, work, and time trade-offs to maximize strategic outcomes

Once this foundation is in place, you can layer on tools, techniques, and methodologies tailored to your organization's needs. The key principles of **wiring for action** remain constant:

1. **Cultivate the Right Mindset:** Embrace transparent silos and thoughtful processes that empower autonomy while preserving alignment.
2. **Clarify the Vision:** Articulate the "why" behind every action. Prioritize effectively, and balance short-term execution with long-term sustainability.
3. **Set Clear Objectives:** Define goals that align with strategy. Gather insights, establish effective interlock, and enable alignment across the organization.
4. **Make Smart Trade-Offs:** Weigh competing priorities with clarity. Minimize dependencies, and create adaptable systems that foster agility.
5. **Prioritize Continuous Improvement:** Build lightweight feedback loops to refine processes, learn from experience, and optimize execution flow.

THE REWARD OF BEING WIRED FOR ACTION

When you're wired for action, teams don't work in silos—they work in sync. Everyone knows what the other groups are doing, how well it's working, and what they've learned. The result is a system that drives:

1. **Improved Decision-Making:** Every decision aligns with strategy, supported by clear priorities and real-time insights.
2. **Clarity on Objectives:** Teams know exactly what to focus on—and why it matters—enabling sharper execution and faster progress.
3. **A Culture of Learning and Adaptation:** Reflection becomes routine. Teams get better, smarter, and faster with every cycle.

Start now. Build the systems, foster the mindset, and empower your teams to deliver with clarity, agility, and purpose.

Because when you're wired for action, progress isn't just possible—it's inevitable. 🚀

SUMMARY

Winners turn strategy into action.

Organizations that thrive don't just set ambitious goals—they align every team, decision, and resource to deliver real results. Alignment is the bridge between strategy and execution, ensuring vision translates into progress.

Alignment connects bold ideas to measurable outcomes.

It turns silos into accelerators.

It balances freedom with focus.

When teams understand priorities, they execute with confidence.

When teams communicate clearly, they adapt with speed.

When teams align, execution flows.

And when execution flows, progress becomes unstoppable.

Wiring for action isn't about rigid processes—it's about building systems that empower teams to move quickly while staying aligned:

- **Clarify the Vision:** Inspire teams with a clear "why" that drives purpose and focus.
- **Strike the Balance:** Foster autonomy while ensuring alignment through trust, shared goals, and transparency.
- **Act on Insights:** Use real-time signals to adapt plans, resolve dependencies, and maintain momentum.
- **Build Cadence and Flexibility:** Establish rhythms for alignment while staying agile enough to realign as conditions change.
- **Prioritize Continuous Improvement:** Capture lessons, refine processes, and turn reflection into progress.

The payoff? Execution accelerates. Teams innovate, align, and adapt with confidence. Misalignment disappears, and every decision propels the organization forward.

Organizations wired for action don't just keep up—they pull ahead. Progress compounds, momentum builds, and strategy turns into results.

Start now. Align your vision, empower your teams, and build systems that transform ideas into unstoppable progress. 🚀

DECISION POINTS

Consider This Scenario: A rapidly growing firm faces a critical challenge. While its product development teams thrive on creative freedom, this autonomy has led to misalignment with strategic goals. Teams delivered technologically advanced projects, but the market rejected them. The root cause? Data and insights were not effectively shared across products, services, and functions. This resulted in duplicated efforts, wasted resources, and a costly financial setback from a poorly received product launch. Leadership agrees: The organization needs a system to improve data flow, align teams, and ensure innovation matches market needs.

WHICH PATH WOULD YOUR ORGANIZATION CHOOSE?
Path 1: Address the Immediate Issues

- Introduce a new weekly sync meeting to focus on alignment across silos.
- Escalate misaligned projects as they emerge, addressing gaps case by case.
- Improve cross-team communication to highlight progress and resolve issues faster.

The Result: Immediate misalignment reduces, and short-term coordination improves. However, systemic gaps remain: Silos persist, data flows inconsistently, and duplicated efforts resurface, keeping innovation out of step with strategy.

Path 2: Build a Sustainable System

- Invest in centralized processes and tools to streamline data sharing across all levels of the organization.
- Define mandatory core metrics to align objectives, ensure visibility, and establish a cadence for tracking progress.
- Create a structured feedback loop: Teams share learnings from project outcomes, aligning creativity with market demands.
- Proactively map dependencies to ensure projects build on shared knowledge instead of duplicating efforts.

The Result: Data flows seamlessly across teams, aligning innovation with strategy and market needs. In short, Path 2 future-proofs the organization by ensuring every ounce of creativity aligns with market needs. Resources are optimized, duplication disappears, and creativity drives measurable value. Product launches gain traction, and the organization transforms its agility, accountability, and results.

Your Turn: If this were your organization, would you choose the quick fixes of Path 1—or commit to lasting transformation with Path 2?

Our Take: Short-term solutions provide temporary relief, but sustained progress requires systems that work. Path 2 connects innovation to strategy, aligning teams, optimizing resources, and ensuring creative breakthroughs deliver real impact. Because when data flows, innovation aligns—and results follow. Ultimately, quick fixes may steady the ship, but they rarely chart a course for true growth. Sustainable systems do both—resolving immediate fires while steering the company toward lasting transformation.

KEY TAKEAWAYS AND DISCUSSION QUESTIONS
1. STRATEGIC ALIGNMENT DRIVES EXECUTION

Alignment connects vision to action, ensuring every decision, priority, and resource pushes the organization forward. Without it, efforts splinter, silos deepen, and momentum stalls.

Questions to Reflect On:

- How can we ensure our strategic goals translate into clear, actionable steps across every level of the organization?
- Where do silos or misaligned priorities slow execution, and what steps can we take to resolve them?
- What processes can improve communication and collaboration to keep teams aligned on shared goals?
- Which metrics or indicators will help us measure alignment and assess its impact on performance?
- What can we learn from aligned, high-performing organizations to strengthen our execution?

2. BALANCE AUTONOMY AND ALIGNMENT TO EMPOWER TEAMS

Success lies in the balance: Autonomy fuels innovation, while alignment ensures progress flows toward shared objectives. Transparent silos allow teams to act independently while staying connected to the big picture.

Questions to Reflect On:

- How can we foster trust and transparency to empower teams while maintaining alignment with strategy?
- Are teams clear on their role in achieving organizational goals, and how can we strengthen accountability?
- What strategies can improve information flow across teams to prevent silos and encourage collaboration?
- How can leaders better communicate shared goals while allowing teams the flexibility to decide *how* to achieve them?
- What indicators will measure our success in balancing autonomy and alignment effectively?

3. CONTINUOUS IMPROVEMENT BUILDS MOMENTUM

Progress compounds when teams reflect, adapt, and improve with each cycle. Continuous improvement embeds learning into execution, turning small tweaks into sustained growth and efficiency.

Questions to Reflect On:

- What mechanisms currently support continuous improvement, and how can we better prioritize them amid daily operations?
- How can we build a culture where teams routinely reflect, share lessons, and adapt processes?
- How effectively are we capturing and acting on feedback loops to improve flow and outcomes?
- What processes or tools can enable us to adapt quickly as new opportunities or challenges arise?
- Which indicators will help us measure and sustain the impact of continuous improvement over time?

KNOWLEDGE MAP

Wire for Action: Alignment transforms strategic intent into execution, ensuring decisions flow smoothly across the organization. When alignment thrives, teams move faster, adapt confidently, and create lasting impact.

PHASE 1: DEFINE CLEAR OBJECTIVES

- **Clarify the Vision:** Reinforce the "why" to inspire and guide teams.
- **Make Bold Choices:** Define where to play, how to win, and the trade-offs required.
- **Turn Strategy into Measurable Goals:** Use frameworks like OKRs to provide clarity and focus.
- **Balance Horizons:** Address today's priorities while investing in tomorrow's growth.

PHASE 2: TRANSLATE VISION INTO ACTION

- **Act on Insights:** Spot trends, test assumptions, and adapt mid-cycle to stay aligned.
- **Manage Dependencies:** Map workflows to untangle complexity and unlock progress.
- **Balance Trade-Offs:** Prioritize decisions that align resources with strategic goals.
- **Stay Agile with Interlock:** Use rhythms and realignment capabilities to stay flexible while maintaining focus.

PHASE 3: ENABLE CONTINUOUS IMPROVEMENT

- **Reflect and Adapt:** Use lightweight feedback loops to identify wins, blockers, and opportunities for improvement.
- **Prioritize Impact:** Focus on changes that enhance flow, alignment, and efficiency.

- **Embed Learning:** Capture lessons and apply them to drive smarter, faster execution every cycle.

ALIGNMENT TOOLS AND SYSTEMS TO DRIVE ACTION

- **Alignment Frames:** Evaluate decisions from multiple perspectives—financial, operational, customer-centric, and talent management.
- **OKRs and Clear Metrics:** Translate strategy into measurable outcomes that align teams and build accountability.
- **Realignment Structures:** Adapt plans dynamically to stay responsive and focused as signals emerge.
- **Feedback Loops:** Build quick, iterative mechanisms to refine execution continuously.

THE REWARDS OF ACTION AND ALIGNMENT

- **Clarity:** Every decision and action ties directly to strategic priorities.
- **Confidence:** Teams move decisively and adapt without hesitation.
- **Momentum:** Execution accelerates as alignment deepens and success compounds.
- **Resilience:** The organization thrives amid uncertainty, responding with focus and agility.

When action is wired into the organization, teams act decisively, progress compounds, and vision transforms into results. 🚀

PART 3

STAY DECISIVELY ALIGNED

Architecting a decisive organization is a powerful step forward. We've wired for context, flow, and action.

But what keeps this momentum alive over the long term? Decisions may flow, teams may move quickly, but without continuous alignment, progress stalls, silos reemerge, and opportunities slip away.

In this section, I'll show you how to stay aligned as you grow.

You'll learn how to integrate decision architecture into your organization's DNA, ensuring clarity and accountability at every level. You'll explore how agile principles can enhance decision-making, enabling teams to adapt and execute with speed. You'll uncover strategies to overcome cognitive biases—those hidden forces that derail even the best decisions—and ensure your teams think clearly under pressure.

Because staying aligned isn't just about keeping pace. It's about maintaining focus, moving as one, and turning decisions into unstoppable momentum.

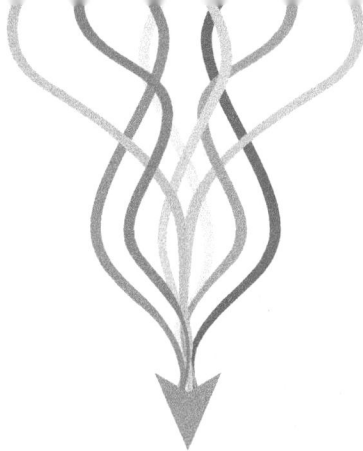

CHAPTER 7

MAKE DECISIONS CLEAR AND ACCOUNTABLE

"The great enemy of communication…is the illusion of it."

—WILLIAM H. WHYTE

Decisions thrive in systems—not chaos.

Picture this: A decision is made. The team leaves the room, but everyone walks away with a different idea of what happens next. Sound familiar? That's what happens when decisions stay implicit—unspoken, unclear, and unowned. Confusion spreads, progress stalls, and accountability disappears.

But when decisions become **explicit**? Everything changes. Roles are defined. Responsibilities are clear. Decisions don't just get made—they get done.

In this chapter, I'll show you how to build decision systems that bring clarity, consistency, and action:

- Systems that define **who** decides what.

- Systems that ensure **how** decisions are made.
- Systems that make **what happens next** clear to everyone.

STANDARDIZE YOUR DECISION ARCHITECTURE

Decisions thrive in structure. A standardized decision architecture eliminates ambiguity and transforms chaos into clarity. Here's how:

1. ALIGN DECISIONS WITH STRATEGY

Every decision is a step. But are those steps leading somewhere?

To keep decisions connected to your big picture:

- Communicate the vision—**relentlessly.**
- Train teams to see how their choices build toward strategic goals.
- Connect decisions to measurable objectives.

Alignment isn't just about goals—it's about purpose. Teams don't just decide—they decide **why it matters.**

2. DEFINE WHO DECIDES

We've already discussed the importance of deciding who decides—defining this across the organization is a key step in designing your decision architecture.

Imagine a relay race where no one knows who carries the baton—or where to pass it. That's decision-making without clear roles.

Use tools like **RAPID** or **DACI** across the organization to define:

- **Who decides?**
- **Who contributes** input?
- **Who approves** the decision?
- **Who gets informed** afterward?

When everyone knows their role, decisions move quickly and accountability becomes a promise—not an afterthought.

3. MAKE DECISION CRITERIA CLEAR

Consistency drives confidence. Establish simple, repeatable criteria for evaluating decisions:

- What's the ROI?
- What are the risks?
- Do we have the resources?
- What are the potential long-term impacts?
- Who will be affected by the decision, and how?

The result? Trade-offs become clearer. Priorities align. Success stops being subjective and starts becoming measurable.

4. STAY FLEXIBLE WITHOUT LOSING STRUCTURE

Rigid systems break. Great ones adapt.
Incorporate regular check-ins:

- Is this process still working?
- What needs to change?
- What new signals are emerging?
- What tools from previous chapters can improve our decision-making process?

Think of it as fine-tuning. The core holds firm, the edges flex, and the system adapts to what's next.

5. CAPTURE DECISIONS FOR THE FUTURE

Decisions fade without a record. Imagine losing the "why" behind a critical choice or forgetting who contributed game-changing insight. Capture it all:

- The "why" behind the decision.
- The contributors who shaped it.
- The context at the time.
- The alternatives you debated before landing on the best path forward.

Decision logs build your organizational memory. Leaders learn faster. Patterns emerge. Mistakes aren't repeated—they're avoided.

WHY STANDARDIZED DECISION SYSTEMS WIN

When decisions follow a clear, standardized process:

- **Confusion** turns into clarity.
- **Guesswork** turns into confidence.
- **Bottlenecks** turn into momentum.

Decisions stop being accidental. They become deliberate, structured, and aligned.

Clarity fuels progress, but maintaining it requires momentum. A dedicated team clears bottlenecks and keeps decisions flowing seamlessly.

WHO KEEPS DECISIONS MOVING?

Decisions slow when no one's clearing the path. Bottlenecks pile up. Frustration grows.

A decision-operations team clears the clutter, fixes the flow, and keeps decisions moving.

1. BUILD A DEDICATED CROSS-FUNCTIONAL TEAM

This isn't a committee. It's a cross-functional team: Finance keeps decisions aligned to the numbers, operations simplifies workflows, and IT ensures systems flow as fast as data. Compliance flags risks, while strategic planners connect every choice to the big picture. Together, they keep decisions moving.

2. MEASURE, IMPROVE, REPEAT

What gets measured gets better. Track key metrics:

- **Decision Velocity:** How fast are decisions made?
- **Decision Quality:** Are outcomes improving?
- **Efficiency Gains:** How much time and cost are saved?

Celebrate the wins and share the impact—when decision-making time drops by 20 percent, make it known. Progress builds confidence, and confidence builds momentum.

3. BUILD TRANSPARENT SILOS

Closed silos make slow decisions. Transparency aligns them.
Make transparency the standard:

- **Share Openly:** Centralize decisions in one accessible platform.
- **Host Alignment Sessions:** Bring departments together regularly.
- **Celebrate Successes:** Recognize collaboration to inspire deeper investment.

When people see their impact, they invest more deeply. Transparency builds momentum.

4. LESS TALK, MORE ACTION

Replace endless meetings with action by adopting tools like scrum boards, sprints, and stand-ups to drive frequent accountability while leveraging asynchronous updates and shared dashboards to keep everyone aligned.

The result? Decisions flow.

A decision-operations team isn't bureaucracy—it's the fuel for clarity and momentum. They simplify processes, measure impact, and keep progress on track. **When decisions flow, the organization does too.**

A decision-operations team is the accelerator of momentum—the group that ensures decisions keep moving forward. Now that decisions are moving, we can focus on knowledge management to ensure they're right.

CENTRALIZE STRATEGIC AND OPERATIONAL KNOWLEDGE

When knowledge is scattered, decisions stall. The solution? **Centralize it.** Make it accessible. Make it actionable. Make it work for you. Here's how:

1. BUILD A SINGLE SOURCE OF TRUTH

Make knowledge easy to find and use. Add search tools, clear tags, and intuitive dashboards. Train teams to share insights through quick sessions, turning lessons and challenges into collective progress.

2. TURN DATA INTO ACTIONABLE INSIGHTS

Data is just noise without insights. Tools like machine learning and predictive analytics can transform raw data into actionable insights, including:

1. Trends to follow.
2. Risks to avoid.
3. Opportunities to seize.

Imagine dashboards that show not just where you've been but **where you're headed.** When data works for you, decisions get smarter—and so do your teams.

3. MAKE IT ACCESSIBLE AND USER-FRIENDLY

If teams can't use the system, they won't. Period.

1. Design clean dashboards.
2. Add powerful search functions.
3. Offer mobile access for teams on the move.
4. Set up guardrails to keep noise out of your repository.

Train people to navigate the system. Support them. Make it simple. When knowledge flows, decisions follow.

4. UPDATE AND REFRESH YOUR KNOWLEDGE SYSTEM

Data gets stale. Keep it alive. This includes:

1. Keeping the data fresh with regular updates.
2. Listening to user feedback and making refinements.
3. Using governance policies to maintain accuracy.

Good decisions require good information. Keep it clean. Keep it current. Keep it sharp.

WHY IT WORKS

Centralized knowledge transforms chaos into clarity, reducing uncertainty and empowering confident action.

No more digging or delays—just fast, informed decisions that drive progress today while fueling lessons for tomorrow.

CENTRALIZE DECISION LOGS

Decisions are like footprints: They show where you've been and how you got there.

But too often, footprints get washed away—lost in emails, buried in notebooks, or locked in forgotten files. Teams move on. Lessons disappear.

The solution? **Centralize your decision logs.** Build a single place where decisions live, breathe, and teach.

When decisions are documented, organized, and accessible, something powerful happens: The past stops being a mystery. It becomes a **map for the future.** Here's how to do it.

1. TURN DECISIONS INTO INSIGHTS

Every decision tells a story. Why it was made. How it was made. What happened next.

When you centralize decision logs, you see the patterns—what works, what doesn't, and what you can do better next time.

- Did we act too slowly?
- Did we miss a signal?
- Did one small change lead to a big win?

By analyzing these decisions in context, teams uncover strengths to replicate and mistakes to avoid. This isn't just history—it's fuel for better choices tomorrow.

2. FOSTER A CULTURE OF LEARNING

When decision logs are centralized, learning becomes part of the culture.

New team members no longer start from scratch. They learn from what came before—what worked, why it worked, and how they can build on it.

Existing employees gain something too: reflection. Instead of plowing forward blindly, they pause to reflect critically, asking, "What could we do differently? What would we repeat?"

Learning from decisions—both good and bad—turns your organization into a **smarter, sharper, more resilient team**.

3. MAKE DECISION LOGS EASY TO USE

A system that's hard to use doesn't get used. Period.

For decision logs to work, they must be:

- **Accessible:** Make them available on any device at any time.
- **Organized:** Add filters and search tools so anyone can find what they need in seconds.
- **Intuitive:** Design a clean, user-friendly interface that makes navigation simple.

Teach teams how to use the system. Hold quick training sessions. Show them how to log decisions, find past insights, and turn history into action.

When it's easy, they'll use it. When they use it, decisions will improve.

4. KEEP LOGS FRESH AND RELEVANT

A stale log is a useless log. Make regular updates part of your process:

- After every major decision, record the **what, why,** and **how**— along with key outcomes.
- Use automated prompts to remind teams to document decisions while they're fresh.
- Assign ownership: Who updates the logs? Who ensures consistency?

Conduct periodic audits to clean up outdated information and reinforce accuracy.

5. TURN LOGS INTO A STRATEGIC ASSET

Centralized decision logs can speed up work. They save teams from repeating debates and chasing forgotten reasons. Leaders make better choices. Past decisions offer a roadmap for smarter, faster calls. Culture improves as reflection and learning become habits, not afterthoughts.

Logged decisions create a lasting legacy that fuels future success. Your decisions are valuable. Treat them as such.

While decision logs anchor your past, clear communication connects teams to what comes next—ensuring everyone knows where they're headed.

CENTRALIZE COMMUNICATION

Decisions don't move in isolation. They flow. And when communication breaks down, alignment breaks.

Centralized channels don't share. They clarify. They connect. They drive action. Here's how.

1. MAKE DECISIONS VISIBLE AND UNDERSTOOD

When teams can't see decisions, they get confused. Context gets lost.

Here's the fix:

- Share decisions in **one place**—no scattered emails, no hunting across platforms.
- Document the **"why"** so teams understand the purpose.
- Tie decisions to goals so alignment feels natural.

When decisions are visible, teams act with clarity and purpose.

2. OVERCOME ROADBLOCKS

Centralizing communications isn't easy. You'll face resistance and scattered tools.

Here's the fix:

- Connect silos by integrating platforms.
- Protect sensitive data with secure access.
- Show the value—explain the "why" behind centralization.

This isn't about control. It's about connection.

3. KEEP TOOLS SIMPLE

Tools must be:

- **User-Friendly:** Intuitive and clean.
- **Powerful:** Searchable, filterable, and accessible.
- **Actionable:** Built for real-time progress.

Train teams. Make adoption easy. The simpler it is, the faster teams align.

4. KEEP COMMUNICATION FRESH

Outdated information kills alignment.

- Automate reminders for updates.
- Assign owners to keep systems clean.
- Audit information regularly for accuracy and relevance.

If accessible communication keeps teams aligned, **risk management prepares them for adversity.**

TURN RISK INTO RESILIENCE

A good definition of risk is "uncertainty that matters."[94]

Risk isn't mysterious; **it's manageable uncertainty that, when ignored, can steer your organization off course**—like driving blindfolded.

By anticipating risks early, great organizations assess the impact of the risks, take decisive action, and transform uncertainty into opportunity. Here's how.

1. INTEGRATE RISK INTO DECISIONS

Risk management isn't separate from decision-making. It's embedded.

Spot risks before they strike. Use checklists, train teams to flag threats early, and embed checkpoints into every stage. See problems coming—and stay ahead of them.

When risks are part of the process, you're not reacting—you're anticipating.

---

94 Yu Yanjuan, "Risk Is Uncertainty That Matters: Interview with Dr. David Hillson," *PM World Journal* 8, no. 9 (October 2019), https://pmworldlibrary.net/wp-content/uploads/2019/10/pmwj86-Oct2019-Yanjuan-Interview-with-David-Hillson.pdf.

2. ALLOCATE RESOURCES BASED ON RISK

Risk tells you where resources matter most:

- Prioritize budgets and resources where risk is greatest.
- Prioritize risk-reducing efforts that create stability.

This isn't about avoiding risks—it's about protecting progress.

3. BUILD STAKEHOLDER CONFIDENCE

Trust comes from transparency:

- Share risks, mitigation plans, and updates clearly.
- Use dashboards to keep stakeholders informed.
- Own the narrative—communicate before questions arise.

Preparation builds credibility.

4. SEE RISKS EARLY, ACT FASTER

Early warning systems change everything:

- Use tools to monitor risks in real time—shifting data, market signals, delays.
- Develop contingency plans that teams can activate instantly.

The faster you respond, the easier it is to minimize the damage. Risk is inevitable, but managing it turns uncertainty into opportunity. Embed it. Measure it. Act on it. **The earlier you act, the stronger your edge.**

BRINGING IT ALL TOGETHER

After working through the steps to make decisions clear and accountable, we see that:

- Standardized systems make decisions clear and actionable.
- Decision-operations teams sustain flow and momentum.
- Centralized knowledge and communication accelerate progress.
- Proactive risk management builds resilience and protects outcomes.

Now your systems are clear and your teams aligned. But alignment isn't static—it's dynamic and ever-evolving. In Chapter 8, we'll explore how learning loops and agile principles keep you adaptive and ahead of change. Thriving organizations don't stand still—they move with the world, sustaining momentum to stay ahead.

SUMMARY

Thriving organizations don't leave decisions to chance—they make them clear, consistent, and actionable.

Clarity transforms chaos into momentum by defining roles, connecting decisions to strategy, and ensuring accountability.

Strong decision systems create purpose-driven teams:

- **Clear Roles:** Everyone knows who decides, contributes, and acts.
- **Strategic Alignment:** Every choice drives measurable progress.
- **Empowered Action:** Teams have the insights to decide confidently.

But decisions don't flow on their own. A dedicated **decision-operations team** clears bottlenecks, simplifies processes, and ensures momentum never stalls:

- They keep decisions moving fast and free of friction.
- They measure, refine, and improve the systems that make decisions possible.
- They break silos with transparency, turning collaboration into a force multiplier.

Centralized knowledge fuels smarter decisions:

- A **single source of truth** eliminates guesswork.
- Decision logs capture lessons, enabling teams to learn, adapt, and improve.
- Clear, accessible communication keeps teams aligned and informed.

When risk is embedded into decisions, uncertainty becomes manageable:

- Spot risks early.
- Allocate resources where they matter most.
- Build stakeholder trust through transparency and preparation.

The result? Resilient systems. Confident teams. Smarter decisions.

Decisions no longer slow you down—they drive you forward. Progress becomes deliberate, momentum accelerates, and accountability turns clarity into action.

Organizations that master decision systems don't just keep up—they lead.

Make decisions clear, make them accountable, and watch progress flow.

DECISION POINTS

Consider This Scenario: A fast-paced company is grappling with repeated project delays and missed deadlines. The root cause? Decision-making processes are unclear, leaving roles and responsibilities ambiguous. Teams are unsure who owns critical decisions, resulting in finger-pointing, stalled progress, and frustration. Leadership realizes that if it doesn't address these challenges, inefficiencies will persist, accountability will erode, and project outcomes will continue to suffer. The organization must establish clear and explicit decision-making systems to drive efficiency and accountability.

WHICH PATH WOULD YOUR ORGANIZATION CHOOSE?
Path 1: Clarify Decision-Making Roles and Responsibilities

- Implement a standardized decision-making architecture that eliminates ambiguity.
- Introduce decision frameworks like RAPID or DACI to clarify roles: who decides, who contributes input, who approves, and who gets informed.
- Ensure every project includes a decision matrix to outline ownership, accountability, and communication flow.

The Result: Ambiguity disappears. Decisions move faster, bottlenecks decrease, and accountability strengthens. Teams execute with confidence, knowing exactly who owns what. However, without a system to continuously review and improve decision processes, the organization risks returning to old patterns as complexity grows.

Path 2: Build a Decision-Operations Team
for Continuous Improvement

- Create a dedicated decision-operations team to oversee and optimize decision-making processes.

- Regularly review decision outcomes to identify bottlenecks, measure efficiency, and refine systems.
- Align decisions with strategic objectives by ensuring teams connect choices to measurable goals.
- Foster transparency and cross-team alignment by centralizing decision logs, sharing knowledge, and improving communication flow.

The Result: Decision-making becomes a strategic advantage. Processes adapt and improve over time, driving faster, clearer, and more accountable decisions. Teams collaborate seamlessly, bottlenecks are proactively cleared, and decisions consistently align with the organization's strategic goals. Efficiency compounds, momentum accelerates, and projects deliver real results.

Your Turn: If this were your organization, would you choose the quick clarity of **Path 1**—or commit to lasting transformation with **Path 2**?

Our Take: Path 1 provides immediate clarity but lacks the continuous improvement needed for long-term success. Path 2 doesn't just fix today's delays—it builds a future where decisions fuel innovation and progress at scale. Because when decisions flow, progress accelerates, accountability thrives, and organizations don't just keep up—they lead.

KEY TAKEAWAYS AND DISCUSSION QUESTIONS
1. STANDARDIZED DECISION ARCHITECTURE BUILDS CLARITY AND ACCOUNTABILITY

Structured decision-making eliminates ambiguity and ensures roles, responsibilities, and processes are clear. When decisions are explicit, teams move with speed and confidence.

Questions to Reflect On:

- How can we clearly define decision-making roles (e.g., who decides, contributes, and approves) to eliminate ambiguity and improve accountability?

- What criteria should we establish to consistently assess trade-offs, risks, and alignment with strategy?
- How can we keep decision-making processes adaptable to changing circumstances while maintaining efficiency?
- How can we better document and communicate decisions to ensure teams act with clarity and focus?
- What frameworks (e.g., RAPID, DACI) can we adopt to make decision responsibilities clear and repeatable?

2. DECISION-OPERATIONS TEAMS DRIVE CONTINUOUS IMPROVEMENT

A dedicated team streamlines decision flow, clears bottlenecks, and ensures decisions align with strategy. This ongoing optimization turns decision-making into a competitive advantage.

Questions to Reflect On:

- What expertise should be represented in a decision-operations team to ensure decisions are efficient, strategic, and aligned across the organization?
- How can we measure and communicate the impact of the decision-operations team to stakeholders and leadership?
- What processes can the decision-operations team implement to proactively identify and resolve decision-making bottlenecks?
- How can we foster transparency and collaboration to break down silos and streamline decision flow?
- How can we optimize this team's work to focus on value-added improvements without adding unnecessary bureaucracy?

3. CENTRALIZED KNOWLEDGE POWERS SMARTER, FASTER DECISIONS

When knowledge is consolidated, teams save time, gain context, and act confidently. A single source of truth ensures decisions are rooted in accurate, up-to-date information.

Questions to Reflect On:

- What steps can we take to centralize organizational knowledge into a single, reliable source of truth?
- How can we facilitate quick and easy access to this knowledge so teams spend less time searching and more time acting?
- What tools or platforms can help transform raw data into actionable insights that guide decisions?
- How can we promote knowledge sharing to ensure lessons learned are captured and applied across teams?
- What governance processes should we adopt to maintain the quality, accuracy, and relevance of contextual knowledge?

4. CENTRALIZED DECISION LOGS FUEL LEARNING AND ACCOUNTABILITY

Documenting decisions and their reasons creates a learning loop. It speeds up improvement, helps teams avoid past mistakes, and builds organizational memory.

Questions to Reflect On:

- How can we effectively centralize and standardize decision logs to ensure decisions are recorded, searchable, and accessible?
- What processes can we adopt to capture the "why" behind decisions, including alternatives considered and lessons learned?
- How can decision logs contribute to building a culture of reflection and continuous improvement?
- What challenges might arise when centralizing decision logs, and how can we overcome them to encourage adoption?
- How can we ensure decision logs are regularly updated, maintained, and leveraged to drive smarter choices?

5. CENTRALIZED COMMUNICATION ENHANCES DECISION VISIBILITY

When decision rationale is communicated clearly through centralized channels, alignment improves, silos dissolve, and teams execute with shared purpose.

Questions to Reflect On:

- What communication tools or platforms can ensure decisions are visible, accessible, and consistently shared?
- How can we streamline decision-related communication to reduce conflicting narratives and provide clear context?
- How can shared communication channels improve inclusivity and foster buy-in across departments?
- What strategies can minimize unnecessary meetings by leveraging centralized communication for updates and alignment?
- How can we ensure the rationale behind decisions is effectively communicated to drive understanding and results?

6. EMBEDDING RISK MANAGEMENT STRENGTHENS RESILIENCE

Proactively identifying and addressing risks ensures decisions are high quality, resources are protected, and teams respond with confidence and speed.

Questions to Reflect On:

- How can we embed proactive risk-assessment frameworks into decision-making processes?
- What strategies can ensure risk mitigation is addressed at every stage of critical decisions?
- How can we allocate resources more effectively based on risk exposure and potential impacts?
- How can transparent risk communication strengthen stakeholder trust and confidence?

- What tools or processes can help identify early warning signals to mitigate risks before they escalate?

KNOWLEDGE MAP

BENEFITS TO STANDARDIZING YOUR DECISION ARCHITECTURE

- Aligns decisions with strategic goals.
- Defines roles and responsibilities clearly.
- Establishes consistent decision criteria.
- Enhances accountability and follow-through.
- Adapts processes to changing needs.
- **Adds flexibility to handle dynamic conditions.**
- **Balances structure with clear, measurable standards.**

DECISION-OPERATIONS TEAM BENEFITS

- Speeds up decision-making by removing bottlenecks.
- Improves efficiency with continuous process optimization.
- Enhances collaboration through cross-silo transparency.
- Reduces friction in decision workflows.
- Tracks and measures decision impact.
- **Creates transparency across teams and silos.**
- **Optimizes flow with measurable improvements.**

CONSOLIDATED CONTEXTUAL KNOWLEDGE BENEFITS

- Speeds up decisions with centralized data.
- Reduces time spent on knowledge transfer.
- Provides actionable insights from raw data.
- Captures lessons to improve future decisions.
- **Creates a single, reliable source of truth.**

CENTRALIZED DECISION LOG BENEFITS

- Tracks decisions to enhance accountability.
- Improves decisions by learning from past actions.
- Avoids repeating mistakes through captured insights.
- Enables faster access to decision rationale.
- **Identifies patterns for strategic improvement.**

CENTRALIZED COMMUNICATION BENEFITS

- Reduces confusion through unified communication.
- Improves team alignment with clear updates.
- Streamlines decision sharing to minimize delays.
- Increases visibility into decision-making.
- **Connects teams with integrated tools and systems.**

EMBEDDED RISK MANAGEMENT BENEFITS

- Identifies risks early to avoid escalation.
- Prioritizes resources based on risk impact.
- Builds resilience through proactive management.
- Strengthens stakeholder trust with transparency.
- **Responds quickly with real-time risk monitoring.**

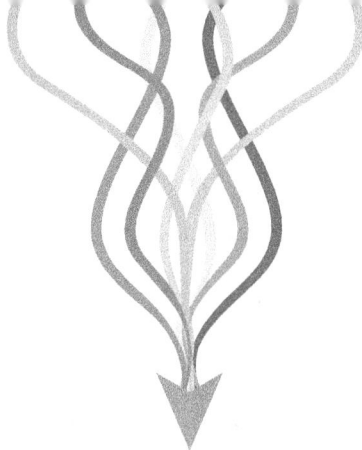

CHAPTER 8

EMBED LEARNING LOOPS

"In a time of drastic change it is the learners who inherit the future. The learned usually find themselves equipped to live in a world that no longer exists."

—Eric Hoffer

Your competitor moves first. The market shifts overnight. Your strategy suddenly feels stale, your teams unsure how to react. What went wrong? The answer isn't speed—it's adaptability.

Now, picture a different scenario. Your teams are wired for learning. Feedback flows seamlessly, insights fuel quick adjustments, and strategies evolve in real time. Your teams don't just respond to change—they anticipate it. They learn, adapt, and thrive.

In this chapter, we'll explore how to build **learning loops**—feedback cycles that transform your organization into a system that's always improving, evolving, and staying ahead. Because in a world of constant disruption, adaptability isn't optional—it's survival.

ADAPTABILITY IS A COMPETITIVE SUPERPOWER

Adaptability is no longer just a competitive advantage—it's the foundation for survival and growth. Today's world demands speed, agility, and a willingness to evolve. Whether it's responding to market shifts, embracing new technologies, or outmaneuvering competition, organizations that **learn faster** lead the way.

Take **Uber**. From its humble beginnings as a ride-hailing app, Uber revolutionized urban mobility by relentlessly adapting to changing consumer needs and market dynamics. It didn't stop at transportation; it expanded into **Uber Eats** for food delivery and **Uber Freight** for logistics, proving adaptability isn't a one-time decision—it's a mindset.[95]

Uber succeeded not just because it had a bold idea but because it continuously:

1. Collected **real-time feedback** from users and markets.
2. Pivoted quickly when faced with new challenges.
3. Tested, refined, and scaled its innovations with agility.

The lesson? Adaptable organizations don't wait for change—they build systems that anticipate it.

WHY LEARNING LOOPS MATTER

Building **learning loops** enables teams, programs, and entire organizations to continuously gather feedback, extract insights, and turn every success or failure into momentum for the next move.

Learning loops turn feedback into momentum, embedding a rhythm of reflection, action, and growth—so you're never caught off guard.

---

95 Bold Narratives, "Redefining the Category: How Uber Disrupted a Market and Redefined Transportation," *The Bold Blog*, February 20, 2024, https://www.boldnarratives.com/knowledge-center/how-uber-disrupted-a-market-and-redefined-transportation.

When adaptability becomes part of your culture, your teams won't fear change—they'll harness it.

Big strategies often crumble under real-world complexity. Teams hesitate, unsure where to start. But what if you could break those big decisions into smaller, testable steps—each one sharpening your focus and reducing uncertainty?

THE POWER OF LEARNING LOOPS

In a fast-moving world, big decisions can feel overwhelming—complex, risky, and slow to deliver results. Learning **loops** for **decisions** simplifies the process. By breaking large decisions into smaller, more manageable parts, organizations can validate assumptions, test solutions, and adapt quickly based on real feedback.

For example, look at Amazon's relentless experimentation with Prime membership benefits. From adding streaming services to expanding same-day delivery, each iteration responds to real-time feedback, keeping the strategy fresh and aligned with customer expectations.[96]

Decisions spark action, but progress thrives on evolving strategies. **Learning loops for decisions takes adaptability to the next level**—ensuring alignment, agility, and innovation.

---

96 Jason Del Rey, "The Making of Amazon Prime, the Internet's Most Successful and Devastating Membership Program," *Vox*, May 3, 2019, https://www.vox.com/recode/2019/5/3/18511544/ amazon-prime-oral-history-jeff-bezos-one-day-shipping.

LEARNING LOOPS FOR DECISIONS

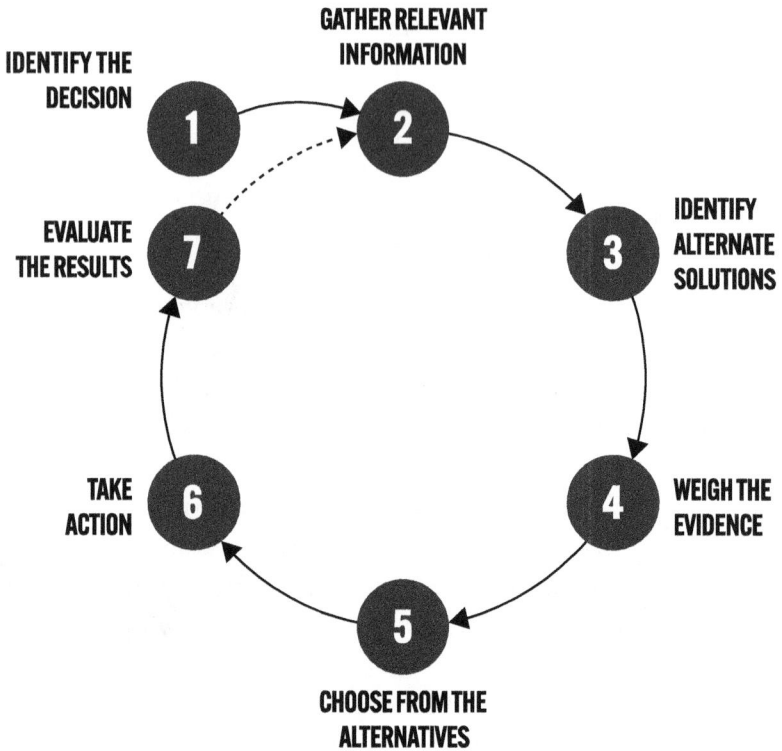

GATHER RELEVANT
INFORMATION

IDENTIFY THE
DECISION

1

2

IDENTIFY
ALTERNATE
SOLUTIONS

3

EVALUATE
THE RESULTS

7

TAKE
ACTION

6

4

WEIGH THE
EVIDENCE

5

CHOOSE FROM THE
ALTERNATIVES

The learning loops for decisions pictured above is a sample framework. While your steps may vary, the principle remains the same: **Iterate as fast as possible to inform the next decision.**

A SIMPLE FRAMEWORK FOR SMARTER, FASTER DECISIONS

Here's how to make learning loops for decisions work in your organization.

1. Identify the Decision

Clearly define the decision you're tackling. Is it **strategic, tactical,** or **operational?**

- Strategic decisions shape long-term direction.
- Tactical decisions refine programs, projects, or functions.
- Operational decisions address day-to-day execution.

Understanding the type of decision you're facing ensures you collect the right amount of information and maintain focus.

2. Gather Relevant Information

Collect data and insights that matter. Pull from:

- Internal reports and performance metrics
- Market research and competitive analyses
- Customer feedback and real-time signals

Agile decision-making prioritizes **what's essential**—enough to act confidently without overanalyzing. Keep it concise to avoid **analysis paralysis.**

3. Identify Alternative Solutions

Brainstorm possible solutions or actions. Involve diverse perspectives to challenge assumptions and uncover creative options.

- Ask: "What else could we try?"
- Encourage quick idea generation over perfect plans.

Decision loops thrive on options—because the first idea isn't always the best one.

4. Weigh the Evidence

Evaluate each alternative quickly:

- What are the potential benefits?
- What are the risks?
- What's most feasible given our resources?

Agile decision-making emphasizes speed without sacrificing thoughtfulness. Assess trade-offs decisively to maintain momentum.

5. Choose from Alternatives

Select the option that aligns best with your goals, minimizes risks, and delivers the highest impact.

- Don't let perfection delay action.
- Embrace "good enough to test" when the stakes are lower.

Decision loops are about progress, not perfection.

6. Take Action

Implement your decision swiftly.

- Start small: a pilot project, a limited rollout, or an experiment.
- Move from decision to action as seamlessly as possible.

The faster you execute, the sooner you gather real-world data on the solution's effectiveness.

7. Evaluate the Results

Review outcomes honestly and objectively:

- Did the decision deliver the expected results?
- What worked? What didn't?
- What can we learn to improve future decisions?

Insights from evaluation fuel the next loop, systematically reducing uncertainty and sharpening your process.

WHY LEARNING LOOPS FOR DECISIONS WORKS

Decision loops create a dynamic, adaptive decision-making process. Instead of locking into rigid plans, teams operate with agility—testing ideas, learning from outcomes, and refining strategies with every cycle.

- They **accelerate progress** by breaking big decisions into small, actionable steps.
- They **build confidence** through continuous feedback and improvement.
- They **remove uncertainty** over time, turning complexity into clarity.

When organizations adopt decision loops, they foster a culture of learning and adaptation. Teams don't wait for change to disrupt them—they stay ahead of it, making decisions that are timely, informed, and resilient.

Ready to build decision loops into your organization? Start small, act fast, and refine continuously. Because in an unpredictable world, the ability to **decide, adapt,** and **iterate** is your greatest advantage.

APPLY LEARNING LOOPS TO STRATEGY

Strategies that stand still get left behind. The most successful organizations know that strategy isn't a one-and-done plan—it's a living process. By adopting **iterative strategy loops,** companies create a system that constantly learns, adapts, and evolves based on real-world feedback.

Elon Musk captures the importance of learning loops best in his quote:[97]

> I think it's very important to have a feedback loop, where you're constantly thinking about what you've done and how you could be doing it better.

Strategy loops are iterative cycles that refine and adjust organizational strategies across **business practices, product development, team dynamics, and discovery initiatives.**

You may be wondering if one learning loop can inform other learning loops in your organization.

Yes, it can! And when connected, strategy loops become a force multiplier.

Learning loops for strategy can **flow together**—connected by continuous learning, feedback, and communication.

When linked, learning loops for strategy can seamlessly connect insights from external business operations to products, teams, and even small-batch deliveries, like a product feature in the discovery loop.

Here's how multiple loops can work together to drive success.

---

97 Lance Ulanoff, "Elon Musk: Secrets of a Highly Effective Entrepreneur," Mashable, April 13, 2012, https://mashable.com/archive/elon-musk-secrets-of-effectiveness#dHzYc5SgAaqH.

LEARNING LOOPS FOR STRATEGY

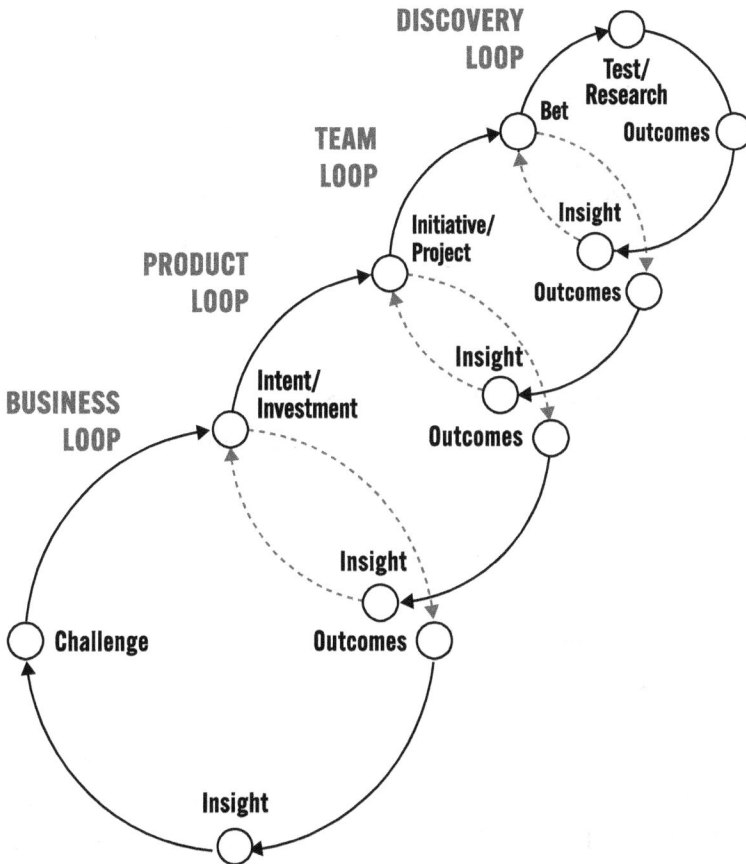

Credit: John May

THE FOUR LOOPS OF STRATEGIC ADAPTATION

1. The Business Loop

This core learning loop focuses on solving specific organizational challenges through strategic investments. Each cycle strengthens alignment with shifting market dynamics and internal priorities. Here's how:

- **Start with a Challenge:** Identify a pain point or opportunity that needs addressing.
- **Make a Strategic Investment:** Allocate resources—time, money, and people—to tackle the challenge.
- **Measure Outcomes:** Evaluate whether the investment delivered the desired results.
- **Feed Insights Forward:** Use the lessons learned from addressing this challenge and its outcomes to refine the next challenge or opportunity. Appendix H provides insights by role and context to guide your insight-development approach.

Why It Works: The business loop keeps organizations nimble. Instead of rigid strategies, leaders iterate continuously, refining investments to drive better outcomes every cycle.

2. The Product Loop

This loop is informed by the business loop to build products that stay relevant. Here's how:

- **Challenge:** Define clear goals for new or existing products.
- **Invest:** Allocate resources to specific projects or experiments.
- **Measure:** Track key metrics, like customer satisfaction, adoption rates, and ROI.
- **Adapt:** Use feedback to refine features and adjust priorities for the next iteration.

Why It Works: Product loops ensure rapid adjustments. They help teams test, learn, and pivot quickly—delivering products that stay relevant and valuable.

3. The Team Loop

This loop is fed by the product loop to foster a culture of experimentation and collaboration. Teams should act, reflect, and adjust in compressed time spans. Here's how:

- **Bet on Solutions:** Empower team members to propose and test potential solutions.
- **Implement and Test:** Put ideas into action and gather real feedback.
- **Review Outcomes:** Analyze what worked, what didn't, and why.
- **Sharpen Team Effectiveness:** Use insights to enhance collaboration, decision-making, and problem-solving.

Why It Works: Team loops empower people to think boldly and act confidently. By iterating on solutions, teams innovate faster and learn together—strengthening both performance and morale.

4. The Discovery Loop

This loop is fed by the team loop to fuel bold exploration of new ideas, technologies, and innovations. It's about taking smart bets on each feature or deliverable. Here's how:

- **Make Short-Term Bets:** Identify and explore promising ideas, trends, or technologies.
- **Test and Validate:** Conduct rigorous experiments to assess their viability and impact.
- **Review Results:** Determine what shows potential—and what doesn't.
- **Plan the Next Bet:** Use insights to guide future exploration and innovation.

Why It Works: Discovery loops reduce the risks of innovation by testing ideas early and often. Organizations learn fast, fail small, and scale only what works.

THE POWER OF LOOPS FOR STRATEGY

While each loop drives its own outcomes, their true power emerges when they work as one interconnected system, joined together by clear, timely communication. Insights from one loop feed into the next, creating a dynamic feedback system that keeps the entire organization learning, adapting, and improving.

For example:

- A discovery loop might uncover a bold new idea that informs the business loop's next strategic investment.
- Insights from a product loop could highlight a team-level challenge, sparking solutions in the team loop.

This continuous flow of feedback ensures every part of the organization stays aligned and agile—moving together toward shared goals.

Here's why the loops matter:

1. **Adaptability:** Loops allow organizations to spot changes early, test ideas quickly, and respond with confidence.
2. **Alignment:** Every effort connects back to overarching goals, turning scattered initiatives into focused momentum.
3. **Innovation:** Loops encourage bold experimentation and informed risk-taking, turning small tests into game-changing ideas.
4. **Risk Management:** Iterative cycles limit downsides by enabling small, controlled bets, reducing the need for high-stakes gambles.
5. **Resource Optimization:** Each loop improves decision-making, ensuring time, budgets, and talent flow to where their utility will be maximized.

By adopting strategy loops, organizations become proactive rather than reactive—learning, adapting, and staying ahead of change. Start small, measure impact, and let every loop fuel smarter, sharper, and stronger decisions.

USE WARDLEY MAPS FOR MORE STRATEGIC CLARITY

With decision and strategy loops driving your agility, you're adapting faster than ever. But without a clear view of the bigger picture, even your best efforts can feel scattered. How do you align every moving part into a cohesive vision for the future? **Wardley Maps** provide the **situational awareness** leaders need to navigate change with precision and confidence, and they work hand in hand with decision loops.[98]

Wardley Maps offer a clear blueprint to navigate your business landscape. By mapping the evolution of key components, leaders move from reacting to anticipating—aligning strategies with confidence.

THE ORIGINS OF WARDLEY MAPS

Simon Wardley created Wardley Maps after identifying a critical gap in traditional strategic thinking: It lacked situational awareness. Inspired by military strategy—where understanding the landscape is key to gaining a competitive edge—Wardley developed a mapping tool that gives business leaders clarity and direction in complex environments.

Wardley Maps provide a **visual representation** of an organization's value chain and the evolution of its components. By mapping out this progression, leaders gain a shared understanding of their position, the competitive landscape, and the opportunities (or threats) ahead.

---

98 John May, "Wardley Maps," The Uncertainty Project, accessed April 21, 2024, https://www.theuncertaintyproject.org/tools/wardley-maps.

WARDLEY MAPS IN ACTION

AWS effectively employed Wardley Maps to gain situational awareness of the competitive environment at the market level, improving its overall chances of success. By mapping out the landscape, AWS was able to identify customer needs and align its cloud services accordingly, ensuring its offerings remained relevant and valuable in a rapidly evolving market.

HOW TO CREATE WARDLEY MAPS

A Wardley Map breaks a business or service into its **key components** and illustrates their **value** and **maturity** over time:

- The **vertical axis** represents value, from foundational elements at the bottom to user-facing, high-value components at the top.
- The **horizontal axis** tracks evolution, from early-stage innovations on the left to widespread, commoditized solutions on the right.

Think of it as a strategic blueprint—**one that connects what your users need, where you deliver value, and how components evolve over time.**

WHY WARDLEY MAPS MATTER

While they don't prescribe strategy, these maps **reveal it.** By visualizing the business landscape, leaders can:

1. **Clarify Complexity:** Break down interdependencies and identify the true value of each component.
2. **Prioritize Investment:** Spot critical areas for investment, innovation, or protection.
3. **Optimize Resources:** Determine which components can be outsourced or commoditized.

4. **Anticipate Change:** Track how components evolve and stay ahead of market shifts.
5. **Improve Collaboration:** Align leadership teams around a shared understanding of the landscape, fostering more precise and connected decision-making.

These maps transform ambiguity into insight, enabling teams to move faster and adapt smarter.

The power of Wardley Maps lies not just in the map itself but in the process of creating it. Building a map requires iteration, discussion, and reflection—refining strategies, uncovering blind spots, and reducing biases along the way. Leaders don't just see the landscape—they align around it.[99]

This collaborative approach fosters ownership and trust, ensuring everyone understands not just **what** the strategy is but **why** it matters. Teams gain confidence to innovate, adjust, and execute with precision.

Clarity. Confidence. Results.

Wardley Maps help leaders:

- Visualize complexity.
- Align decisions with value.
- Navigate change with confidence.

WHAT'S NEXT

Your teams are moving fast, learning faster, and adapting with agility. But speed without clarity risks mistakes, misalignment, and wasted effort. In Chapter 9, we'll uncover how to eliminate biases, sharpen decisions, and move from motion to momentum. Because the difference between **motion** and **momentum** lies in the clarity of your decisions.

---

99 May, "Wardley Maps."

SUMMARY

Adaptability fuels progress. **Learning loops make it inevitable.**

Organizations that thrive don't wait for change to disrupt them—they build systems that learn, adapt, and improve. Learning loops ensure organizations don't just respond to change—they anticipate it, turning uncertainty into opportunity.

Feedback drives momentum.

It transforms challenges into growth.

It turns decisions into progress.

It connects strategy to action.

When learning loops are embedded, teams move with confidence:

- **Decisions Adapt Faster:** Small, testable steps replace slow, high-risk plans.
- **Strategies Evolve Continuously:** Real-world feedback sharpens direction with every cycle.
- **Teams Stay Resilient:** Learning becomes a habit—failure fuels progress, and success scales faster.

Decision loops accelerate action.

They break big decisions into smaller, testable parts.

Iterate quickly. Learn faster. Remove uncertainty with every loop.

Strategy loops drive alignment and innovation.

Four interconnected loops—**business, product, team,** and **discovery**—refine strategies and unlock bold solutions.

- Business loops solve challenges and invest resources strategically.
- Product loops build what customers need faster.
- Team loops empower collaboration, experimentation, and learning.
- Discovery loops reduce risk by testing bold ideas early and often.

Together, they form a dynamic flow of feedback—aligning every decision, action, and investment.

Iteration turns agility into advantage—test small, adapt continuously, and stay ahead of change. The result? Organizations that don't fear change—they thrive in it.

When learning loops are strong:

- Teams act boldly and adapt quickly.
- Strategies stay relevant and resilient.
- Innovation becomes a rhythm, not a risk.

Progress is no longer accidental—it's intentional, iterative, and unstoppable.

Lead with learning. Build feedback into every action. Adapt faster than the world around you changes. And watch your organization thrive.

DECISION POINT

Consider This Scenario: A rapidly growing company is struggling to keep pace with its competitors. While market leaders quickly adapt to new technologies and shifting customer demands, this company's hierarchical decision-making structure has become a bottleneck. Opportunities are missed, product launches are delayed, and momentum is slowing. Leadership recognizes that without improving adaptability, the company risks falling behind in an increasingly dynamic environment.

WHICH PATH WOULD YOUR ORGANIZATION CHOOSE?

Path 1: Build Cross-Functional Teams for Innovation

- Form agile, cross-functional teams tasked with experimenting, testing, and refining new ideas.
- Establish regular review cycles to evaluate innovations, inte-

grating successful experiments into the organization's broader strategy.

- Empower teams to move quickly on smaller bets while providing leadership oversight of larger, high-stakes initiatives.

The Result: Innovation accelerates as teams are freed to experiment and act quickly. Successful ideas feed into the company's strategy, ensuring adaptability without losing control. However, without a structured system for feedback and iteration, progress may remain uneven, and promising opportunities risk being overlooked.

Path 2: Implement Decision Loops for Rapid Adaptation

- Adopt an iterative decision loop system where large, strategic decisions are broken into smaller, manageable components.
- Encourage teams to test reversible decisions quickly, gather real-world feedback, and refine actions with each loop.
- Continuously review outcomes to ensure decisions stay aligned with the company's broader goals while maintaining the flexibility to adapt to market changes.

The Result: Adaptability becomes a competitive advantage. Teams make decisions faster with less risk and course-correct in real time based on real-world feedback. Small, iterative cycles enable rapid learning, ensuring decisions remain both agile and strategic. The organization doesn't just respond to change—it stays ahead of it.

Your Turn: If this were your organization, would you foster innovation with cross-functional teams but risk uneven progress without structured feedback with Path 1—or embed adaptability through decision loops with Path 2, aligning speed, learning, and strategy in every move?

Our Take: Path 2 is the future. It transforms adaptability into a repeatable advantage, ensuring every decision fuels momentum and alignment. Why just react when you can lead?

KEY TAKEAWAYS AND DISCUSSION QUESTIONS

1. ADAPTABILITY AS A STRATEGIC IMPERATIVE

Adaptability isn't just about survival—it's the foundation for growth in a dynamic business environment. Organizations that learn faster, pivot smarter, and integrate feedback more effectively thrive amid disruption. Adaptability turns market fluctuations, technological advancements, and competitive pressures into opportunities for innovation and progress.

Questions to Reflect On:

- How do we currently measure our organization's ability to adapt to market changes and competitive pressures?
- What specific barriers inhibit us from learning and improving based on our successes and failures?
- How can our current organizational structure better support continuous innovation and adaptability?
- What steps can we take to foster a culture that embraces change rather than resists it?
- How can we ensure internal and external feedbacks effectively inform our strategic planning?

2. IMPLEMENTATION OF DECISION LOOPS

Decision loops enhance adaptability by breaking complex decisions into smaller, iterative cycles. Teams test, act, and refine quickly, building momentum and reducing uncertainty with each loop. This agile approach ensures decisions are fast, feedback-driven, and continuously improving.

Questions to Reflect On:

- How can we customize decision loops to address the specific needs of different departments or teams?
- What training or resources will ensure our teams effectively contribute to and benefit from decision loops?

- How do we evaluate whether decision loops are accelerating adaptability or adding unnecessary layers of process?
- What mechanisms can help us share learnings from decision loops across the organization in real time?
- How can technology help us track, analyze, and optimize decision-loop outcomes for continuous improvement?

3. BENEFITS OF ITERATIVE STRATEGY LOOPS

Strategic loops ensure organizations stay agile, aligning decisions and actions with business goals through continuous cycles of learning, testing, and improvement. By focusing on business operations, product innovation, team performance, and discovery, strategy loops drive progress and resilience.

Questions to Reflect On:

- Which areas of our organization would benefit most from the implementation of strategic loops, and why?
- How can we ensure insights from one loop (e.g., product) effectively influence other areas (e.g., team or discovery)?
- What metrics should we track to measure the success and impact of each type of strategic loop?
- How can we encourage teams to see strategic loops as opportunities for growth and learning rather than extra work?
- How do we balance the need for quick decisions with the thorough analysis required to optimize strategic loops?

KNOWLEDGE MAP
ADAPTABILITY AS A STRATEGIC ADVANTAGE

- Respond faster to market shifts.
- Integrate feedback for continuous improvement.
- Turn failures into learning opportunities.
- Support continuous innovation.

- Enable growth through change.

DECISION LOOP BENEFITS

- Fast, iterative decision-making.
- Reduced complexity through smaller cycles.
- Improved feedback integration.
- Continuous adaptation to real-world changes.
- Enhanced momentum and confidence in execution.

FOUR STRATEGIC DECISION LOOPS

- **Business Loop:**
  - Solve organizational challenges.
  - Align investments with priorities.
  - Improve outcomes through iteration.
- **Product Loop:**
  - Respond rapidly to customer needs.
  - Test and scale product innovations.
  - Refine product features with feedback.
- **Team Loop:**
  - Foster collaboration and bold experimentation.
  - Empower teams to solve problems iteratively.
  - Strengthen team learning and morale.
- **Discovery Loop:**
  - Explore and validate bold ideas.
  - Reduce risks in early-stage innovations.
  - Guide future strategic bets with data.

STRATEGIC ITERATION BENEFITS

- Connected insights across loops.
- Alignment of teams and actions.
- Resilience to disruption.

- Faster innovation and iteration.
- Improved risk management and resource use.

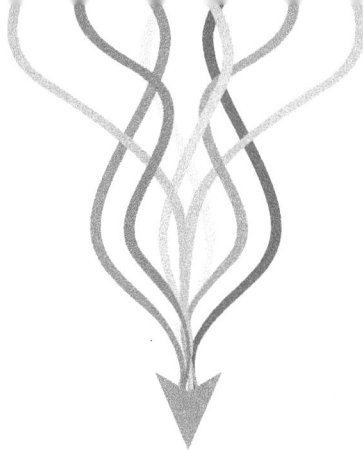

CHAPTER 9

THINK SHARPER, DECIDE SMARTER

"The emotional tail wags the rational dog."

—JONATHAN HAIDT

Bias clouds judgment. Noise distorts decisions. Together, they erode the sharp thinking organizations need to succeed.

We like to think we're rational, logical, and clear. But we're not. Our brains are wired to take shortcuts. Shortcuts that save time. Shortcuts that feel efficient. These shortcuts—**cognitive biases**—work like silent influencers, nudging our decisions off course. And unless we design for them, they will affect every choice we make.

Elon Musk often highlights how cognitive biases—if unexamined—sabotage organizations.[100] Leaders who study these forces,

---

100 Jessica Stillman, "Elon Musk Thinks Every Child Should Learn About These 50 Cognitive Biases," *Inc.,* January 3, 2022, https://www.inc.com/jessica-stillman/elon-musk-cognitive-biases.html.

design processes to reveal them, and confront them can think sharper and decide smarter.

The truth is you can't eliminate bias. It's part of being human. But you **can** reduce it. You can design processes that limit its power. And when you do, your decisions will improve.

Take hiring, for example. An interviewer might favor a candidate because they both went to the same college. That's **affinity bias**. It feels harmless, but it can lead to missed opportunities and unfair outcomes. Now, imagine a better process—one where every candidate answers the same set of questions in the same order.

Better processes shrink bias. Better decisions follow.

Organizations that acknowledge bias and actively design processes to counter it don't just make better decisions—they build trust. Their processes inspire confidence. They deliver outcomes people believe in.

In this chapter, we'll focus on the eight fundamental biases that most disrupt strategy development. These biases don't just affect individuals—they affect systems, plans, and results. I'll show you how to spot them, measure their impact, and design processes to keep them in check.

Thinking sharper and deciding smarter isn't about being perfect. It's about being aware. It's about revealing the unseen forces that shape our choices—and designing systems to stay one step ahead of them.

ANCHORING BIAS

The first impression is rarely the full story.

Imagine this: You're building a house. The first brick you lay seems sturdy, so you use it as your guide. Every brick after that aligns with the first. But what if the first brick wasn't level? What if that single mistake throws off the whole foundation?

That's **anchoring bias**. It's the "first impression syndrome" of decision-making, and it's everywhere.

Amos Tversky and Daniel Kahneman, pioneers of behavioral psychology, first identified this bias. They showed how one piece of initial information—**the anchor**—can skew every decision that follows. Instead of evaluating new information independently, we compare it to the anchor. The anchor dominates our thinking, whether it's accurate or not.[101]

THE COST OF ANCHORING: KODAK'S DOWNFALL

For decades, Kodak was *the* name in photography—a giant that defined the industry. They invented the first digital camera. **Invented it!** But instead of embracing the future they helped create, Kodak anchored itself to its past.

Kodak's leadership clung to its film business like a life raft, convinced digital cameras were a niche market. Film was their anchor. It was safe. Familiar. Profitable. For a while, at least.

Meanwhile, digital technology raced forward. Competitors like Canon and Sony sprinted ahead. Smartphones put cameras in every pocket. And Kodak, still pushing film, fell further behind.

In 2012, Kodak filed for bankruptcy. The company that once ruled photography became a cautionary tale. A titan toppled by its inability to let go of a bad anchor.[102]

Anchoring bias doesn't just cloud small decisions. It can derail entire strategies, locking companies into outdated thinking while competitors sprint ahead.

---

101 Amos Tversky and Daniel Kahneman, "Judgement Under Uncertainty: Heuristics and Biases," in *Judgement Under Uncertainty: Heuristics and Biases*, eds. Daniel Kahneman, Paul Slovic, and Amos Tversky (Cambridge University Press, 1982), 14–18.

102 Nick Brown and Tanya Agrawal, "Kodak Emerges from Bankruptcy with Focus on Commercial Printing," Reuters, September 3, 2013, https://www.reuters.com/article/us-eastmankodak-emergence/kodak-emerges-from-bankruptcy-with-focus-on-commercial-printing-idUSBRE98213220130903.

- **Shine a Light:** Educate teams on anchoring bias and its impact.
- **Independent Inputs:** Use blind estimates to prevent the first idea from becoming the anchor.
- **Standardize:** Evaluate options with consistent tools, like scoring systems or predefined criteria.

Key Insight: Challenge the first impression. Build systems that test its reliability.

Anchoring bias locks decisions to early impressions, while authority bias magnifies leadership influence. Together, they reveal how initial conditions and power dynamics can skew judgment. To make smarter decisions, question the first impression and challenge the loudest voices.

AUTHORITY BIAS

When power speaks, judgment fades.

Imagine sitting in a meeting. The CEO shares a bold idea—exciting, revolutionary. The room goes silent. Heads nod. No one questions it. Why? **Because the idea came from the CEO.** Authority carries weight, even when it shouldn't.

That's authority bias. It's the tendency to trust and follow the opinions of authority figures more than we should. It's human nature. From an early age, we're taught to respect authority—parents, teachers, leaders.[103] Over time, that respect hardens into assumption: **If they're in charge, they must be right.**

But what happens when they're not?

---

103 Lindsay Morgia, "Authority Bias: When We Irrationally Trust the Judgment of Experts," Ness Labs, accessed April 21, 2024, https://nesslabs.com/authority-bias.

ENRON: WHEN AUTHORITY LED TO COLLAPSE

For years, Enron was a Wall Street darling. Innovation, growth, power—they had it all. Or so it seemed. Behind closed doors, CEO Kenneth Lay and CFO Andrew Fastow were cooking the books, hiding billions in debt behind complex accounting tricks.

And people believed their tricks.

Employees trusted their leaders. Investors trusted the numbers. Auditors—including **Arthur Andersen,** one of the most reputable accounting firms in the world at the time—rubber-stamped the financials. No one dared question the executives at the top. **Unchecked power leads to unchecked mistakes.**

Then, one reporter asked a simple question: **How does Enron make money?**

That question—combined with an internal whistleblower—shattered the illusion. Investigations revealed fraud on a massive scale. Enron's empire collapsed into one of the largest bankruptcies in US history. Thousands lost their jobs. Investors were out billions. And the world learned a harsh lesson: Blind faith in authority can be catastrophic.[104]

KEY MITIGATION STRATEGIES

- **Focus on Ideas, Not Titles:** Remove names from brainstorming and reviews to let ideas stand on merit.
- **Build Safety:** Foster psychological safety, where dissent is encouraged and mistakes are learning opportunities.[105]
- **Invite Disagreement:** Use devil's advocates and critical questions to challenge leadership assumptions.

---

104 Paul M. Healy and Krishna G. Palepu, "The Fall of Enron," *Journal of Economic Perspectives* 187, no. 2 (Spring 2003): 3–26, https://doi.org/10.1257/089533003765888403.

105 Amy Gallo, "What Is Psychological Safety?," *Harvard Business Review*, February 15, 2023, https://hbr.org/2023/02/what-is-psychological-safety.

Key Insight: Trust in leadership matters, but unchecked authority can distort judgment. Focusing on ideas, not titles, keeps decisions objective.

Authority bias isn't all bad. Leaders exist to guide, inspire, and make hard calls. But when authority goes unchecked, bad decisions go unchallenged. Enron proved that.

The best organizations strike a balance. They respect leadership but trust the process more. They challenge ideas, not individuals. They build cultures where truth matters more than titles.

Because when authority bias fades, judgment clears. Decisions improve. And organizations don't just follow leaders—they challenge them to be better.

If authority bias clouds our judgment by amplifying powerful voices, availability bias distorts it by focusing on what's easiest to recall. The loudest or most recent information often drowns out what truly matters.

AVAILABILITY BIAS

When the obvious clouds the possible.

Think of the last time you made a quick decision. Maybe it was choosing a familiar restaurant or recalling a piece of advice you once heard. Why did it come to mind so easily? Because it was **available.** Vivid memories and easy-to-recall information feel true, even when they're not the full story.

That's availability bias. It's what happens when we rely on what's **easiest** to remember rather than what's **most accurate.** A recent event, a dramatic failure, a news headline—all of these distort how we see the world.[106]

When leaders fall into this trap, decisions get skewed. The obvious becomes the anchor. The overlooked becomes the threat.

---

106 A. Banerjee and D. Nunan, "Availability Bias," Catalogue of Bias, 2019, https://catalogofbias.org/biases/availability-bias/.

BLOCKBUSTER: A DECISION THAT COST BILLIONS

Once upon a time, Blockbuster ruled the world of Friday-night entertainment. Thousands of stores. Millions of customers. Endless shelves of DVDs and VHS tapes. They were untouchable—until they weren't.

In 2000, Netflix approached Blockbuster with an offer: **Buy us for $50 million.**

Blockbuster laughed. Why would they take a risk on a small, unproven company when their stores were packed with customers? Why would they bet on a future they couldn't see when the present was so profitable?

That's availability bias at work.

The executives saw the evidence they **wanted** to see—full parking lots, long checkout lines, and rows of rentals—because the obvious feels safe. But the overlooked holds the truth: The rise of the internet and shifting consumer habits signaled the future they failed to see.

Netflix grew. It embraced streaming. Consumers embraced convenience. Blockbuster, meanwhile, clung to its stores, blind to the storm on the horizon. In 2010, Blockbuster filed for bankruptcy. Netflix became a multibillion-dollar juggernaut.[107]

What happened? Did Blockbuster fail because they couldn't see the future—or because they refused to? Availability bias **made the present feel safe**, but safety doesn't win in a world driven by change.

KEY MITIGATION STRATEGIES

- **Widen the Lens:** Conduct risk assessments and audits to uncover overlooked data.
- **Seek Hidden Insights:** Encourage curiosity and exploration beyond surface-level information.

---

107 Greg Satell, "A Look Back at Why Blockbuster Really Failed and Why It Didn't Have To," *Forbes*, September 5, 2014, https://www.forbes.com/sites/gregsatell/2014/09/05/a-look-back-at-why-blockbuster-really-failed-and-why-it-didnt-have-to/?sh=74de7fd41d64.

- **Broaden the Debate:** Invite diverse perspectives to identify nonobvious risks and opportunities.

Key Insight: The obvious is not always the full story. Broaden perspectives and dig deeper to avoid mistaking what's easy to recall for what's true.

Blockbuster's story wasn't just a failure—it was a lesson. The world changes. Technologies shift. Customer habits evolve. But availability bias locks us into the present, distorting the future.

Great organizations fight back. They challenge assumptions, hunt for hidden insights, and explore what's **not obvious**. Because the decisions that matter most aren't based on what's easy to see— they're based on what others miss.

So, look deeper, think further, and never let the obvious cloud your judgment.

While availability bias makes us rely on what's easiest to remember, confirmation bias narrows our focus further by filtering out information that challenges our beliefs. Seeing only what we want to see can prove costly.

CONFIRMATION BIAS

When what you believe clouds what you see.

Think of confirmation bias as a filter for your mind. It lets in what **agrees** with your beliefs and shuts out what doesn't. It's comforting, reassuring, and efficient—but it's also dangerous.

Confirmation bias happens when leaders seek, interpret, or recall information that supports what they already believe to be true. It's the boardroom nodding in agreement with an untested plan. It's executives dismissing bad news because it doesn't fit their narrative. It's data being selectively chosen to reinforce a decision, not challenge it.[108]

---

108 *Britannica*, "confirmation bias," last updated February 11, 2025, https://www.britannica.com/science/confirmation-bias.

And in business, when the world is changing, confirmation bias doesn't just hold you back—it sets you up to fail.

BLACKBERRY: THE COST OF SEEING ONLY WHAT YOU WANT TO SEE

Once upon a time, BlackBerry **owned the smartphone market.** Its signature QWERTY keyboard was iconic. Its loyal customers swore by it. Its executives believed physical keyboards were **essential** to BlackBerry's success.

In 2007, Apple launched the iPhone—sleek, elegant, and radically keyboard-free. Consumers loved it, but BlackBerry's leadership dismissed it as a fad. They clung to their belief in the supremacy of physical keyboards, ignoring data and trends that showed otherwise. By the time they pivoted, it was too late.[109]

The BlackBerry Storm, a compromise between a touchscreen and a physical keyboard, failed. By the time BlackBerry finally released a full-touchscreen phone in 2013, Apple, Samsung, and others had already won the market.

What went wrong?

BlackBerry saw what it **wanted** to see. It believed what it **wanted** to believe. Confirmation bias blinded it to the truth: The market had moved on.

KEY MITIGATION STRATEGIES

- **Challenge Assumptions:** Assign devil's advocates to expose blind spots and test beliefs.
- **Blind Reviews:** Evaluate proposals or ideas anonymously to avoid preloaded judgments.

---

109 Shobhit Seth, "BlackBerry: A Story of Constant Success and Failure," Investopedia, April 14, 2024, https://www.investopedia.com/articles/investing/062315/blackberry-story-constant-success-failure.asp.

- **Seek Honest Feedback:** Invite knowledgeable peers to challenge your thinking and refine decisions.

Key Insight: Seeing only what you want to see is dangerous. Systems that invite dissent and test assumptions ensure decisions are grounded in reality.

BlackBerry's story is more than a cautionary tale—it's a call to action. Confirmation bias doesn't announce itself. It hides in the **data you ignore,** the challenges you dismiss, and the assumptions you cling to.

But businesses that thrive know the truth matters more than their comfort. They question themselves. They test their beliefs. And they seek out the evidence they don't want to see.

Because when you fight confirmation bias, you don't just make smarter decisions—you make decisions that keep you **ahead of the curve.**

So, challenge yourself, ask the hard questions, and always look beyond what you want to believe.

You'll notice some strategies—like encouraging dissent or building psychological safety—show up across multiple biases. That's because the same strategies can strengthen decision-making against multiple invisible forces. These solutions build habits of clarity, critical thinking, and objectivity that ripple across your organization.

Confirmation bias is dangerous when individual leaders ignore inconvenient truths, but groupthink amplifies the problem to the team level. When harmony replaces debate, the illusion of consensus can lead to disaster.

GROUPTHINK

When consensus becomes the enemy of progress.

Think of groupthink as the hidden cost of team harmony. It feels comfortable, safe, and unified—but it comes at a price. When groupthink takes hold, dissent disappears. Independent ideas are silenced. Decisions go unchallenged. And teams mistake **agreement** for **wisdom**.

Irving Janis, the psychologist who coined the term in the 1970s, defined groupthink as a phenomenon where group members prioritize consensus over critical thinking.[110] It creates the illusion that the group is:

- **Invulnerable:** "We can't fail."
- **Morally Right:** "Our way is the only way."
- **Superior:** "They just don't get it."

But in reality, groupthink **undermines** creativity, blinds teams to risks, and weakens problem-solving. It replaces thoughtful debate with surface-level agreement—and when the stakes are high, that can be catastrophic.

SWISSAIR: A STORY OF UNQUESTIONED CONSENSUS

Swissair was once a model of success. Known as the "Flying Bank" for its financial stability, it dominated the skies and inspired confidence worldwide.

In the late 1990s, Swissair pursued the **Hunter Strategy**— an aggressive, debt-heavy acquisition plan. Confidence ran high, and groupthink stifled dissent. Warnings were ignored, and unity replaced scrutiny. When the **9/11 attacks** disrupted the airline industry, Swissair, overleveraged and unprepared, collapsed into **bankruptcy.**[111]

A company once revered for its stability was undone by unchallenged decisions and an illusion of invulnerability.

---

110 Derek Schaedig, "Groupthink: Definition, Signs, Examples, and How to Avoid It," Simply Psychology, last modified July 31, 2023, https://www.simplypsychology.org/groupthink.html.

111 Patrick Richter, "The Collapse of Swissair," World Socialist Web Site, October 13, 2001, https://www.wsws.org/en/articles/2001/10/swis-013.html.

The lesson? Teams that silence dissent and avoid tough conversations don't avoid failure—they accelerate it.

KEY MITIGATION STRATEGIES

- **Encourage Debate:** Model leadership behavior that welcomes dissent and critical analysis.
- **Break It Up:** Form independent subgroups to develop alternative solutions.
- **Debrief Honestly:** Review decisions to identify overlooked concerns and improve future processes.

Key Insight: Harmony feels safe, but conflict fuels progress. Dissent sharpens ideas and exposes risks before they become failures.

Swissair's story isn't just a cautionary tale—it's a reminder that **tough conversations make teams stronger.** The best decisions don't come from agreement—they come from healthy conflict, diverse ideas, and teams unafraid to **challenge the status quo.**

So, embrace dissent. Encourage debate. And when everyone agrees too quickly, ask: **"What are we missing?"**

Because teams that challenge each other don't just make smarter decisions—they **lead the way forward.**

Groupthink stifles dissent and creativity for the sake of agreement, but overconfidence bias takes it one step further—convincing leaders they're invincible. Confidence without humility can blind even the best organizations to risk.

OVERCONFIDENCE BIAS

When confidence clouds judgment.

Think of overconfidence bias as **believing you're invincible—** until reality proves otherwise.

Overconfidence bias occurs when individuals **overestimate** their **abilities, knowledge, or control** over a situation. It's the voice that says, "I've got this," even when the evidence disagrees.[112]

It leads people to underestimate risks, overcommit to deadlines, and ignore the possibility of failure. For example, a leader might believe a project will finish early because they're **certain** of their team's speed—only to realize the hard way that reality doesn't match their optimism.

NOKIA: CONFIDENCE TO COMPLACENCY

Nokia was once untouchable. The king of mobile phones. The brand on everyone's lips.

But **overconfidence** turned success into downfall.

When Apple introduced the iPhone and Samsung followed with multifunctional, user-friendly smartphones, the market shifted overnight. Consumers wanted touchscreen devices, sleek interfaces, and app ecosystems.

Nokia saw the trend. It knew the competition was rising.

But it **believed** it was too strong to fail.

It underestimated the smartphone revolution, dismissing it as a temporary disruption. Leadership was so confident in Nokia's **innovation capabilities** and market position that they moved **too slowly** to adapt. By the time they responded, it was too late. Apple and Samsung had taken the lead. Nokia's delayed efforts couldn't close the gap.[113]

The result? Nokia's market share plummeted. Profitability evaporated. And the industry giant became a cautionary tale.

Overconfidence blinded Nokia to the threat smartphones posed to its market dominance. Nokia delayed its response to disrup-

---

112 Kassiani Nikolopoulou, "What Is Overconfidence Bias?: Definition & Examples," Scribbr, March 18, 2023, https://www.scribbr.com/research-bias/overconfidence-bias/.

113 Brand Minds, "Why Did Nokia Fail and What Can You Learn from It?," *Multiplier Magazine*, Medium, July 24, 2018, https://medium.com/multiplier-magazine/why-did-nokia-fail-81110d981787.

tion. And it proved **confidence without humility** is a dangerous combination.

- **Make Assumptions Explicit:** State assumptions and the odds of success clearly to ground optimism in data.
- **Seek Feedback:** Regularly review past decisions and align confidence with reality.
- **Prioritize Data:** Test ideas with evidence, not intuition alone.

Key Insight: Overconfidence blinds decision-making. Testing assumptions against data keeps leaders grounded and adaptable.

Nokia's story reminds us that **success breeds overconfidence.** It's easy to assume today's strengths will carry us through tomorrow's challenges. But the market changes. Competitors emerge. Trends evolve.

The solution isn't to lose confidence—it's to **balance it with humility.**

Test assumptions. Seek feedback. Question certainty. And remember: **Confidence doesn't come from ignoring risks—it comes from understanding them.**

Overconfidence bias keeps leaders overestimating their abilities, while the sunk-cost fallacy traps them in past investments. When confidence meets attachment, even failing paths can feel hard to abandon.

SUNK-COST FALLACY

When past investments pull you backward.

Think of the sunk-cost fallacy as **chasing losses**—pouring good money, time, and effort after bad simply because you've already invested so much.

The sunk-cost fallacy occurs when decision-makers feel compelled to continue with failing initiatives because of **costs already incurred.** These costs—financial, emotional, or otherwise—become

anchors that distort judgment. Rather than focus on what lies ahead, leaders cling to what's already gone.[114]

HP AND THE $11 BILLION MISTAKE

In 2011, Hewlett-Packard (HP) made a bold move: They acquired UK software company Autonomy for **$11.1 billion.**

It was supposed to be transformative, strengthening HP's foothold in software.

But critics were skeptical. Many believed the deal was **wildly overvalued.**

HP pushed forward anyway. They had invested millions in negotiations. Their leadership was committed. The costs—both financial and reputational—felt too high to walk away from.

But when the deal closed, reality struck. Autonomy's accounting practices came under scrutiny. Within a year, HP wrote off **$8.8 billion** of the acquisition. What started as a transformative bet turned into a **financial disaster**—one that damaged HP's reputation and triggered years of legal battles.[115]

HP's mistake? They let the **sunk costs of negotiations** outweigh the evidence. Instead of reassessing when warning signs emerged, they doubled down—because they'd already come so far.

The sunk-cost fallacy traps leaders in this way. It convinces them quitting equals failure, when in truth, **letting go** of a bad investment is the smarter move.

KEY MITIGATION STRATEGIES

- **Reassess Value:** Regularly evaluate projects based on future potential, not past costs.

---

114 Dan Pilat and Sekoul Krastev, "Why Are We Likely to Continue with an Investment Even If It Would Be Rational to Give It Up?: The Sunk Cost Fallacy, Explained," The Decision Lab, accessed February 15, 2025, https://thedecisionlab.com/biases/the-sunk-cost-fallacy.

115 Peter Sayer, "The HP–Autonomy Lawsuit: Timeline of an M&A Disaster," CIO, September 5, 2024, https://www.cio.com/article/304397/the-hp-autonomy-lawsuit-timeline-of-an-ma-disaster.html.

- **Focus Forward:** Ask, "Would I invest again today?" to make decisions without emotional attachment.
- **Seek Objectivity:** Consult fresh perspectives to cut through emotional biases.

Key Insight: What's spent is spent. Letting go of past investments frees resources for future value and better opportunities.

The sunk-cost fallacy makes walking away feel like **defeat**. It makes quitting seem like a failure of leadership.

But the truth is this: **Holding on to bad investments costs more**—in money, time, and energy—than letting go ever will.

The smartest leaders understand this. They evaluate every decision with **fresh eyes**. They ask, "What's the value **now**, and what can we gain from here?"

Because success isn't about clinging to the past. It's about **investing in the future**—and knowing when to walk away.

The sunk-cost fallacy ties us to the past, but zero-risk bias tempts us with the illusion of certainty. Eliminating one small risk often distracts us from greater opportunities—and bigger threats.

ZERO-RISK BIAS

The false comfort of eliminating one risk.

Think of zero-risk bias as the **lure of certainty**—a preference for reducing a single, small risk to **zero**, even when larger risks remain or greater overall risk reductions are possible elsewhere.

Zero-risk bias tempts us with a clear win: **Eliminate this risk, and you're safe.** But it's a trap. It shifts focus from the bigger picture to a narrow point of certainty, leading to **short-sighted decisions** that overlook more significant benefits.[116]

---

116 Dan Pilat and Sekoul Krastev, "Why Do We Seek Certainty in Risky Situations?: Zero Risk Bias, Explained," The Decision Lab, accessed February 15, 2025, https://thedecisionlab.com/biases/zero-risk-bias.

WHEN CERTAINTY BECAME COSTLY: CITIGROUP AND THE FINANCIAL CRISIS

The 2007–2008 financial crisis shattered global markets. Citigroup, like many others, suffered enormous losses—writing off **$18.1 billion** in risky assets as the subprime-mortgage bubble burst.

Faced with chaos, Citigroup responded swiftly. They slashed costs and adopted "zero-risk" solutions. They cut **forty-two hundred jobs** and sold off risky assets—moves designed to eliminate immediate risks.[117]

At first glance, this approach seemed rational. Cutting costs and reducing exposure created an illusion of control amid uncertainty. But the **zero-risk bias** blinded Citigroup.

Instead of exploring more balanced strategies—like enhancing risk-assessment systems or diversifying assets—Citigroup clung to certainty. They missed opportunities to invest for the future, focus on nuanced risk management, or reposition themselves strategically.

The crisis eventually passed, but the damage was done. Citigroup's short-term pursuit of **zero risk** came at the cost of long-term growth, leaving it behind more resilient competitors.

Citigroup's story reveals a critical truth: Eliminating one risk doesn't make you safe. **Ignoring bigger opportunities—or bigger threats—can hurt far more.**

KEY MITIGATION STRATEGIES

- **Think Big Picture:** Quantify risks and benefits objectively to prioritize overall value.
- **Highlight Inaction's Cost:** Make the hidden dangers of doing nothing explicit.
- **Learn and Balance:** Review past decisions to balance short-term risk reduction with long-term gains.

---

117 William D. Cohan, "How Citigroup Escaped Financial Disaster in 2008," *New York Times*, August 6, 2018, https://www.nytimes.com/2018/08/06/books/review/james-freeman-vern-mckinley-borrowed-time.html.

Key Insight: Eliminating small risks can create bigger blind spots. Balance certainty with strategic risk-taking to maximize long-term outcomes.

Zero-risk bias is seductive because it feels safe. But safety doesn't come from eliminating small risks—it comes from managing **all risks effectively.**

The best leaders don't seek certainty—they seek balance. They ask:

- "Where can we create the most value?"
- "Which risks are worth taking?"

Because true progress lies not in avoiding all risk but in navigating uncertainty with **clarity, courage,** and **confidence.**

This chapter covered common biases, but there's much more to explore. Understanding traps and biases is the first step to control, so I've included deeper dives for further exploration: Appendix E covers decisiveness traps, Appendix F lists common biases, and Appendix G offers practical bias-mitigation strategies you can start using immediately.

While these strategies tackle biases effectively, decision-making systems also face another challenge: noise. Unlike bias, which skews decisions in predictable ways, noise introduces random inconsistencies. To ensure decisions remain consistent and aligned, we need tools to uncover and manage this hidden chaos.

A TOOL KIT FOR SMARTER DECISIONS

The invisible forces of bias may vary, but their antidotes share common threads: clarity, discipline, and inclusion. Whatever the challenge, universal principles can cut through complexity and empower teams to think boldly and decide smarter. These "universal" strategies are the backbone of smarter decision-making systems. Here's a consolidated tool kit to apply across your organization:

1. ENCOURAGE DISSENT

- **How to Implement:**
  - Foster a culture of psychological safety, where teams feel comfortable challenging ideas.
  - Appoint a devil's advocate in key discussions to surface blind spots.
  - Reward constructive dissent to demonstrate its value to the organization.
- **What It Solves:** Groupthink, authority bias, confirmation bias.

2. STANDARDIZE DECISION PROCESSES

- **How to Implement:**
  - Use predefined criteria for evaluations (e.g., scoring systems or decision matrices).
  - Develop templates for decision-making processes to ensure consistency.
  - Incorporate structured frameworks, such as RAPID or DACI, for clear accountability.
- **What It Solves:** Anchoring bias, availability bias, noise, sunk-cost fallacy.

3. DIVERSIFY PERSPECTIVES

- **How to Implement:**
  - Assemble cross-functional teams for brainstorming and decision reviews.
  - Include voices from outside the immediate team for fresh viewpoints.
  - Actively solicit opinions from underrepresented or dissenting stakeholders.
- **What It Solves:** Groupthink, availability bias, confirmation bias, anchoring bias.

4. FOCUS ON DATA OVER INTUITION

- **How to Implement:**
  - Ground decisions in metrics and measurable outcomes.
  - Regularly test assumptions with real-world data.
  - Leverage dashboards, analytics tools, or external benchmarks for evidence-based decisions.
- **What It Solves:** Overconfidence bias, zero-risk bias, anchoring bias, availability bias, confirmation bias, sunk-cost fallacy.

5. USE BLIND REVIEWS

- **How to Implement:**
  - Remove names, titles, or identifying details from proposals during evaluations.
  - Conduct anonymous surveys to gather team input before open discussions.
  - Analyze options without initial context to avoid anchoring on first impressions.
- **What It Solves:** Authority bias, anchoring bias, confirmation bias.

6. EVALUATE DECISIONS REGULARLY

- **How to Implement:**
  - Schedule routine reviews of key decisions to reassess their value and outcomes.
  - Use trip wire metrics—predefined thresholds that prompt a reevaluation.
  - Incorporate lessons learned into future decision-making frameworks.
- **What It Solves:** Sunk-cost fallacy, overconfidence bias, noise.

If biases pull decisions in the wrong direction, noise scatters them entirely. Reducing noise ensures consistency, helping teams stay focused and aligned even in the face of uncertainty.

REDUCING NOISE

Bias is predictable. Noise is chaos.

The biases we've explored—anchoring, authority, availability, confirmation, groupthink, overconfidence, sunk costs, and zero-risk—distort judgment in consistent ways. Noise, on the other hand, scatters decisions randomly, making them inconsistent, unreliable, and harder to trust.

WHAT IS NOISE?

Noise isn't just variability—it's chaos hiding in plain sight. Unlike bias, which creates systematic errors, noise introduces random deviations, eroding trust and weakening outcomes.[118]

Key Question: Is your organization applying the same standards to every decision?

Key Insight: Random noise scatters good decisions. Structure and discipline eliminate chaos, creating outcomes teams can trust.

Consider these examples of noise in the real world:

1. Two hiring managers evaluate the same candidate. One sees potential; the other sees failure—why? Noise.
2. Did you know a judge's lunch break might determine your sentence? Studies reveal that judges are significantly more lenient after eating and harsher before meals—same case, same facts, same judge, but wildly different outcomes based on hunger.[119]

Sixty-one percent of executives admit their organizations struggle to bridge the gap between strategy and implementation—often

---

118 Daniel Kahneman et al., *Noise: A Flaw in Human Judgment* (Little, Brown Spark, 2021), 4.

119 Shai Danziger et al., "Extraneous Factors in Judicial Decisions," *PNAS* 108, no. 17 (2011): 6889–6892, https://doi.org/10.1073/pnas.1018033108.

because noise fills that gap.[120] Random inconsistency wastes time, undermines clarity, and derails progress.

HOW TO REDUCE NOISE

Random variability thrives in unstructured environments, but it can be mitigated by implementing structured processes and engaging decision observers. Here's how:

1. **Standardized criteria and repeatable frameworks** replace randomness with clarity, ensuring consistency and reliability.
2. **Neutral third parties acting as decision observers** monitor processes to spot inconsistencies and confirm alignment with stated criteria.

Together, these measures act as quality control—shining a light on variability and keeping decisions consistent.

Noise isn't harmless—it wastes time, erodes trust, and weakens strategy. Thriving organizations actively hunt for noise, expose it, and implement processes—like decision observers—to eliminate it. The result? Clearer, fairer, and far more reliable decisions.

Less Noise. Better Decisions. Stronger Results. When noise is silenced, teams focus, strategies align, and decisions shift from chaos to clarity.

SUMMARY

Sharp thinking fuels smart decisions. Systems that reduce bias and noise make sharp thinking inevitable.

Organizations that thrive don't trust decisions to chance—they design processes that uncover truth, limit bias, and eliminate chaos.

---

120 Larry Wolff, "The Strategy–Execution Gap," LinkedIn, January 24, 2021, https://www.linkedin.com/pulse/strategy-execution-gap-larry-wolff.

Reducing bias keeps decisions focused. Reducing noise keeps them consistent. Together, they create clarity, confidence, and progress.

Bias distorts judgment. Noise scatters decisions.

Both demand control.

- **Anchoring bias** locks decisions to the first impression.
- **Authority bias** amplifies powerful voices and silences critical judgment.
- **Availability bias** prioritizes the familiar over the feasible.
- **Confirmation bias** filters out truths that challenge beliefs.
- **Groupthink** replaces debate with harmony—and progress stalls.
- **Overconfidence bias** blinds leaders with certainty when humility is needed.
- **Sunk-cost fallacy** traps teams in failing investments instead of future value.
- **Zero-risk bias** tempts leaders to eliminate small risks while ignoring greater opportunities.

Bias pulls decisions off course. Noise turns strategy into chaos.

But great organizations don't just fight back—they design clarity into every decision, ensuring progress isn't left to chance. They:

- **Build Awareness:** Name the biases. Spot the patterns.
- **Design Systems:** Standardize processes, challenge assumptions, and encourage dissent.
- **Hunt for Noise:** Replace inconsistency with structure. Decision observers bring clarity where chaos hides.

When biases are addressed and noise is reduced:

- **Decisions Improve:** Objectivity replaces shortcuts.
- **Teams Act Smarter:** Dissent fuels progress. Truth rises to the surface.

- **Strategies Align:** Systems of clarity scale across the organization.

Progress isn't about perfection—it's about awareness and action. Bias distorts. Noise distracts. But sharp thinking and decisive systems create momentum that no competitor can match. Build awareness, design clarity, and empower action. The best decisions don't just happen—they're engineered by leaders who refuse to settle for mediocrity.

Clarity scales. Noise fades. Organizations thrive.

DECISION POINTS

Consider This Scenario: A product development team at a leading organization is preparing to launch a new flagship product. The team's experienced and confident manager firmly believes the product will be a game changer, despite limited market testing and minimal external feedback. Some team members have raised concerns about potential flaws and the product's readiness for launch, but the manager dismisses these concerns, convinced of its inevitable success. Leadership now faces a critical decision: proceed with the launch as planned or delay to address these concerns and reduce risk.

WHICH PATH WOULD YOUR ORGANIZATION CHOOSE?

Path 1: Delay the Launch to Strengthen Market Readiness

- Postpone the product launch to address concerns raised by team members.
- Conduct additional market testing to gather real-world data and feedback.
- Make necessary adjustments to improve the product and reduce the risk of failure driven by **overconfidence bias**.

The Result: The product benefits from additional validation and refinement, reducing the chance of failure in the market. However, delaying the launch comes with trade-offs: lost momentum, additional costs, and the risk that competitors could gain an edge while adjustments are made.

Path 2: Proceed with Launch, but Mitigate
Risks with Trip Wire Metrics

- Proceed with the product launch as scheduled to capitalize on momentum.
- Clarify success metrics and desired outcomes to measure product performance in real time.
- Establish live tracking metrics and **trip wire triggers**—specific thresholds that, if crossed, automatically prompt a reassessment of the product's market performance and strategic direction.

The Result: The organization moves forward without delay, testing the product in the real world and gathering live feedback. Trip wire metrics provide a safety net, ensuring leadership can quickly detect issues and pivot as needed. This approach maintains momentum while balancing agility and accountability. However, proceeding without deeper prelaunch testing still carries the risk of overconfidence and potential flaws impacting success.

Your Turn: If this were your organization, would you delay for thorough validation with Path 1—or proceed with momentum while managing risks through live metrics and trip wires with Path 2?

Our Take: Path 1 prioritizes caution and reduces the risk of overconfidence bias by leveraging real-world testing to strengthen the product's market readiness. However, delays could slow momentum and hand competitors an advantage.

Path 2 embraces action but adds safety measures, balancing speed with accountability. Trip wire metrics and live tracking ensure the organization can pivot decisively if assumptions are proven wrong. This approach mitigates the risk of overconfidence while keeping teams agile and focused.

How will you transform the way your organization thinks, decides, and leads?

KEY TAKEAWAYS AND DISCUSSION QUESTIONS
1. STRUCTURED DECISION-MAKING PROCESSES

Systematic and structured decision-making processes limit the influence of personal biases by introducing transparency and clear criteria. Objective frameworks ensure decisions are grounded in data and rational analysis, not intuition or subjective impressions.

Questions to Reflect On:

- How can we redesign our decision-making processes to make them more structured, transparent, and bias-resistant?
- What objective criteria should we use to make critical decisions, and how can we ensure consistency across teams?
- How can we balance the need for speed with the rigor of structured, data-driven decision-making?
- What tools or frameworks could help us improve the objectivity and repeatability of our decisions?
- How do we encourage teams to prioritize processes over personal preferences or intuition?

2. DIVERSE PERSPECTIVES AND INCLUSION

Diversity of thought helps expose biases by bringing unique experiences, viewpoints, and ideas into the decision-making process. Inclusive environments ensure decisions are well-rounded, creative, and less susceptible to blind spots.

Questions to Reflect On:

- How can we create systems that ensure diverse perspectives are considered in every decision?
- What steps can we take to encourage participation from voices that might otherwise go unheard?
- How can we measure whether diverse viewpoints are actively improving the quality of our decisions?
- How can we ensure decision-framing considers a broader range of experiences and insights?
- What role does leadership play in fostering inclusion and valuing dissenting viewpoints?

3. AWARENESS AND EDUCATION

Awareness is the first step to managing bias. Training and education programs help teams identify common cognitive biases and develop strategies to counteract their impacts. Bias awareness empowers individuals to approach decisions with greater self-awareness and discipline.

Questions to Reflect On:

- How can we integrate bias-awareness training into our ongoing leadership and development programs?
- What tools or workshops could make bias awareness engaging and actionable across all levels of the organization?
- How can we measure the effectiveness of bias training and ensure it translates into improved decision-making?
- How do we embed bias-awareness principles into our day-to-day processes, not just formal training sessions?
- How can we encourage teams to identify and challenge biases in real time?

KNOWLEDGE MAP

- **Bias:** Systematic errors that distort judgment.
- **Noise:** Random variability that causes inconsistent decisions.
- **Solution:** Structured, repeatable decision-making processes to improve clarity, consistency, and trust.

EIGHT KEY BIASES AND MITIGATION STRATEGIES

1. **Anchoring Bias**
   A. **Effect:** Overrelying on initial information.
   B. **Fix:** Blind estimates, standardized evaluations, and education.
2. **Authority Bias**
   A. **Effect:** Blindly trusting leaders.
   B. **Fix:** Focus on ideas (not names), build psychological safety, and encourage dissent.
3. **Availability Bias**
   A. **Effect:** Relying on easily recalled information.
   B. **Fix:** Conduct risk assessments and audits, and seek hidden insights.
4. **Confirmation Bias**
   A. **Effect:** Favoring information that aligns with beliefs.
   B. **Fix:** Play devil's advocate, conduct blind reviews, and invite diverse feedback.
5. **Groupthink**
   A. **Effect:** Prioritizing consensus over critical analysis.
   B. **Fix:** Independent subgroups, debriefings, and leadership modeling dissent.
6. **Overconfidence Bias**
   A. **Effect:** Overestimating abilities and control.
   B. **Fix:** Test assumptions, establish feedback systems, and rely on data.
7. **Sunk-Cost Fallacy**

A. **Effect:** Clinging to failing investments.
B. **Fix:** Reassess projects, focus on future value, and seek objective advice.
8. **Zero-Risk Bias**
   A. **Effect:** Over-prioritizing the elimination of small risks.
   B. **Fix:** Balance risks with objective analysis, and highlight the cost of inaction.

NOISE-REDUCTION STRATEGIES

- **What Is Noise?** Random variability eroding decision quality.
- **Solutions:**
  - Implement structured, repeatable processes.
  - Use **decision observers** to monitor and standardize outcomes.
  - Apply consistent criteria to eliminate chaos.

KEY PRINCIPLES FOR SMARTER DECISIONS

1. **Recognize Bias and Noise:** Awareness is the first step to control.
2. **Adopt Disciplined Approaches:** Standardize frameworks for clarity and consistency.
3. **Encourage Diverse Perspectives:** Challenge assumptions and reduce blind spots through inclusion.
4. **Leverage Feedback Loops:** Measure, refine, and improve decisions iteratively.
5. **Build Critical-Thinking Culture:** Empower teams to question and challenge confidently.

Outcome: Reduce bias, silence noise, and design decision systems that drive clarity, consistency, and progress. Smart decisions become systematic, turning complexity into competitive advantage.

PART 4

ACTIVATE STRATEGIC OPERATIONAL INTELLIGENCE

Imagine a decision-making system so precise, so aligned that every choice becomes a competitive advantage. This section is about more than optimization—it's about transformation. Your systems will no longer just support progress—they will propel your organization to lead the charge.

You've learned how to reduce bias, silence noise, and align decision-making across your organization. But what if that's just the beginning? Imagine decisions powered by unmatched insights, real-time context, and pinpoint accuracy—turning every choice into a catalyst for success.

This is where strategic operational intelligence (SOI) takes the stage. SOI isn't just a system upgrade—it's the blueprint for greatness.

By filling gaps, connecting the dots, and harnessing your team's full potential, SOI transforms fragmented efforts into a unified, unstoppable strategic asset. With stronger organizational memory and critical intelligence, every action becomes a step closer to your shared vision.

In this section, you'll find a step-by-step roadmap to implementing SOI and achieving unparalleled alignment with your organization's most critical goals. With each insight, you'll gain the tools to build a smarter, stronger, and more unified enterprise—one decision at a time.

Let's get started.

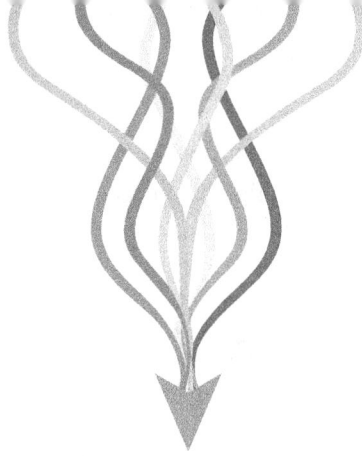

CHAPTER 10

BUILDING THE NERVOUS SYSTEM FOR STRATEGIC INTELLIGENCE

"Just as a calculator can assist us in mathematical tasks, so AI can support our decision-making process, freeing up cognitive space for more complex thoughts."

—DANIEL KAHNEMAN

WHAT IS THE NEXT LEVEL OF DECISION-MAKING?

Imagine an organization where everything works in harmony. Goals are aligned. Actions are connected. Insights flow seamlessly. Decisions are sharp, fast, and always on point.

Little wasted energy. Less scattered information. No hesitation.

That's what **SOI** delivers. It builds a **nervous system for your strategy**—interconnected layers that bridge your long-term vision with real-time execution. SOI provides the clarity, context, and momentum you need. It creates an environment where every team can make smarter, more effective decisions—at every level.

The result?

- **Clarity** replaces chaos.
- **Context** replaces confusion.
- **Momentum** replaces hesitation.

Right now, most organizations are drowning in disconnected data, fragmented tools, and broken processes. Leaders are trying to steer the ship with half the map and outdated coordinates. Decisions are reactive, opportunities slip through the cracks, and agility feels elusive.

But what if your data didn't just sit in silos—what if it connected, evolved, and learned with you? What if your systems not only collected information but also wove context into every piece, delivering insights with traceability and accuracy?

That's where SOI steps in. It automates workflows, leverages assistive AI, and builds dynamic context graphs. It taps into **organizational memory** and merges it all into a unified rhythm. **The result?** Actionable intelligence that never loses momentum.

It doesn't just connect the dots—it keeps them connected. It evolves as your business grows, aligning every action with your strategy.

HOW TO GET THERE

Leaders face relentless complexity—expanding markets, rising risks, and million-dollar decisions made faster than ever before. Gut instincts aren't enough. Success demands foresight, clarity, and precision.

Strategy isn't chess—it's poker. You don't get perfect information. You get signals, probabilities, and choices under pressure.

But AI and dynamic context graphs can change the game.

Think of how complexity scales: At first, decisions feel small and linear. But over time, exponential possibilities emerge. **SOI unlocks that second half for organizations.**

It starts with knowledge collection—but the real power comes when that data turns into intelligence. AI processes vast datasets, identifies hidden patterns, and surfaces insights humans alone would **miss,** but only if you are intentional about how knowledge is harvested, connected, and shared.

The result?

Organizations that don't just react to change—they shape it.

THE DATA CHALLENGE

Here's the truth: **Data without context is just static crackling in the background—distracting and, ultimately, useless.**

Imagine a marketing team struggling to align campaigns with sales data stored in siloed systems. This disconnection wastes time, creates friction, and limits results. SOI bridges these gaps, unlocking the hidden power of their data.

According to Accenture, only **32 percent of companies** see measurable value from their analytics programs.[121] Why?

- Data is scattered.
- Context is missing.
- Insights disappear.

To unlock the promise of data, organizations must solve four core challenges.

---

121 Accenture, *The Human Impact of Data Literacy* (Accenture, 2020), 4, https://www.accenture.com/content/dam/accenture/final/a-com-migration/r3-3/pdf/pdf-118/accenture-the-human-impact-data-literacy.pdf.

1. UNSTRUCTURED DATA

Your business generates data everywhere—emails, images, videos, documents. **Unstructured data is chaos without a compass.** It's valuable but messy.

- No format. No consistency. No rules.
- Teams waste resources cleaning the mess.
- Insights stay buried, accessible only with technical intervention.

The Fix: Organizations need tools that process and connect unstructured data—turning chaos into clarity.

2. DATA SPRAWL

Is your critical data scattered and siloed? Information can hide across cloud drives, email threads, and disconnected systems.

- Data becomes invisible.
- Silos stall decision-making.
- Governance and security break down.

The Fix: Centralize your data. A single source of truth ensures leaders make decisions with the full picture—not incomplete fragments.

3. MISSING ONTOLOGY

An **ontology** is a formal framework that defines and organizes concepts, relationships, and rules within a specific domain to enable shared understanding and reasoning. Every team speaks its own language, uses its own tools, and interprets relationships differently.

- Misaligned goals create friction.
- Communication gaps waste resources.

- Leaders struggle to connect strategy with action.

The Fix: Build a shared ontology—a universal language for your business. Here's how:

1. **Define Critical Terms:** Identify the core words and phrases each department uses, and create a shared glossary.
2. **Map Relationships:** Show how these terms link to products, customers, and processes.
3. **Enforce Consistency:** Use tools and guidelines that ensure teams adopt the same terminology across meetings, memos, and documentation.
4. **Use Modern Technology:** Utilize AI, context graphs, and human-in-the-loop processes to identify and address gaps in your ontology, decreasing the need for manual mapping exercises.

With a shared ontology, you're not just using the same words— you're creating a connected, organization-wide understanding of every goal, project, and result.

4. LOST INSIGHTS

Insights from data analysis are valuable—until they're lost.

- Scattered across reports.
- Buried in slide decks.
- Forgotten when team members leave.

The Fix: Surface insights in context to the right people at the right time. Create a centralized catalog of insights. Insights become searchable, accessible, and reusable, fueling smarter decisions and continuous innovation.

The Bottom Line

Solve these challenges, and your data becomes a living asset—a foundation for action, not noise.

CONNECTING THE DOTS

Modern organizations generate vast amounts of knowledge and insights. But without connection, it's meaningless. SOI builds the connective tissue between your systems, turning raw data into relational insights. Here's how.

PHASE 1: BUILD A CONTEXT GRAPH

Think of this as the foundation of your organization's nervous system. By mapping entities and their relationships, you transform scattered data into a structured, actionable map for decision-making.

BUILDING THE GRAPH LAYER

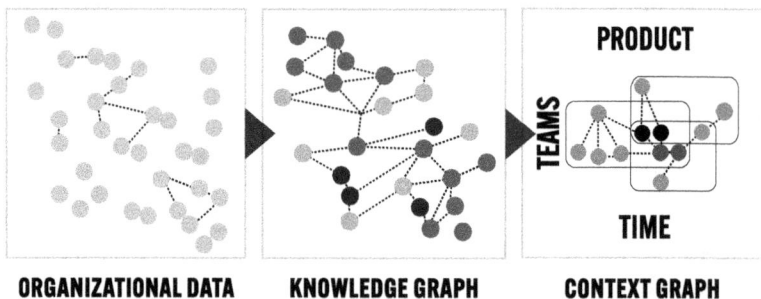

ORGANIZATIONAL DATA   KNOWLEDGE GRAPH   CONTEXT GRAPH

Building a graph layer matters because it:

1. Unveils patterns and connections in data, giving leaders deep context for confident decision-making.

2. Improves search, integration, and strategic alignment.
3. Adapts fluidly as the organization evolves.
4. Derives meaningful relationship chains that offer richer context than tabular data.
5. Captures time-based information to reveal how strategy evolves over time.

The Result

Improved search capabilities, better data integration, and smarter, faster decisions.

PHASE 2: DIGITIZE YOUR DECISION ARCHITECTURE

Most organizations rely on ad hoc decision-making. Meetings end, slides get shared, and the decision trail disappears.

Digitizing decisions changes everything.

- Explicit decisions—big moves like market entries—are captured.
- Implicit decisions—like budget approvals—are logged.

The Result

- Teams align around a single source of truth.
- Leaders spot patterns, biases, and opportunities for improvement.
- Decisions become transparent, consistent, and scalable.

PHASE 3: BUILD ORGANIZATIONAL MEMORY

Your organization's memory is one of its greatest competitive tools. It holds your history, decisions, and lessons learned.

STRATEGIC DECISION INTELLIGENCE

AUTOMATION

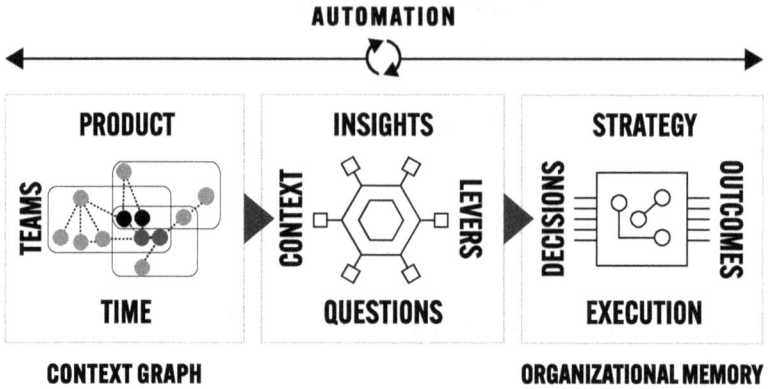

PRODUCT	INSIGHTS	STRATEGY
TEAMS	CONTEXT	DECISIONS
TIME	QUESTIONS	EXECUTION

CONTEXT GRAPH   ORGANIZATIONAL MEMORY

But most of it is scattered across silos and systems. Context disappears, and patterns go unnoticed.

The impact of adding a system to digitize your organizational memory:

1. Avoid repeating mistakes and chasing previously exploited dead ends.
2. Strengthen strategy with historical context.
3. Support decision-making by leveraging collective organizational knowledge.
4. Build an invaluable source of legible knowledge for future AI-driven analytics.

Here's how to do it:

1. Document recent decisions, strategies, and outcomes.
2. Connect them into a unified framework.
3. Track trends over time to replicate successes and avoid mistakes.

The Result

Organizational memory becomes a self-improving engine that guides teams, strengthens strategy, and informs every action.

PHASE 4: SIMPLIFY COLLABORATION

Collaboration works best when it's seamless—where teams work naturally, without friction or complexity. Yet tools often force rigid structures, slowing creativity and adoption.

The solution? A free-form collaboration experience powered by large language models (LLMs).

Teams can work in familiar, document-like spaces—brainstorming ideas, capturing plans, or strategizing together—while AI works behind the scenes. LLMs extract meaning, structure data, and connect inputs to your context graph, keeping everything organized without excessive manual effort.

Why It Matters

1. **Work Your Way:** Teams collaborate naturally, with no need to learn new systems or tools.
2. **Automatic Structure:** AI organizes data in real time, turning ideas into actionable insights.
3. **Instant Context:** LLMs surface relevant information and automate updates through natural interactions.

The Result

Free-form collaboration becomes powerful and productive. Teams move faster, creativity flows, and every action connects to your strategy. Unstructured input transforms into structured intelligence—without teams ever needing to think about it.

AUTOMATE INTELLIGENCE FLOW

Data is omnipresent, but insights are elusive. How do you turn this noise into clarity? It starts with smart automation:

1. **Gather Dots:** Collect strategically and operationally relevant information from across your organization.
2. **Assign Meaning:** Align data with your goals and priorities, transforming raw numbers into actionable knowledge.
3. **Add Dimensions:** Create hierarchies and networks that reflect your organization's complexity.
4. **Surface Relationships:** Uncover hidden connections and insights that change how you see the big picture.
5. **Unlock Insights:** Deliver real-time, contextual intelligence directly to decision-makers, empowering them to act with confidence.

AUTOMATED INSIGHTS

GATHER DOTS	ASSIGN MEANING	ADD DIMENSIONS	SURFACE RELATIONSHIPS

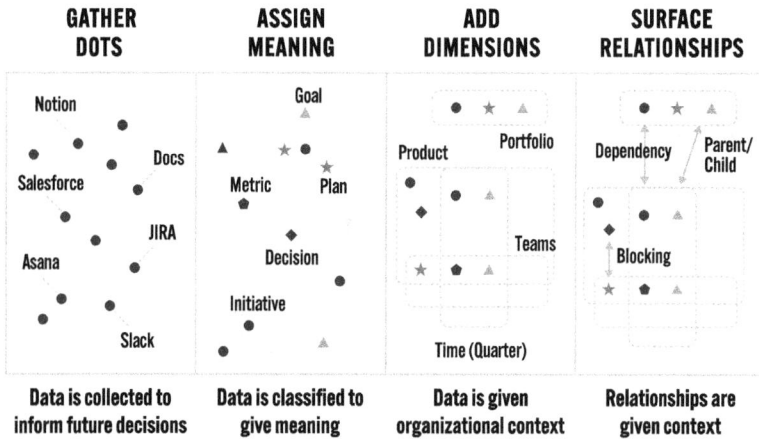

Data is collected to inform future decisions	Data is classified to give meaning	Data is given organizational context	Relationships are given context

UNLOCK INSIGHTS

☑ If we don't make this decision, we can't plan for the next quarter.

☑ In the past five years, we've made eight similar decisions, reversing four and achieving the related OKR once out of the remaining six.

☑ Delaying the related initiative impacts 259 customers, constituting 59% of next quarter's revenue, and is a top-five request for 82% of them this year.

Strategic effectiveness is bolstered

Bringing all components together, a flow is established from raw data to contextualized data with centralized relationships, leading to organizational memory. This process offers a significant advantage when making decisions. The true potential of centralized ontology is realized when these elements are integrated seamlessly.

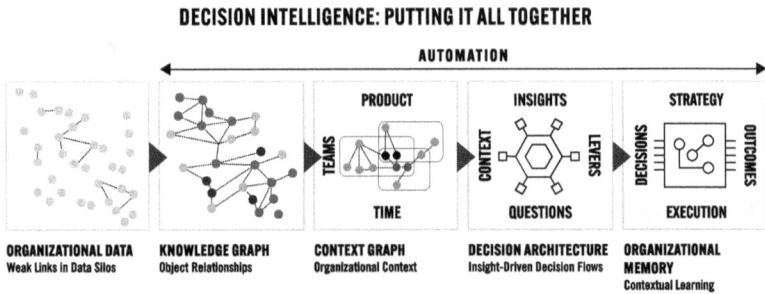

DECISION INTELLIGENCE: PUTTING IT ALL TOGETHER

DECISION-FLOW AUTOMATION

Repetitive decisions—like inventory or scheduling—can be fully automated, freeing human minds for creativity and strategy.[122] Complex decisions rely on **Human-in-the-Loop (HitL)** models, where AI provides support and humans apply judgment.

The outcome?

- Decisions are faster.
- Errors are fewer.
- Productivity soars.

---

122 Marcin Kapuściński, "Boosting Productivity: Using AI to Automate Routine Business Tasks," *TTMS* (blog), September 5, 2024, https://ttms.com/boosting-productivity-using-ai-to-automate-routine-business-tasks/.

THE FUTURE OF SOI

Imagine a world where tools for strategic operations don't just serve but anticipate. Where they adapt as your team evolves, fitting seamlessly into workflows as if designed uniquely for you. Picture a system that understands the rhythm of your organization, supporting complex models with grace, never missing a beat. Tools that grow with you, flex with you, but never overwhelm you. They enhance what you already rely on, unlocking hidden potential rather than demanding reinvention. They guide change gently, never abruptly. They feel crafted for your challenges, built for your pace, designed for your context. These tools don't ask you to compromise; they let you embrace uncertainty with confidence, turning chaos into clarity and making strategy as dynamic as the world it shapes.

This is the promise of the next generation of solutions. The next frontier of decision-making is advanced operational intelligence. It's **a single system that aligns goals, actions, and insights—your organization's true nervous system.** By capturing and sharing critical context in real time, it empowers more-informed decisions. Every step aligns with strategy, every action supports the big picture, and every leader can respond to change with agility. This is how you bridge long-term vision with day-to-day execution.

SOI transforms everything. It integrates assistive AI, builds dynamic context graphs, and develops an evolving organizational memory. It doesn't just connect the dots—it keeps them meaningful as your organization scales.

THE FUTURE OF DECISION-MAKING

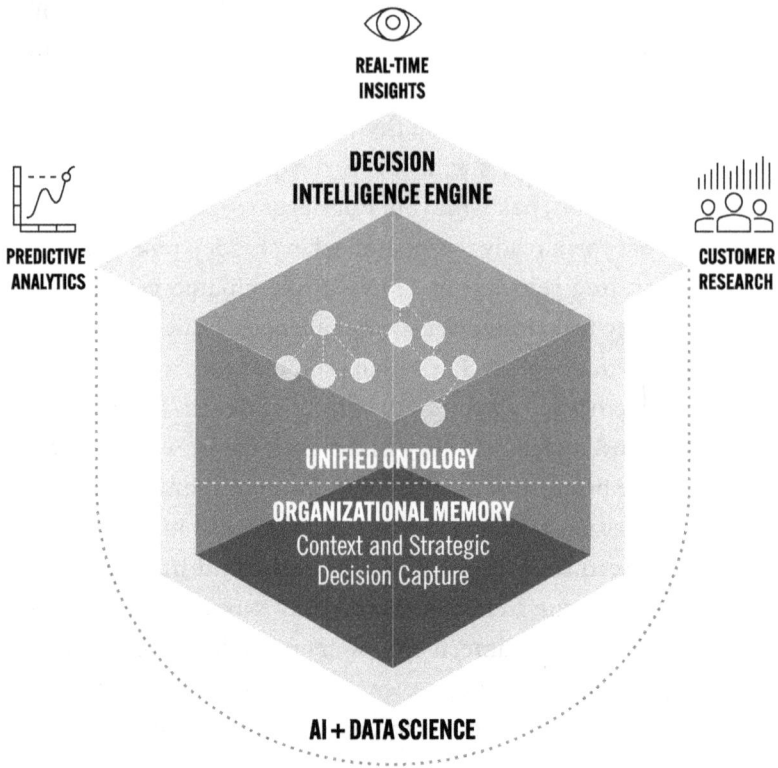

The integration of **context graphs, organizational memory, and contextual automation** will make this leap possible, enabling:

- Real-time contextual insights.
- Predictive analytics that are pushed, not searched for.
- Systems that flex with your organization.
- Unmatched decision-making clarity.

POWERING NEXT-LEVEL DECISIONS

Organizations face decisions that range from straightforward to overwhelmingly complex. Understanding the nature of these decisions is critical to ensuring the right approach is applied. The Cynefin Framework, developed by Dave Snowden, provides a powerful lens for categorizing decision-making scenarios based on knowledge and uncertainty. When paired with advanced systems, like context graphs, organizational memory, and context-fueled AI, SOI becomes a transformative force for organizations striving to navigate uncertainty and complexity.

The Cynefin Framework divides decision scenarios into five key domains, each with its own characteristics and appropriate approaches:[123]

- **Simple:** High agreement and high certainty. Decisions are straightforward and well-understood. Best practices apply.
- **Complicated:** Moderate certainty and agreement. Solutions exist but require expert analysis. Good practices are needed.
- **Complex:** Low certainty but moderate agreement. Decisions involve unknowns, and outcomes emerge through iterative learning. Probe–sense–respond is the best approach.
- **Chaotic:** Low agreement and low certainty. Decisions are made in rapidly changing, high-pressure environments where immediate action is needed. Act–sense–respond is critical.
- **Disorder:** When the situation is unclear and the domain needs to be identified before action is taken.

SOI must be flexible to support diverse decision-making scenarios, adapting its function based on the decision's domain within the Cynefin Framework. When integrated with tools like dynamic

---

123 David J. Snowden and Mary E. Boone, "A Leader's Framework for Decision Making," *Harvard Business Review*, November 2007, https://hbr.org/2007/11/a-leaders-framework-for-decision-making.

context graphs, organizational memory, and AI, SOI enables leaders to make decisions with unmatched clarity and confidence.

SOI IN SIMPLE AND COMPLICATED DOMAINS

In these domains, where certainty is higher, SOI focuses on providing direct, actionable support:

- **Specific Recommendations:** SOI uses its context graph to analyze reliable data and predictable patterns, delivering clear guidance.
- **Automated Insights:** Streamlined workflows help leaders make fast, effective decisions.
- **Minimized Human Effort:** AI identifies optimal solutions, freeing teams to focus on strategic challenges.
- **Leveraged Organizational Memory:** SOI retrieves lessons from past decisions and outcomes, ensuring established best practices guide current choices.

Example: A manufacturing company relies on SOI to optimize production schedules. The system integrates inventory data, supply-chain patterns, and market demand within its context graph. It references past successful scheduling strategies stored in its organizational memory, delivering precise recommendations, eliminating delays, and ensuring efficiency.

SOI IN COMPLEX DOMAINS

In the complex domain, where uncertainty prevails, SOI shifts to enabling informed judgment. Here, the power of a context graph and organizational memory becomes indispensable:

- **Context-Rich Insights:** SOI connects disparate datasets, unveiling relationships that help leaders grasp broader implications.

- **Highlighting Consequences:** AI models scenarios, showing the ripple effects of potential decisions and enabling adaptive learning.
- **Cross-Functional Collaboration:** SOI maps interdependencies, fostering teamwork and presenting a unified strategic view.
- **Building on Experience:** Organizational memory ensures insights from previous complex scenarios inform current strategies, reducing the risk of repeating mistakes.

Example: A retail chain considering a new market entry uses SOI to model economic trends, consumer behavior, and logistical challenges. By surfacing hidden connections in its context graph and referencing lessons from prior market entries, the system equips leaders with the clarity to make confident decisions.

SOI IN CHAOTIC DOMAINS

In the chaotic domain, where urgency and uncertainty dominate, SOI stabilizes decision-making:

- **Critical Context:** SOI cuts through noise to identify immediate priorities.
- **Quick-Win Actions:** SOI highlights actions that mitigate risks and restore order.
- **Real-Time Updates:** As conditions evolve, SOI adjusts strategies dynamically, ensuring alignment.
- **Historical Comparisons:** Organizational memory provides insights from past crises, enabling quicker identification of effective responses.

Example: During a cybersecurity breach, SOI integrates real-time threat data with historical breach patterns stored in its organizational memory and context graph. It identifies vulnerable systems, recommends immediate containment measures, and references successful mitigation strategies from similar incidents, enabling swift and decisive action.

SOI IN DISORDER DOMAINS

In situations where the domain is unclear, SOI helps leaders move from confusion to clarity through:

- **Sensemaking Tools:** Leveraging AI to identify patterns and classify the situation.
- **Diagnostic Insights:** Mapping data to the appropriate Cynefin domain, guiding the next steps.

Why This Matters

When powered by AI, dynamic context graphs, and organizational memory, SOI revolutionizes decision-making. It tailors support to the specific needs of each domain, empowering organizations to:

- Act decisively in simple and complicated contexts.
- Navigate complexity with informed judgment.
- Restore order and focus in chaotic situations.
- Make sense of disordered scenarios with diagnostic tools.

The context graph's ability to connect, organize, and evolve data amplifies SOI's impact. Organizational memory adds a rich layer of historical knowledge, ensuring decisions are informed not just by the present but by accumulated experience. Together, these elements create a living system of intelligence that guides action with precision.

SOI isn't just a framework—it's the future of decision-making. To see its transformative potential, let's explore how one organization, GlideTech, Inc., leveraged SOI to gain a competitive edge.

EXAMPLE: THE POTENTIAL OF NEXT-GENERATION SOI

Organization: GlideTech, Inc.

Industry: Enterprise software.

Challenge: Scaling decision-making in a fast-growing organization.

Background

GlideTech, an enterprise software company, had grown rapidly over the last five years, expanding into new markets and doubling its product lines. However, this growth created fragmentation across departments, with data silos in marketing, sales, and operations. Leadership struggled to make informed, timely decisions due to disconnected information and a lack of contextual insights.

The Problem

- Marketing campaigns didn't align with sales strategies, leading to missed revenue targets.
- Product teams operated in isolation, duplicating efforts and failing to leverage shared lessons from past launches.
- Leadership decisions relied on outdated reports, with critical insights buried in scattered spreadsheets and siloed systems.

The SOI Solution

GlideTech was at a crossroads. Rapid growth brought opportunity but also chaos. Disconnected teams, silos of data, and missed targets plagued its operations. That's when GlideTech embraced SOI. This wasn't just an upgrade—it was a lifeline. By aligning strategy with execution, GlideTech didn't just survive—it thrived. Here's how it accomplished this:

- Phase 1: Build a Context Graph

- **Action:** GlideTech centralized its data into an AI-driven context graph. This graph mapped relationships between customer profiles, marketing campaigns, sales performance, and product features.
- **Impact:** Hidden patterns emerged, such as which customer segments responded best to specific campaigns and which product features drove the most renewals.

- Phase 2: Digitize Decision Architecture
  - **Action:** The company digitized decision workflows. Budget approvals, go-to-market plans, and roadmap changes were captured and linked within the system.
  - **Impact:** Teams aligned around a single source of truth, reducing decision delays by 40 percent and enabling leadership to trace the impact of every strategic move.

- Phase 3: Build Organizational Memory
  - **Action:** Past product launches, campaign outcomes, and customer feedback were integrated into an evolving organizational memory.
  - **Impact:** Lessons learned from previous initiatives informed future strategies, reducing redundant efforts and improving product launch efficiency by 25 percent.

- Phase 4: Simplify Collaboration
  - **Action:** Teams used free-form collaboration tools powered by LLMs. These tools structured status updates and insight delivery in real time, connecting them to the context graph.
  - **Impact:** Cross-departmental collaboration improved, with 30 percent faster project turnaround times and a noticeable boost in creativity and innovation.

The Measurable Results

Within a year of implementing SOI:

- **Revenue Growth:** A 15 percent increase in revenue due to better-aligned marketing and sales efforts.
- **Efficiency Gains:** A 20 percent reduction in duplicated work and wasted resources.
- **Decision Speed:** Strategic decision-making cycles reduced from weeks to days.
- **Employee Satisfaction:** A 25 percent improvement in employee survey scores for alignment and collaboration.

The Result

With SOI, GlideTech transformed its fragmented systems into a cohesive nervous system, connecting strategy, execution, and decision-making. The result was a smarter, more agile organization capable of thriving in a fast-paced market.

GlideTech's Leadership Summed It Up Best

"SOI didn't just help us make better decisions—it made us a better company. Every action is now connected, every decision aligned, and every team empowered."

THE BOTTOM LINE

Organizations that embrace SOI will turn data into action, decisions into progress, and strategy into success.

SOI enables organizations to turn insights into action, decisions into momentum, and strategy into impact. It's the nervous system for an agile, adaptive, and aligned operating model. This isn't the distant future—it's happening now.

Build your nervous system for strategy. Automate intelligence. Lead the way.

SUMMARY

Organizations today are drowning in chaos—scattered data, fragmented tools, and disconnected decisions. Leaders navigate with outdated maps, chasing clarity in a fog of noise.

But imagine this instead: A system where strategy aligns with execution. Data flows seamlessly, building context as it moves. Decisions are sharp, fast, and impactful.

That's SOI.

SOI isn't a tool—it's a necessity. It transforms how organizations think, decide, and lead. It bridges vision with action, uncovers patterns others miss, and evolves alongside your business. In today's fast-paced world, SOI isn't optional—it's survival.

- Disconnected data becomes a context graph.
- Ad hoc decisions transform into a digitized decision architecture.
- Lost lessons evolve into organizational memory.
- Fragmented collaboration turns into seamless teamwork.

The result?

- Chaos becomes clarity.
- Confusion becomes context.
- Hesitation becomes momentum.

Organizations that implement SOI don't just react to change—they shape it. They anticipate outcomes, allocate resources with precision, and navigate complexity with confidence.

This is the future of decision-making.

It's agile. It's adaptive. And it's happening now.

SOI turns strategy into success, action into momentum, and data into your greatest advantage.

Ready to build your nervous system for strategy?

DECISION POINTS

Consider This Scenario: An organization has heavily invested in AI-driven SOI to enhance operations and drive innovation. While the AI systems have provided significant insights and streamlined various processes, the company faces challenges with data silos across departments. This fragmentation limits the potential of AI by restricting integrated data analysis, leading to suboptimal strategic decisions. Leadership must decide on the best path to address these challenges and unlock the full potential of SOI.

WHICH PATH WOULD YOUR ORGANIZATION CHOOSE?
Path 1: Break Down Silos with a Cross-Departmental Task Force

- Create a cross-departmental AI task force to address data silos and ensure seamless data flow.
- Focus on identifying bottlenecks, promoting interdepartmental collaboration, and establishing data-sharing protocols.
- Align processes to reduce fragmentation and enable better integration for decision-making.

The Result: A coordinated effort improves data integration incrementally, enhancing decision-making without major infrastructure investments. However, progress may depend heavily on cross-departmental cooperation and time-intensive collaboration.

Path 2: Build an AI-Driven Context Graph for Unified Insights

- Invest in an AI-driven context graph to centralize essential data, context, and organizational memory into a unified repository.
- Connect the dots between departments, providing real-time insights and facilitating strategic decision-making across all levels.
- Train employees on using the system to ensure adoption and effective utilization.

The Result: A unified platform accelerates decision-making with integrated, real-time insights. The investment in infrastructure and training enhances collaboration and alignment across departments but requires up-front resources and commitment.

Your Turn: If this were your organization, would you prioritize the collaborative, incremental approach of Path 1—or invest in transformative infrastructure and training with Path 2?

Our Take: Path 1 emphasizes collaboration and addresses silos step by step, making it a practical approach for organizations seeking incremental improvements. Path 2, while requiring a larger up-front investment, positions organizations for long-term success with integrated, context-rich insights that support faster, smarter decisions.

The smartest decisions are those informed by the most complete picture—whether through gradual integration or bold transformation.

KEY TAKEAWAYS AND DISCUSSION QUESTIONS
1. INTEGRATION OF ADVANCED TECHNOLOGIES

Organizations should integrate AI, machine learning, and advanced analytics into their strategic decision-making processes. These tools unlock patterns, generate actionable insights, and transform raw data into a competitive advantage.

Questions to Reflect On:

- What types of relational data would provide the most impactful insights for our strategic decision-making?
- What infrastructure is needed to support the integration of a context graph, and how can we ensure scalability and security?
- How can we create a culture that balances AI-driven decision-making with the value of human judgment and expertise?

2. CENTRALIZATION AND STANDARDIZATION OF CONTEXT

Centralizing context into a unified graph with a shared ontology improves accessibility, consistency, and alignment across an organization. This enables data to be analyzed efficiently and ensures decisions are based on a complete picture.

Questions to Reflect On:

- What challenges do our current data silos create, and how could a unified graph and shared ontology help overcome these issues?
- How can we design a centralized repository that balances data accessibility with security and privacy concerns?
- What processes can we implement to ensure consistent and accurate data entry into our unified graph?
- How can we incentivize departments to adopt and adhere to a shared ontology?

Enhancing Decision-Making Agility

Building a decision-intelligence framework enables organizations to anticipate future challenges, assess risks, and make informed decisions quickly and effectively. This approach fosters agility and empowers organizations to adapt in dynamic environments.

Questions to Reflect On:

- What types of intelligence would most enhance our current decision-making processes?
- How can predictive analytics help us anticipate future conditions and potential risks?
- What steps can we take to ensure our decision intelligence framework remains flexible and responsive to changing business environments?
- How can we measure the effectiveness of our decision-intelligence framework in improving speed, accuracy, and strategic impact?

KNOWLEDGE MAP

SOI

A system for aligning goals, actions, and insights—connecting strategy, execution, and decision-making into a unified flow.

Core Idea: SOI acts as the nervous system of the organization, providing the clarity, context, and momentum to invest in environments for more informed, effective decision-making at every level.

FOUR KEY INGREDIENTS OF SOI

1: Build a Context Graph

- **Purpose:** Organize and connect data to reveal relationships and meaning.
- **What It Does:** Maps entities (nodes) and relationships (edges) across people, projects, and outcomes.
- **Impact:**
  - Surfaces hidden insights and patterns.
  - Brings deep context to complex decision-making.
  - Improves search, integration, and strategic alignment.
  - Adapts fluidly as the organization changes.
  - Derives meaningful relationship chains that provide more valuable context than tabular data.
  - Captures time-based information, not just point-in-time data, to better understand how the strategy has evolved in context.

2: Digitize Your Decision Architecture

- **Purpose:** Capture and structure decisions to build a single source of truth.
- **What It Does:** Logs explicit (big, strategic moves) and implicit (tactical approvals) decisions.
- **Impact:**
  - Aligns teams around a shared, explicit decision stream.

- Increases transparency, consistency, and scalability.
- Helps leaders identify patterns, biases, and opportunities for improvement.
- Enables every team to know how and why their work matters

3: Build Organizational Memory

- **Purpose:** Preserve knowledge, decisions, and lessons learned as an evolving resource.
- **What It Does:** Integrates past goals, outcomes, and insights into a connected framework.
- **Impact:**
  - Avoids repeating mistakes and chasing previously exploited dead ends.
  - Strengthens strategy with historical context.
  - Supports decision-making by leveraging collective organizational knowledge.
  - Builds an invaluable source of legible knowledge for future AI-driven analytics.

4: Simplify Collaboration

- **Purpose:** Enable seamless, free-form collaboration while maintaining structure and context.
- **What It Does:** Uses LLMs to organize unstructured input and connect it to the context graph.
- **Impact:**
  - Allows teams to collaborate naturally without learning new systems.
  - Ensures ideas are structured, connected, and actionable.
  - Flows context in real time, keeping decisions aligned with strategy.
  - Saves time for each person involved in planning.

AUTOMATE INTELLIGENCE FLOW

Automation of the journey from raw data to actionable insights.
How It Works:

1. **Gather Dots:** Pull from all internal and external sources.
2. **Assign Meaning:** Align data to goals, metrics, and priorities.
3. **Add Dimensions:** Build networks by linking data to teams, products, and timelines.
4. **Surface Relationships:** Map connections and surface patterns.
5. **Unlock Insights:** Deliver real-time, contextualized intelligence.

The Result: Faster analysis, clearer decisions, and continuous improvement through automated workflows.

STRATEGIC OPERATIONS AUTOMATION

- **What It Does:** Delegates routine planning and alignment tasks to AI and automates decision support for strategic moves.
- **Impact:**
  - Frees teams for creative, high-value work.
  - Reduces human errors and decision delays.
  - HitL ensures complex decisions balance automation with judgment.

THE FUTURE OF SOI

- **Unified Context Graphs:** Connect data, decisions, and goals for unmatched clarity.
- **Organizational Memory:** Guide strategy with lessons from the past.
- **Contextual Insights:** Surface contextual trends and predictions as data evolves.

KEY PRINCIPLES FOR SOI

- **Connect the Dots:** Build relational insights through context graphs.
- **Unify Decisions:** Digitize processes for transparency and alignment.
- **Preserve Knowledge:** Strengthen decision-making with organizational memory.
- **Collaborate Seamlessly:** Let AI structure data while teams work naturally.
- **Automate Intelligence:** Move from raw data to actionable insights with speed and precision.

OUTCOME

SOI enables organizations to turn insights into action, decisions into momentum, and strategy into impact. It's the nervous system for an agile, adaptive, and aligned operating model.

Connected knowledge systems. Clear decisions. Sustainable success.

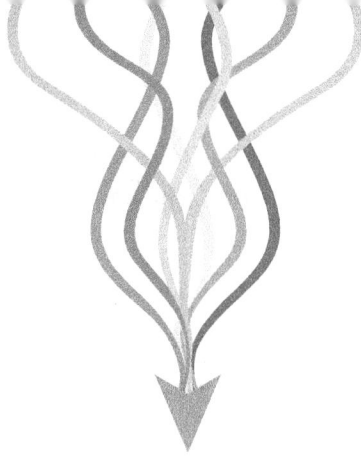

THE STATUS QUO CONUNDRUM

"If you're good at course correcting, being wrong may be less costly than you think, whereas being slow is going to be expensive for sure."

—JEFF BEZOS

The world's leading organizations aren't lucky. They're decisive.

In every organization, there's a silent force working against change: the **status quo conundrum**. It's the weight of entrenched processes, cultural inertia, and the illusion of safety in doing what's familiar. Past successes build comfort, and comfort breeds complacency. Teams stick to what's easy. Leaders hesitate to disrupt what works "well enough."

But here's the truth: **The status quo is the most dangerous choice of all.** In a world that moves faster every day, standing still isn't neutral—it's falling behind. Organizations clinging to the familiar will wake up disrupted. Those that choose action will thrive.

Your organization's future will be shaped by the decisions you make today, not by the decisions you **avoid**. Jean-Paul Sartre asserts that we are our choices. The same is true for your company.

Your culture, your reputation, your success—all are products of the choices you make and decisions you empower your teams to make.

SO EMBRACE DECISIVENESS

Decisiveness isn't reckless. It's not about rushing or skipping due diligence. It's about moving **deliberately** when others hesitate. The greatest leaders don't chase perfection—they chase progress. They take bold, informed action, knowing the cost of indecision far outweighs the cost of an occasional misstep.

Decisiveness builds momentum. It turns hesitation into clarity, action into outcomes.

When leaders choose decisiveness, organizations become more agile, aligned, and innovative. Employees gain confidence. Teams rally around a common purpose. Customers notice the difference. Competitors feel the pressure.

SHAPING THE FUTURE THROUGH DISRUPTION

The future belongs to the disruptors, to leaders willing to disrupt the status quo and reimagine how organizations think, decide, and act.

The work of leaders is to make decisions—big, small, and everything in between. Those who design systems, tools, and cultures that **enable decisiveness** will shape the future. Those who hesitate will be shaped by it.

Ask yourself:

- Will you let the status quo slow you down?
- Or will you lead the way with clarity, action, and momentum?

Your organization is a collection of decisions—who you hire, what you build, how you operate, and how you impact the world. Each choice defines who you are. So be exceptional at making those choices.

HOW TO GET STARTED

We've explored the tools, principles, and frameworks to help you drive smarter decisions and sharper execution. So, where do you begin?

Start small, but start now:

- Wire your organization for **context** (Chapter 4), **flow** (Chapter 5), and **action** (Chapter 6).
- Build systems to **standardize your decision architecture, centralize your knowledge,** and **streamline learning** while reducing **bias** and **noise** (Chapters 7, 8, and 9).
- Add **SOI** (Chapter 10) to align strategy and execution through modern AI, collaboration, and graph technology instead of manually hacking it together every quarter.

QUICK-START CHECKLIST FOR DECISIVE ACTION

1. **Commit to One Bold Move This Month:**
   A. Identify a single high-impact decision you've been postponing—like streamlining a process, reprioritizing a key project, or phasing out an underperforming product.
   B. Set a firm deadline, and block out any meetings or distractions until you finalize the call.
   C. Make it public—tell your team (or your peers) the decision date to hold yourself accountable.
2. **Map Your Stakeholders:**
   A. List the critical voices and influencers who need to be aligned—from frontline teams to senior leadership.
   B. Schedule quick, focused check-ins to gather their perspectives. Keep each conversation under thirty minutes to stay nimble.
   C. Document insights in a shared space (like an online whiteboard or digital hub) to maintain clarity.
3. **Implement One Decision-Velocity Tool:**

A. Pick a simple decision-making framework (e.g., RAPID, DACI, or a short decision template) and standardize its use for at least one upcoming project.

B. Keep it visible—post the flowchart or roles matrix in your team's communication channel.

C. Practice strict adherence for the next two weeks then refine together if needed.

4. **Schedule a "Decisiveness Debrief":**
A. Set aside fifteen minutes for a quick retrospective two weeks from now.

B. Ask, "Which decisions went well? Which ones dragged? Why?"

C. Encourage honest feedback. If a decision got bogged down, figure out which step—lack of data, misalignment, or communication gaps—caused the holdup.

5. **Reward Swift, Thoughtful Action:**
A. Publicly acknowledge a team or individual who made a timely, well-informed decision (even if the outcome wasn't perfect).

B. Signal through praise that decisive action is valued, reinforcing a culture that chases momentum rather than avoids risk.

Progress doesn't happen overnight, but small, deliberate steps compound. Wire your organization to observe, align, and act—and momentum will follow.

PARTING THOUGHTS

As leaders, our work is to decide—and ensure our organizations are wired to make better, faster decisions. Every choice we make shapes our organization's path forward. An organization's journey is largely defined by its people's decisions and commitment to execute those decisions.

Your journey begins now. Challenge the status quo. Build a culture of decisiveness. Invest in the systems and tools that enable alignment, clarity, and action. In a world defined by speed and disruption, your ability to decide will define your success.

The future is built one decision at a time. Make them count.

APPENDICES

A. Digital Transformation: A Journey, Not a Destination

B. Hybrid Work: A New Era of Collaboration and Complexity

C. Business Agility: A Key to Thriving in Uncertainty

D. AI Integration: Transforming the Future

E. Decisiveness Traps: Patterns That Slow Decisions

F. Cognitive Bias Index

G. Bias Mitigation Index

H. Insights Index

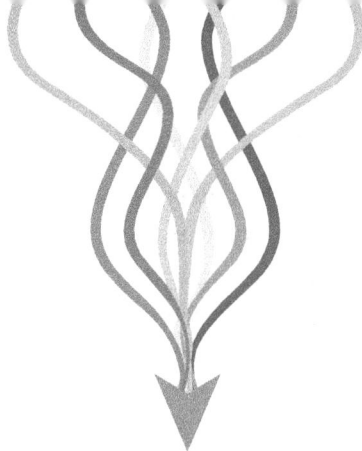

DIGITAL TRANSFORMATION

A JOURNEY, NOT A DESTINATION

"The digital revolution is far more significant than the invention of writing or even of printing."

—Douglas Engelbart

Digital transformation is not a single leap. It's a thousand deliberate steps. It's rethinking everything—how we operate, innovate, and compete. It's the evolution of technology intertwined with the evolution of business.

Every decision shapes the path forward: choosing technology, redesigning processes, managing data, enhancing customer experiences, and safeguarding against cyber threats. It's not just about progress—it's about precision.

But here's the truth: Digital transformation never ends. It shifts, adapts, and grows. The leaders who thrive are those who embrace its relentless pace—not as a challenge but as an opportunity to lead.

THE EVOLUTION OF DIGITAL TRANSFORMATION

It began with simplicity: machines replacing manual work. Early computing automated tasks, saving time and cutting costs.

The 1980s and '90s brought personal computers and the internet. Retail became e-commerce. Advertising turned digital. Companies began to realize that technology wasn't just a tool—it was an edge.

Then came the 2000s. Smartphones and social media redefined connection. Cloud computing gave businesses flexibility. Data analytics transformed decision-making.

In the 2010s, a new wave emerged. Artificial intelligence (AI) optimized processes. The Internet of Things (IoT) connected products, creating ecosystems instead of silos. Companies didn't just adapt—they evolved.

Now, in the 2020s, the rules are being rewritten again. Generative AI, powered by tools like OpenAI and Google Bard, enables personalized customer experiences and predictive insights.

5G drives real-time operations for businesses in almost every industry, from healthcare to logistics.

The blockchain secures transactions and ensures supply-chain transparency.

Augmented reality (AR) and virtual reality (VR) create immersive customer and employee experiences.

This is the era of perpetual transformation. Agility and vision are no longer optional—they are the foundation of survival.

THE CURRENT LANDSCAPE

Today's digital landscape is both volatile and rich with potential.

- **Generative AI** fuels creativity and cross-functional problem-solving.
- **Hybrid work** is stabilizing, powered by AI-driven collaboration tools and immersive AR/VR platforms.

- **Sustainability** has risen as a mandate. IoT, AI, and blockchain drive efficiency and accountability.
- **Edge computing** revolutionizes industries with instant decision-making capabilities.
- **Digital sovereignty** reshapes strategies, emphasizing privacy and localization.

Netflix offers a powerful example. By pivoting to streaming and leveraging AI-driven recommendations, the company transformed itself from a DVD-rental service into a global leader in entertainment. This is the potential of aligning technology and strategy.

In this ever-changing terrain, only those who balance innovation with execution will succeed.

THE ECONOMICS OF TRANSFORMATION

Adapting to change is no longer optional—it's the price of staying relevant.

Digital transformation spending worldwide is predicted to reach almost $4 trillion by 2027.[124] Companies like Walmart and Microsoft are investing billions to remain competitive.[125]

And the payoff is enormous. The World Economic Forum estimates digital transformation could contribute $100 trillion to society and industry globally by 2026.[126]

Yet, the journey is not without its hurdles. Home Depot's $11 billion struggle to integrate in-store and online shopping is

---

124 "Worldwide Spending in Digital Transformation Is Forecast to reach Almost $4 Trillion by 2027, According to New IDC Spending Guide," IDC, May 30, 2024, https://www.idc.com/getdoc.jsp?containerId=prUS52305724.

125 Baburajan Kizhakedath, "Walmart Reveals How Digital Technology Powers Efficiency," InfotechLead, August 18, 2024, https://infotechlead.com/cio/walmart-reveals-how-technology-investment-powers-digital-business-86319; Satya Nadella, "Annual Report 2023," Microsoft, July 27, 2023, https://www.microsoft.com/investor/reports/ar23/index.html.

126 Oliver Cann, "$100 Trillion by 2025: The Digital Dividend for Society and Business," World Economic Forum, January 22, 2016, https://www.weforum.org/press/2016/01/100-trillion-by-2025-the-digital-dividend-for-society-and-business/.

a cautionary tale. Legacy systems created delays. Budgets were stretched.[127]

Research has found that **87.5 percent of digital transformations fail to meet their goals.**[128] Why? Misalignment. Leaders fail to grasp technology's potential. Teams fail to account for operational realities.

Transformation isn't just about adopting new tools—it's about aligning strategy, technology, and execution.

THE DECISIVENESS DILEMMA

In the digital age, every decision is more connected—and more complex.

Changes ripple across systems, delaying progress and creating unforeseen challenges. Decisions that once relied on intuition now demand input from security, compliance, legal, and technology teams.

Dependencies can paralyze progress.

But here's the paradox: While complexity slows decisiveness, digital transformation also delivers tools to accelerate it:

- **Data-driven insights** reduce uncertainty.
- **Agile frameworks** balance speed with rigor.
- **Collaboration platforms** streamline alignment and decision-making.

Organizations that master these tools move faster, adapt better, and stay ahead.

---

127 Martin Giles, "Home Depot's $11 Billion Digital Rebuild Hits a Legacy-Tech Speed Bump," *Forbes*, November 20, 2019, https://www.forbes.com/sites/martingiles/2019/11/20/home-depot-digital-transformation-speed-bump/?sh=4cfe6f1c5bc2.

128 Didier Bonnet, "3 Stages of a Successful Digital Transformation," *Harvard Business Review*, September 20, 2022, https://hbr.org/2022/09/3-stages-of-a-successful-digital-transformation.

THE ROAD AHEAD

Digital transformation isn't slowing down—it's accelerating.

By 2025, structured automation will grow from 20 percent adoption to 70 percent.[129] AI alone is expected to contribute $13 trillion to the global economy by 2030.[130]

5G will redefine worldwide connectivity.

Quantum computing could tackle problems once deemed unsolvable.

AR and VR are projected to generate $80 billion by 2025, revolutionizing industries from retail to healthcare.[131]

The future belongs to organizations that see transformation not as a goal but a mindset.

THE BIG PICTURE

Digital transformation fuels innovation. But it also amplifies uncertainty. It creates dependencies and complexity that challenge traditional leadership models.

Yet, within that complexity lies an opportunity:

- To make sharper decisions faster.
- To build systems that thrive on agility.
- To turn uncertainty into an advantage.

129 Itential, "Itential Recognized in Six Gartner® Hype Cycle™ Reports for Its Innovative Infrastructure Automation & Orchestration Technology," press release, August 8, 2023, https://www.itential.com/news/itential-recognized-in-six-gartner-hype-cycle-reports-for-its-innovative-infrastructure-automation-orchestration-technology/.

130 Jacques Bughin et al., *Notes from the AI Frontier: Modeling the Impact of AI on the World Economy* (McKinsey Global Institute, 2018), 13, https://www.mckinsey.com/~/media/mckinsey/featured%20insights/artificial%20intelligence/notes%20from%20the%20frontier%20modeling%20the%20impact%20of%20ai%20on%20the%20world%20economy/mgi-notes-from-the-ai-frontier-modeling-the-impact-of-ai-on-the-world-economy-september-2018.pdf?shouldIndex=false.

131 Heather Bellini, "The Real Deal with Virtual and Augmented Reality," Goldman Sachs, February 1, 2016, https://www.goldmansachs.com/intelligence/pages/virtual-and-augmented-reality.html.

The key is balance. Leaders must embrace both sides of the equation: **Transformation is chaos and clarity.** Success isn't about reaching the end of the journey—it's about mastering the journey itself.

Because in a world that never stops evolving, neither can we.

SUMMARY

Digital transformation is more than a buzzword—it's a force reshaping how businesses operate, innovate, and lead. While it introduces complexity, dependencies, and challenges, it also offers unparalleled tools for clarity and speed.

The choice is simple: **Adapt or be left behind.** Seize the tools, embrace the chaos, and lead your organization into a world of perpetual transformation. In a world of constant change, only those who evolve will thrive.

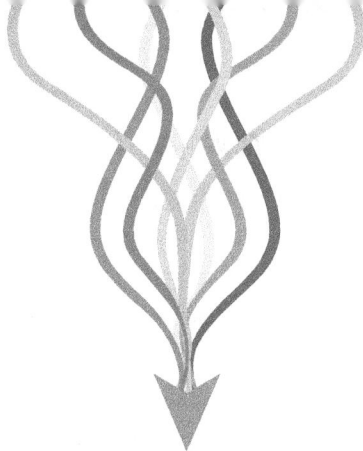

HYBRID WORK

A NEW ERA OF COLLABORATION AND COMPLEXITY

"The digital age has brought us a wealth of new ways to communicate, but none of them can beat an old-fashioned face-to-face conversation."
—RICHARD BRANSON

We are in a new era of collaboration.

Working outside the office isn't new. What's new is how it's redefining work itself. Remote work once meant independence and flexibility. Today, hybrid work represents a delicate balance: flexibility without losing connection, autonomy without isolation.

Hybrid work blends remote efficiency with the energy of in-person collaboration. It's about integrating technology, culture, and community to create a seamless work experience—anywhere, anytime.

THE EVOLUTION OF REMOTE WORK

Hybrid work didn't start with the pandemic. The pandemic was just the latest chapter in a rich history.

- **1970s:** Telecommuting was born out of necessity during energy crises and urban congestion.
- **1980s–1990s:** The internet and email made remote work feasible. IBM led the way, with 40 percent of its workforce working remotely by 2009.[132]
- **2010s:** High-speed internet, smartphones, and collaboration tools enabled remote work at scale, driven by demand for better work–life balance.
- **2020s:** The pandemic forced a global experiment in remote work, with 62 percent of Americans working from home in 2020. This accelerated hybrid models into the mainstream.[133]

By 2024, the initial excitement about remote work has settled into hybrid models that balance productivity with collaboration.

THE ECONOMICS OF HYBRID WORK

Hybrid work brings clear advantages:

- **Flexibility** enhances job satisfaction.
- **Broader talent pools** reduce geographic constraints.
- **Cost savings** result from reduced office space and commuting expenses.

Yet, the costs are more complex:

---

132 Nathan Allen, "The Pioneers of Modern Remote Work," wrkfrce, November 10, 2020, https://wrkfrce.com/the-pioneers-of-modern-remote-work/.

133 Megan Brenan, "U.S. Workers Discovering Affinity for Remote Work," Gallup News, April 3, 2020, https://news.gallup.com/poll/306695/workers-discovering-affinity-remote-work.aspx.

- **Cultural challenges** amplify feelings of disconnection, particularly for fully remote employees.
- **Managerial skepticism** persists. While 87 percent of employees report being productive at home, only 20 percent of managers agree.[134]

These challenges reveal hybrid work isn't a universal productivity booster—it's an evolving experiment requiring deliberate adjustments.

THE REALITY CHECK: IS REMOTE WORK THE PRODUCTIVITY BOOSTER WE THOUGHT?

The early pandemic narrative celebrated remote work as a productivity revolution. But as the dust settles, the reality is more nuanced:

1. **Innovation Slowed:** Spontaneous office interactions—the "weak ties" crucial for creativity—disappeared.
2. **Collaboration Struggled:** Without in-person synergy, teams found it harder to solve complex problems.
3. **Cultural Alignment Frayed:** Employees felt disconnected from corporate missions and values.

By 2023, companies like Goldman Sachs and JPMorgan reversed remote policies, citing weakened culture and diminished innovation. Leaders began questioning whether fully remote environments could sustain high performance over time.[135]

---

134 Simon Jack, "Bosses Think Workers Do Less from Home, Says Microsoft," *BBC*, September 22, 2022, https://www.bbc.com/news/business-62980639.

135 Vicky McKeever, "Goldman Sachs CEO Solomon Calls Working from Home an 'Aberration,'" CNBC, February 25, 2021, https://www.cnbc.com/2021/02/25/goldman-sachs-ceo-solomon-calls-working-from-home-an-aberration-.html.

IMPACT ON DECISIVENESS

Hybrid work has reshaped the way organizations function, but its impact on decisiveness is profound and, at times, **problematic**. A shift to remote work reduced productivity by 4 percent in call centers and slashed feedback among software engineers by 20 percent, according to recent research.[136] Collaboration, mentoring, and culture—the pillars of workplace cohesion—thrive in person, experts argue, yet these are the very elements hybrid work often erodes. Consider culture: In many organizations, a significant portion of the workforce joined after the pandemic, lacking the shared history that fosters trust and familiarity. As Peter Cappelli of Wharton points out, this gap creates a challenge for leaders trying to unify teams and drive quick, effective decisions.[137] Hybrid work doesn't just change where decisions happen—it changes how, and how well, they're made.

Hybrid work introduces new complexities to decision-making:

1. **Collaboration Challenges:**
    A. Decisions now unfold on digital platforms, requiring more structure to prevent misalignment. Nearly 60 percent of employees reported feeling less connected than before the COVID-19 aftermath.[138]
    B. Balancing synchronous (real-time) and asynchronous (flexible) communication complicates teamwork.
2. **Documentation Overload:**
    A. Virtual setups generate a digital paper trail. Without clear organization, unstructured records hinder insights.
3. **Dependencies and Decentralization:**

---

136 Sarah Lynch, "Did 2024 Kill Remote Work?," *Inc.*, December 5, 2024, https://www.inc.com/sarahlynch/did-2024-kill-remote-work/91034949.

137 Peter Cappelli, *The Future of the Office: Work from Home, Remote Work, and the Hard Choices We All Face* (Wharton School Press, 2021), 59.

138 Microsoft, "What We've Lost...and What We've Gained," WorkLab, accessed April 21, 2024, https://www.microsoft.com/en-us/worklab/pandemic-lost-and-gained.

A. Clear ownership and alignment are crucial. Decentralized decision-making empowers employees but risks misalignment unless guided by robust frameworks.

4. Weakening Weak Ties:

A. Research from Microsoft shows a 60 percent drop in weak ties—casual interactions that spark creativity—since hybrid models became more common.[139] Leaders with strong weak ties make better decisions, emphasizing the need to foster cross-team connections.

CASE STUDY: MICROSOFT'S HYBRID SUCCESS

Microsoft exemplifies hybrid work done right.

By integrating tools like Teams with flexible schedules, it has created a culture that blends autonomy with connection. Virtual brainstorming sessions and "digital watercooler" chats mimic casual in-office interactions, fostering collaboration and innovation.

Its approach highlights the importance of aligning technology with culture to maintain productivity and creativity in a hybrid environment.

OPPORTUNITIES FOR MORE DECISIVENESS

Hybrid work offers organizations unprecedented opportunities to improve decision-making:

- **AI-powered tools** streamline workflows, surface insights, and align teams in real time.
- **Structured frameworks** like OKRs ensure alignment, even in decentralized environments.
- **Virtual spaces** for spontaneous interactions rebuild weak ties, sparking innovation and fresh ideas.

---

139 Microsoft, "What We've Lost and Gained."

Quick, informed decisions will define success in this new era. Agile organizations will adapt faster, innovate boldly, and thrive amid uncertainty.

LOOKING AHEAD

Hybrid work isn't a passing trend—it's the foundation of the modern workplace. By 2025:

- Seventy-eight percent of global knowledge workers expect location flexibility, while 95 percent desire schedule flexibility, indicating a shift toward hybrid work arrangements.[140]
- Structured automation will drive decision-making in 70 percent of organizations.[141]
- Enterprise collaboration tools are expected to reach $154 billion by 2032.[142]

The biggest challenge remains culture. Hybrid workforces require leaders who can redefine what it means to belong, connect, and thrive in a distributed organization.

Success will depend on balancing flexibility, collaboration, and decisiveness. Organizations that embrace this reality will gain a competitive edge. Those that resist risk falling behind.

Hybrid work is a test of leadership, agility, and resilience.

---

140 "Leveling the Playing Field in the New Hybrid Workplace," *Slack* (blog), January 25, 2022, https://slack.com/blog/news/leveling-the-playing-field-in-the-new-hybrid-workplace.

141 "The Future of Business Automation in 2024," *Salient Process* (blog), January 19, 2024, https://salientprocess.com/blog/future-of-business-automation-2024/.

142 "Enterprise Collaboration Market Size, Share and Segmentation by Type (Unified Communication and Project Management and Workflow Automation), by Deployment (On-premises and Cloud), by Enterprise Type, by Industry, by Region and Global Forecast 2024-2032," SNS Insider, January 2025, https://www.snsinsider.com/reports/enterprise-collaboration-market-3574.

SUMMARY

Hybrid work isn't just a trend—it's a seismic shift in how we work, connect, and decide. By balancing flexibility and collaboration, organizations can harness its potential.

Opportunities abound for flexibility, cost savings, and broader talent pools within hybrid work. But challenges—weak ties, cultural misalignment, and decision complexity—threaten its success.

Organizations that invest in AI-powered tools, adopt structured frameworks, and rebuild team connections will unlock hybrid work's full potential. It's no longer optional—hybrid work is the future. The organizations that find the balance will thrive.

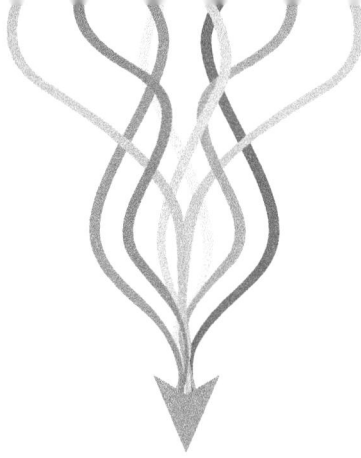

BUSINESS AGILITY

A KEY TO THRIVING IN UNCERTAINTY

"Long-term survival in today's business environment depends upon a company's ability to adapt to change."

—JOHN MAXWELL

Business agility, also called enterprise agility, is more than a buzz-word. It's the ability of an organization to swiftly realign strategies, structures, processes, people, and technology to deliver value and satisfy customers. Business agility connects strategy to execution, creating a seamless flow from high-level objectives to actionable outcomes.

But agility isn't just about reacting. It's about proactively turning challenges into opportunities, driving innovation, improving efficiency, and staying ahead in a competitive landscape.

THE EVOLUTION OF BUSINESS AGILITY

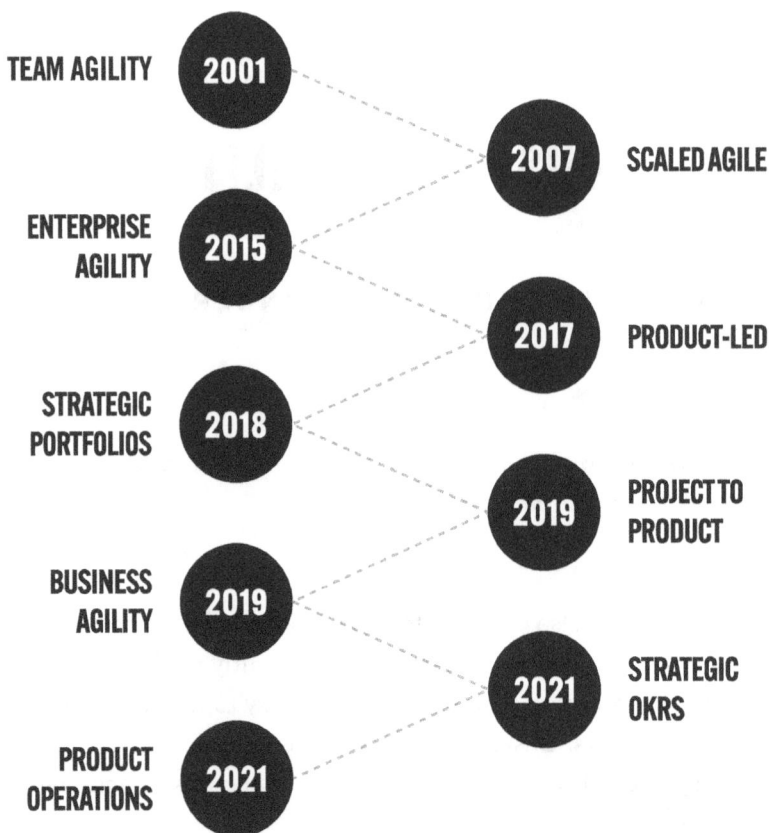

Agility didn't originate in boardrooms—it began in software development.

THE EVOLUTION OF BUSINESS AGILITY

TEAM AGILITY	**2001**
	2007 SCALED AGILE
ENTERPRISE AGILITY	**2015**
	2017 PRODUCT-LED
STRATEGIC PORTFOLIOS	**2018**
	2019 PROJECT TO PRODUCT
BUSINESS AGILITY	**2019**
	2021 STRATEGIC OKRS
PRODUCT OPERATIONS	**2021**

The years denoted are approximations of concept introduction.

- **Team Agility:** It started in 2001 with the *Agile Manifesto*, which emphasized collaboration, adaptability, and customer focus in software development.[143]
- **Scaled Agile:** By 2007, frameworks like SAFe extended agility across teams, improving alignment and coordination.
- **Enterprise Agility:** Agile principles transcended IT, reshaping operations, culture, and leadership into customer-focused, responsive organizations.
- **Product-Led:** Companies like Slack and Zoom used their products as growth engines, proving agility's value in dynamic markets.[144]
- **Strategic Portfolios:** Agility expanded into portfolio management, aligning projects with strategic goals.
- **Project to Product:** The focus shifted to delivering continuous value through product-centric delivery models.
- **Business Agility:** Organizations embraced agility beyond development teams, embedding adaptability, rapid decision-making, and cross-functional collaboration into core business functions to drive resilience and growth.
- **Strategic OKRs:** Objectives and key results emerged as a bridge between goals and execution, driving alignment and focus across entire organizations.[145]
- **Product Operations:** Product operations bridges product, engineering, and customer-facing teams, ensuring strategic alignment and facilitating data-driven decisions.[146]

Today, business agility encapsulates adaptability across all

143 Kent Beck et al., *Manifesto for Agile Software Development* (agilemanifesto.org, 2001), https://agilemanifesto. org/.

144 Hal Koss, "Product-Led Growth: A Guide," Built In, August 3, 2020, https://builtin.com/product/ product-led-growth.

145 John Doerr, *Measure What Matters: How Google, Bono, and the Gates Foundation Rock the World with OKRs* (Portfolio/Penguin, 2018), 7.

146 "Product Ops," ProductPlan, accessed April 22, 2024, https://www.productplan.com/glossary/product-ops/.

functions, making it essential for thriving in an ever-changing environment.

THE ECONOMICS OF AGILITY

Investing in agility isn't optional—it's the cost of staying competitive.

- **Global IT Spending:** Predicted to reach $5 trillion in 2024, driven by agile, digital, and artificial intelligence (AI) initiatives.[147]
- **Organizational Health:** Agile organizations have a 70 percent chance of ranking in the top quartile of performance.[148]
- **Efficiency Gains:** Sony Interactive saved $30 million annually by scaling agile practices.[149]

Yet, not all transformations succeed. Around 70 percent of agile initiatives fail, often due to cultural resistance or misaligned strategies. Success requires more than adopting agile frameworks—it demands cultural shifts, leadership buy-in, and robust execution.[150]

AGILITY'S IMPACT ON DECISIVENESS

Business agility doesn't just improve operations—it transforms decision-making:

---

147 Gartner, "Gartner Forecasts Worldwide IT Spending to Grow 5.5% in 2023," press release, April 6, 2023, https://www.gartner.com/en/newsroom/press-releases/2023-04-06-gartner-forecasts-worldwide-it-spending-to-grow-5-percent-in-2023.

148 Donovan Carreira et al., "Organizing for Speed: Agile as a Means to Transformation in Japan," McKinsey & Company, November 20, 2020, https://www.mckinsey.com/capabilities/people-and-organizational-performance/our-insights/organizing-for-speed-agile-as-a-means-to-transformation-in-japan.

149 Tripp Meister, "PlayStation Network—SAFe: Enabling Value Delivery," Scaled Agile, accessed April 22, 2024, https://scaledagile.com/case_study/playstation-network/.

150 Michael Bucy et al., "Transformation with a Capital T," in *The Next Normal: Transformation with a Capital T* (McKinsey Global Publishing, October 2020), 89, https://www.mckinsey.com/~/media/mckinsey/business%20functions/transformation/our%20insights/the%20path%20to%20true%20transformation/transformation-with-a-capital-t.pdf.

1. **Decentralization:** Teams are empowered to make decisions, enabling faster responses. However, without robust alignment, this can lead to duplication and missteps.
2. **Iterative Risk Management:** Decisions are tested through small, controlled experiments, allowing organizations to fail fast, learn faster, and course correct.
3. **OKRs as a Compass:** Objectives and key results create clarity and ensure decentralized decisions align with overarching goals.
4. **Adaptability over Certainty:** Leaders navigate ambiguity with confidence, making real-time decisions that evolve with new data.

However, agility isn't without challenges. Dependencies between teams and processes can complicate alignment, slowing decisions and increasing the risk of missteps. To harness agility's full potential, organizations must balance flexibility with disciplined coordination.

CASE STUDY: PHILIPS'S AGILE TRANSFORMATION

Philips demonstrates the transformative power of business agility.

Facing a competitive healthcare market, the company restructured around agile principles. By reducing release cycles from eighteen months to just six, Philips accelerated innovation and improved responsiveness to customer needs. This wasn't just a process shift—it was a cultural overhaul that empowered teams to take ownership, align with strategic goals, and deliver value faster.[151]

Philips's success underscores the importance of integrating agility into culture, strategy, and execution.

---

151 "Royal Philips—Adopting SAFe for Agile Transition," Scaled Agile, accessed April 22, 2024, https://scaledagile.com/case_study/royal-philips/.

THE FUTURE OF BUSINESS AGILITY

The pace of change is accelerating, making agility more than a competitive advantage—it's a necessity.

1. **Dynamic Strategy Development:** Annual planning is giving way to continuous strategic planning, where goals are evaluated and adapted often.
2. **Operational Resilience:** Organizations must develop plasticity—the ability to reshape and adapt dynamically to survive disruption.
3. **Technology Integration:** The synergy between human insight and technology, underpinned by OKRs, will define successful enterprises.

Adopting agility requires effort, but the rewards are transformative: faster decisions, smarter strategies, business-to-tech alignment, and empowered teams that drive innovation.

THE BOTTOM LINE

Business agility transforms uncertainty into opportunity. By connecting strategy to execution, decentralizing decisions, and embracing continuous improvement, agile organizations don't just survive change—they thrive on it.

The future belongs to those who are agile enough to adapt, decisive enough to act, and bold enough to innovate.

SUMMARY

Business agility is the ability of organizations to swiftly adapt strategies, structures, and processes to deliver value in a rapidly changing environment. It bridges the gap between strategy and execution, ensuring alignment across all levels of the organization.

The evolution of agility—from the *Agile Manifesto* to enterprise-wide adoption—shows its transformative power. Movements like scaled agile frameworks, product-led growth, and the shift from projects to products have redefined how organizations operate. Agile principles are now set to drive adaptability and innovation across all business functions.

Agility redefines decision-making, emphasizing decentralization, iterative risk management, and adaptability. Teams are empowered to make decisions autonomously, while frameworks like OKRs ensure alignment with strategic goals.

Looking ahead, dynamic strategic planning, operational resilience, and tighter technology integration will define the future of agility. Organizations that embrace agility don't just react to change—they thrive on it, making faster, smarter decisions that empower innovation and resilience.

Agility is no longer a competitive advantage—it's essential for survival in today's dynamic business landscape.

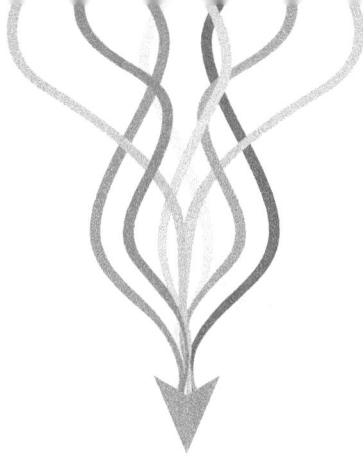

APPENDIX D

AI INTEGRATION

TRANSFORMING THE FUTURE

"Artificial Intelligence will reach human levels by around 2029. By 2045, we will have multiplied our civilization's human biological machine intelligence a billion-fold."

—RAY KURZWEIL

Artificial intelligence (AI) has moved from futuristic speculation to a cornerstone of enterprise strategy. Over the past decade, organizations have increasingly embraced AI to support decision-making, streamline operations, and drive innovation.

AI's value lies in its ability to analyze vast amounts of data, automate processes, and predict outcomes with precision. It transforms how businesses assess risk, plan strategically, and adapt in a competitive landscape. But this transformation comes with challenges. AI demands significant investment, faces cultural resistance, and raises questions about ethics and trust.

Still, for organizations willing to navigate its complexities, AI offers a roadmap to a more innovative, efficient, and decisive future.

THE BUILDING BLOCKS OF AI

At the broadest level is **AI**, encompassing all systems designed to simulate human intelligence. Within AI lies **machine learning (ML)**, a subset focused on algorithms that enable systems to learn and improve from data. Nested within ML is **deep learning**, which leverages neural networks to process large datasets and identify complex patterns. **Generative AI** is a specialized area of AI focused on creating new content, such as text, images, or music, using learned patterns.

BUILDING BLOCKS OF AI

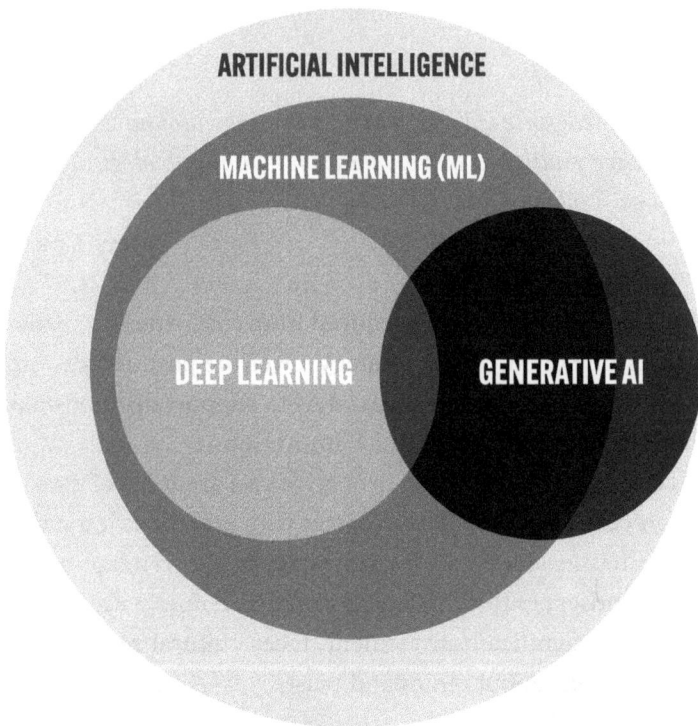

ARTIFICIAL INTELLIGENCE

MACHINE LEARNING (ML)

DEEP LEARNING

GENERATIVE AI

These building blocks have fueled AI's rapid growth and widespread adoption.

AI IN ACTION

Leading companies are leveraging AI to unlock value and gain a competitive edge. Here are a few examples:

- **JPMorgan:** AI analyzes legal documents, saving thousands of hours of manual labor. Generative AI enhances financial forecasting and customer service, delivering precision and personalization.
- **Google DeepMind (AlphaFold):** Revolutionizes drug discovery by predicting protein structures, enabling breakthroughs in treating diseases.
- **Amazon:** AI drives demand forecasting, fraud detection, and personalized shopping experiences. Warehouse automation reduces costs and accelerates deliveries.
- **Microsoft:** With tools like Copilot, AI transforms productivity by drafting reports, summarizing emails, and assisting with presentations.

These examples highlight AI's versatility in industries from healthcare and logistics to finance and retail.

CASE STUDY: PFIZER'S AI-POWERED BREAKTHROUGHS

Pfizer exemplifies AI's transformative potential.

In its quest for life-saving treatments, Pfizer leverages AI to analyze vast datasets, predict disease progressions, and design more effective clinical trials. By integrating generative AI, the company has accelerated timelines, improved patient outcomes, and reduced costs.

Pfizer's success demonstrates the power of combining human

expertise with machine precision, offering a model for other organizations to follow.

ETHICS AND TRUST

Despite its promise, AI adoption is not without risks:

1. **The Black Box Problem:** AI models often operate without transparency, making it difficult to understand how decisions are made.[152]
2. **Bias in Data:** AI reflects the biases of its training data and human-built safety models, potentially perpetuating inequalities.
3. **Job Displacement:** Fears of automation replacing roles create resistance among employees.

Organizations must address these challenges proactively by implementing ethical guidelines, fostering transparency, and emphasizing collaborative AI models like Human-in-the-Loop (HitL) systems.

DECISIVENESS, AGILITY, AND AI

AI enhances decisiveness by integrating predictive, prescriptive, and descriptive analytics into decision-making. Key advantages include:

1. **Data-Driven Insights:** AI reduces uncertainty by identifying patterns and trends in real time.
2. **Iterative Risk Management:** Small-scale experiments allow businesses to test and refine strategies before committing resources.

---

152 Davide Castelvecchi, "Can We Open the Black Box of AI?," *Nature* 538, no. 7623 (2016): 20–23, https://doi.org/10.1038/538020a.

3. **Enhanced Collaboration:** AI tools streamline communication, aligning cross-functional teams and reducing silos.
4. **Descriptive Analytics:** AI is able to rummage through the past, scouring data to spot patterns and trends and show us what has already happened.
5. **Prescriptive Analytics:** AI can look ahead, weighing scenarios with data and models and calculating the best course of action and how to shape future outcomes.
6. **Predictive Analytics:** AI can peer into tomorrow, using statistics and machine learning to forecast events and revealing what might happen next.

However, businesses must balance agility with caution. Dependencies on AI tools can complicate alignment, and overreliance on automation may stifle innovation. Robust frameworks, like OKRs, ensure AI-driven decisions align with organizational goals.

LOOKING AHEAD

AI stands at our doorstep, knocking with a promise of radical change. Experts say generative AI could lift global gross domestic product (GDP) by 7 percent and add $7 trillion to the global economy in just ten years.[153] That's a wave of wealth large enough to stir every industry on Earth. But this power doesn't stop there. Shifts in workflows triggered by AI advances could expose the equivalent of three hundred million full-time jobs to automation.[154] The future looms, brimming with possibility and tinged with uncertainty, daring us to imagine what comes next.

The next decade will see AI intersect with emerging technologies, creating transformative opportunities. A few examples include:

---

153 "Generative AI Could Raise Global GDP by 7%," Goldman Sachs, April 5, 2023, https://www.goldmansachs.com/insights/articles/generative-ai-could-raise-global-gdp-by-7-percent.

154 Joseph Briggs, "Generative AI Could Raise Global GDP by 7%," Goldman Sachs, April 5, 2023, https://www.goldmansachs.com/insights/articles/generative-ai-could-raise-global-gdp-by-7-percent.

- **Quantum Computing:** Exponentially increases AI's processing power, solving previously unsolvable problems.
- **Blockchain Integration:** Secures AI-driven transactions and ensures data integrity.
- **Internet of Things (IoT) Synergy:** Connects AI to real-time data from smart devices, enhancing responsiveness.

In healthcare, companies like the Mayo Clinic are using AI to integrate wearable data for proactive care. In transportation, Tesla and Waymo are advancing autonomous vehicles, attempting to make roads safer and more efficient. AI is reshaping industries, pushing the boundaries of what's possible.

THE PATH FORWARD

Adopting AI requires more than technology—it demands a mindset shift:

1. **Start with Clear Use Cases:** Focus on areas where AI delivers immediate value, like automation and customer personalization.
2. **Emphasize Collaboration:** Use HitL systems to combine human oversight with AI's analytical power.
3. **Invest in Ethics and Transparency:** Establish guidelines to address bias, accountability, and trust.

The journey to AI maturity is complex, but the rewards—faster decisions, smarter strategies, and greater agility—are transformative.

THE BOTTOM LINE

AI is not just a tool—it's a force reshaping industries and redefining how organizations operate. For leaders, the challenge is clear: embrace AI's opportunities while managing its risks.

The future belongs to those who are bold enough to innovate, agile enough to adapt, and ethical enough to ensure AI remains a tool for progress.

SUMMARY

AI has transitioned from speculation to strategy, powering industries by automating processes, driving personalization, and enabling smarter decision-making. Companies like Pfizer, Amazon, and Microsoft demonstrate AI's transformative potential, leveraging it for predictive analytics, drug discovery, and operational efficiency.

However, challenges, such as bias, trust, and resistance, require proactive solutions. Collaborative AI models using HitL systems combine human judgment with machine precision, ensuring ethical and effective decision-making.

Looking ahead, AI will intersect with quantum computing, blockchain, and IoT, creating unprecedented opportunities. Organizations must approach AI with clarity and caution, balancing innovation with ethical considerations.

AI is no longer optional—it's essential. The organizations that succeed will harness its potential to navigate complexity, make faster decisions, and thrive in a rapidly evolving world.

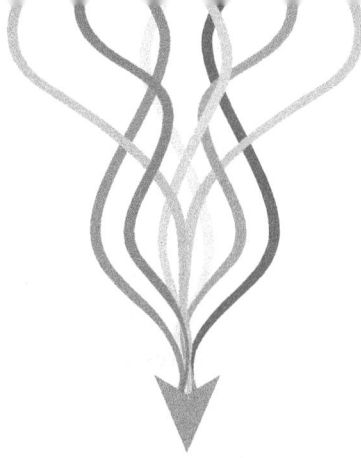

DECISIVENESS TRAPS

PATTERNS THAT SLOW DECISIONS

"Be willing to make decisions. That's the most important quality in a good leader."

—T. Boone Pickens

Organizational decision-making often stumbles into traps that derail progress and undermine strategic goals. **Resulting, complacency,** and **consensus** form a triad of pitfalls that challenge decisiveness. Each trap, when left unchecked, erodes morale, stifles productivity, and suppresses innovation. Together, they create a formidable obstacle course for organizations striving to maintain strategic alignment and agility.

This appendix explores how these traps manifest, their collective impact, and strategies to avoid them.

RESULTING: THE PERIL OF JUDGING DECISIONS BY THEIR OUTCOMES

Resulting is the tendency to evaluate decisions solely by their outcomes rather than the quality of the decision-making process. This bias often skews judgment and penalizes efforts made under uncertain circumstances. Consider the resulting trap in these scenarios:

1. **Performance Reviews:** Employees are judged by results beyond their control rather than the rationale of their decisions.
2. **Project Evaluation:** Success or failure is measured by meeting goals without analyzing the decisions leading to success or failure.
3. **Strategic Decisions:** Leadership evaluates outcomes without accounting for the uncertainty at the decision's inception.

THE DAMAGE

- **Morale:** Employees feel undervalued when judged unfairly, leading to frustration and disengagement.
- **Productivity:** Fear of negative outcomes discourages risk-taking, resulting in a culture of caution.
- **Innovation:** Risk aversion suppresses creative problem-solving and bold ideas.

THE FIX

Shift focus from outcomes to **processes**. Foster a **learning culture**, where failures are treated as growth opportunities. Recognize sound decision-making even when outcomes falter.

SYSTEMIC COMPLACENCY: THE SILENT KILLER
OF ORGANIZATIONAL EFFECTIVENESS

"Good is the enemy of great."

—JIM COLLINS

Complacency breeds stagnation. In large organizations, even isolated complacency can have a ripple effect, undermining adaptability and innovation. Consider the systematic complacency trap when these behaviors arise:

1. **Resistance to Change:** Overreliance on the status quo inhibits progress.
2. **Disregard for Competition:** Overconfidence blinds organizations to emerging threats.
3. **Lack of Initiative:** Employees settle for "good enough," avoiding proactive problem-solving.

THE DAMAGE

- **Morale:** Mediocrity erodes motivation, especially for high-performing employees.
- **Productivity:** Declining attention to detail and enthusiasm compromise output.
- **Innovation:** Fear of disrupting the status quo stifles creativity.

THE FIX

Cultivate a culture of **continuous improvement**. Challenge the status quo, reward initiative, and ensure effective communication of strategic intent.

CONSENSUS THINKING: THE DOUBLE-EDGED SWORD OF COLLECTIVE AGREEMENT

Consensus values inclusivity but risks watering down decisions and slowing progress. Striving for unanimity often sacrifices clarity and innovation. Consider the trap of consensus thinking when evaluating:

1. **Decision-Making Processes:** Complex and time-consuming, leading to delays.
2. **Team Collaboration:** The pursuit of agreement suppresses bold ideas.
3. **Organizational Culture:** Groupthink prevails, diluting diverse perspectives.

THE DAMAGE

- **Morale:** Prolonged debates lead to frustration and decision fatigue.
- **Productivity:** Lengthy consensus-building wastes time and resources.
- **Innovation:** Minority viewpoints are overshadowed, stifling fresh ideas.

THE FIX

Balance **inclusivity** with **efficiency**. Employ consensus only when necessary and foster a psychologically safe environment for dissenting opinions.

THE ROLE OF LEADERSHIP

Leaders play a pivotal role in sidestepping decisiveness traps. Successful leaders share key traits:

1. **Forward-Thinking:** They focus on long-term objectives, evaluating decisions in their strategic context.
2. **Resilience:** They challenge the status quo and champion innovation.
3. **Transparency:** They promote open communication and clarity in decision-making.
4. **Curiosity:** They embrace learning, viewing failures as opportunities.

HOW LEADERS BUILD DECISIVENESS

1. **Encourage Diversity of Thought:** Value differing perspectives to challenge assumptions.
2. **Promote Continuous Learning:** Emphasize growth through reflection on successes and failures.
3. **Reinforce Decision Integrity:** Separate the process from outcomes.
4. **Emphasize Transparency:** Foster openness to build trust and understanding.

HIGH-PROFILE LEADERSHIP EXAMPLES

- **Satya Nadella,** CEO of Microsoft, revitalized the company by fostering a **growth mindset,** embracing diversity, and rejecting complacency. His leadership transformed Microsoft into a beacon of agility and innovation.[155]
- **Indra Nooyi,** former CEO of PepsiCo, avoided resulting by prioritizing long-term health initiatives, even amid criticism. Her decisions demonstrated a commitment to process over immediate outcomes.[156]

---

155 Lina Tran, "The 'Shifts' Satya Nadella Made to Revitalize Microsoft Empire," EnvZone, July 2, 2021, https://envzone.com/the-shifts-satya-nadella-made-to-revitalize-microsoft-empire/.

156 Grant Freeland, "Indra K. Nooyi on Performance with Purpose," Boston Consulting Group, January 14, 2010, https://www.bcg.com/publications/2010/indra-nooyi-performance-purpose.

These leaders exemplify how avoiding decisiveness traps leads to sustained organizational success.

SUMMARY

Decisiveness traps—resulting, complacency, and consensus—can derail strategic decision-making and hinder organizational progress.

- **Resulting:** Judging decisions by outcomes undermines morale and innovation.
- **Complacency:** Maintaining the status quo stifles adaptability and creativity.
- **Consensus:** Seeking unanimity sacrifices speed and bold thinking.

The antidote lies in **effective leadership**. Leaders who champion diversity of thought, foster transparency, and embrace continuous learning can navigate these traps, empowering their organizations to thrive.

Decisiveness is not just about making decisions—it's about making the **right decisions** with clarity, courage, and conviction.

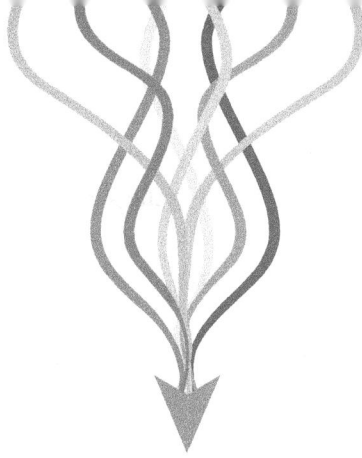

COGNITIVE BIAS INDEX

Action Bias: The tendency to favor action over inaction, even when it might be counterproductive.

Anchoring Bias: The human tendency to rely heavily on the first piece of information offered (the "anchor") when making decisions.

Authority Bias: The tendency to attribute greater accuracy to the opinion of an authority figure and be more influenced by that opinion.

Availability Bias: A mental shortcut that relies on examples that immediately come to mind when evaluating a specific topic, concept, method, or decision.

Availability Cascade: A self-reinforcing process in which a collective belief gains more and more plausibility through its increasing repetition in public discourse.

Bandwagon Effect: The tendency to do (or believe) things because many other people do (or believe) the same.

Base-Rate Fallacy: Ignoring available statistical data in favor of particulars.

Belief Bias: The tendency to judge the strength of arguments based on the plausibility of their conclusion rather than how strongly they support that conclusion.

Bikeshedding: A metaphor to illustrate the tendency to spend excessive time on trivial matters, often glossing over important ones.

Blind Spot Bias: Failing to recognize your cognitive biases is a bias.

Bounded Rationality: When individuals make decisions, their rationality is limited by their information, the cognitive limitations of their minds, and the finite amount of time they have to decide.

Choice Overload: A cognitive process in which people have difficulty deciding when faced with many options.

Cognitive Dissonance: The mental discomfort experienced by a person who holds two or more contradictory beliefs, ideas, or values.

Commitment Bias: The tendency to be consistent with what we have done or said we would do, particularly if this is public.

Confirmation Bias: The tendency to search for, interpret, favor, and recall information in a way that confirms one's preexisting beliefs or hypotheses.

Curse of Knowledge: When better-informed people find it

extremely difficult to think about problems from the perspective of lesser-informed people.

Decision Fatigue: Being tired and less able to make quality decisions when making many decisions in a compressed window.

Dunning–Kruger Effect: The tendency of unskilled individuals to overestimate their ability and experts to underestimate theirs.

Egocentric Bias: The tendency to rely too heavily on one's perspective and have a higher opinion of oneself than reality.

False Consensus: Overestimating how much other people agree with us.

Feature-Positive Effect: A bias toward noticeable, tangible things and away from unnoticeable or transparent things.

The Framing Effect: Drawing different conclusions from the same information depending on how that information is presented.

Functional Fixedness: The tendency to see objects only working in a particular way.

Groupthink: The psychological phenomenon that occurs within a group of people when the desire for harmony or conformity results in an irrational or dysfunctional decision-making outcome.

Halo Effect: The tendency of an impression created in one area to influence opinion in another.

Hard-Easy Effect: The tendency to overestimate the probability of success at a task perceived as hard and underestimate the likelihood of success at a task perceived as easy.

Hindsight Bias: Sometimes called the "I knew it all along" effect; the tendency to see past events as predictable.

Hyperbolic Discounting: The tendency for people to choose a smaller-sooner reward over a larger-later reward.

IKEA Effect: People tend to place a disproportionately high value on objects they have assembled themselves, even if the assembly is partial or the end product is of lower quality than a professionally assembled one.

Illusion of Validity: Believing that our judgments and decisions are accurate, especially when available information suggests they are not.

Illusory Correlation: Perceiving a relationship between variables (typically people, events, or behaviors) even when no such relationship exists.

In-Group Bias: People tend to give preferential treatment to others they perceive as members of their group.

Law of the Instrument: An overreliance on a familiar tool or method, ignoring or undervaluing alternative approaches ("If all you have is a hammer, everything looks like a nail").

Loss Aversion: The tendency to prefer avoiding losses to acquiring equivalent gains.

Mere Exposure Effect: The tendency to express undue liking for things merely because we are familiar with them.

Motivating-Uncertainty Effect: People tend to experience increased motivation and engagement when the outcome of a task or the reward is uncertain. The unpredictability can make the activity more intriguing, leading individuals to put in more effort and persist longer, even when the potential reward is relatively modest.

Naive Allocation: People tend to evenly distribute resources, time, or attention across all available options or tasks, a behavior often referred to as "peanut buttering." This approach reflects a desire to treat all options equally, even when some might deserve more focus or resources due to their greater importance or potential impact. This bias can lead to suboptimal outcomes, as it overlooks the varying significance of different tasks or options.

Observer Expectancy Effect: The tendency for experimenters to believe, certify, and publish data that agrees with their expectations for the outcome of an experiment and disbelieve, discard, or downgrade the corresponding weightings for data that appears to conflict with those expectations.

Optimism Bias: The tendency to be overoptimistic about planned actions' outcomes.

Overconfidence Bias: The tendency to overestimate our abilities, skills, knowledge, or control over a situation.

Planning Fallacy: The tendency to underestimate task-completion times.

Priming: The subtle, unconscious influence on a person's behavior and decisions due to prior experiences or exposures.

Reactive Devaluation: Devaluing proposals only because they are presumed to originate from an antagonist.

Salience Bias: Focusing on the most easily recognizable features of a person or concept.

Status Quo Bias: The preference to keep things as they are or maintain a previous decision.

Strategic Misrepresentation: The planned, systematic distortion or misstatement of factual evidence to serve strategic aims.

Sunk-Cost Fallacy: The phenomenon where people justify increasing investment in a decision based on the cumulative prior investment despite new evidence suggesting the cost, starting today, of continuing the decision outweighs the expected benefit.

Survivorship Bias: Concentrating on the people or things that "survived" some process and inadvertently overlooking those that didn't because of their lack of visibility.

Zeigarnik Effect: The tendency to remember uncompleted or interrupted tasks better than completed ones.

Zero-Risk Bias: The preference to reduce a small risk to zero over achieving a greater reduction not to zero in a larger risk.

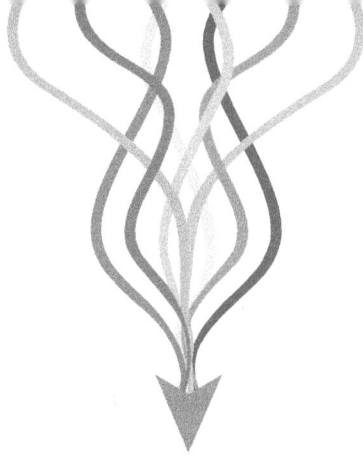

BIAS MITIGATION INDEX

Bias is an inherent part of decision-making. While it cannot be eliminated, organizations can adopt practices, processes, and norms to mitigate its effects effectively. This appendix outlines key biases and actionable strategies to address them.

SURVIVORSHIP BIAS

Definition: Focusing only on successes while ignoring failures, leading to skewed conclusions.

MITIGATION STRATEGIES

- **Analyze Full Data:** Include both successes and failures in evaluations to gain a complete picture.
- **Seek External Perspectives:** Involve third-party consultants or diverse review committees to identify overlooked biases.
- **Encourage Reporting Failures:** Foster a culture where failures are shared openly as learning opportunities.

OPTIMISM BIAS

Definition: Overestimating positive outcomes while underestimating risks.

MITIGATION STRATEGIES

- **Conduct Premortems:** Imagine future failure and identify potential causes to uncover hidden risks.
- **Leverage Third-Party Reviews:** Involve external evaluators for objective assessments.

FEATURE-POSITIVE EFFECT

Definition: Focusing on present features while ignoring what is missing.

MITIGATION STRATEGIES

- **Run SWOT Analyses:** Evaluate strengths, weaknesses, opportunities, and threats to uncover blind spots.
- **Use Balanced Scorecards:** Assess projects holistically, considering both positives and negatives.
- **Promote Critical Thinking:** Encourage employees to challenge assumptions and think beyond what is visible.

BLIND SPOT BIAS

Definition: Recognizing biases in others but not in oneself.

MITIGATION STRATEGIES

- **Institutionalize Feedback:** Use anonymous mechanisms to surface unnoticed biases.

- **Employ Decision Support Tools:** Utilize structured models, like checklists, to guide unbiased decision-making.
- **Practice Self-Reflection:** Encourage regular introspection to identify personal blind spots.

STRATEGIC MISREPRESENTATION

Definition: Distorting facts to achieve a desired outcome.

MITIGATION STRATEGIES

- **Foster Transparency:** Reward honesty, and discourage over-optimistic projections.
- **Implement Audits:** Use independent reviews to validate data and identify distortions.

FALSE CONSENSUS

Definition: Overestimating how much others share one's beliefs or opinions.

MITIGATION STRATEGIES

- **Encourage Dissent:** Create environments where differing opinions are welcomed.
- **Seek Anonymous Feedback:** Use tools that allow team members to express views without fear of backlash.

CURSE OF KNOWLEDGE

Definition: Struggling to see a problem from the perspective of less-informed individuals.

- **Promote Plain Language:** Simplify communication for better understanding.
- **Encourage Questions:** Foster a culture where clarifying questions are welcomed.
- **Use Visual Aids:** Present complex information through diagrams or charts.

BELIEF BIAS

Definition: Judging arguments based on the plausibility of their conclusions rather than their validity.

- **Assign Devil's Advocates:** Ensure opposing viewpoints are explored during discussions.
- **Promote Intellectual Humility:** Encourage openness to revising beliefs in light of new evidence.

AVAILABILITY CASCADE

Definition: Collective beliefs becoming more plausible through repetition.

- **Verify Information:** Base decisions on verified data, not popular narratives.
- **Promote Media Literacy:** Train teams to evaluate information sources critically.

SALIENCE BIAS

Definition: Overweighting prominent or emotionally striking information.

MITIGATION STRATEGIES

- **Take a Holistic View:** Consider all aspects of a situation, not just the most visible.
- **Use Scenario Planning:** Simulate outcomes to understand less apparent factors.

REACTIVE DEVALUATION

Definition: Discounting proposals simply because of their source.

MITIGATION STRATEGIES

- **Involve Neutral Parties:** Use mediators to present ideas objectively.
- **Focus on Interests:** Evaluate proposals based on merit rather than origin.

PRIMING

Definition: The subconscious influence of prior stimuli on decisions.

MITIGATION STRATEGIES

- **Raise Awareness:** Train employees to recognize and counteract priming effects.
- **Base Decisions on Data:** Use structured frameworks to minimize unconscious biases.

PLANNING FALLACY

Definition: Underestimating the time needed to complete tasks.

MITIGATION STRATEGIES

- **Use Historical Data:** Base estimates on past project timelines.
- **Break Tasks Down:** Estimate smaller components for greater accuracy.
- **Add Buffers:** Allocate extra time for unforeseen delays.

OBSERVER EXPECTANCY EFFECT

Definition: The subconscious influence of expectations on outcomes.

MITIGATION STRATEGIES

- **Implement Blind Processes:** Remove identifying details in evaluations to reduce bias.
- **Standardize Protocols:** Use consistent procedures for assessments.

NAIVE DIVERSIFICATION

Definition: Allocating resources equally across options without considering their merits.

MITIGATION STRATEGIES

- **Conduct Needs Assessments:** Prioritize options based on potential impact.
- **Seek Expert Guidance:** Use professional advice for resource allocation.

WISHFUL THINKING BIAS

Definition: Favoring desired outcomes over realistic ones.

MITIGATION STRATEGIES

- **Conduct Peer Reviews:** Ensure findings are validated by independent teams.
- **Promote Objectivity:** Reward fact-based decision-making.

MERE EXPOSURE EFFECT

Definition: Preferring options simply due to familiarity.

MITIGATION STRATEGIES

- **Encourage Experimentation:** Introduce trial periods for new methods or tools.
- **Foster a Growth Mindset:** Emphasize learning and adaptability.

LOSS AVERSION

Definition: Avoiding losses more strongly than pursuing equivalent gains.

MITIGATION STRATEGIES

- **Reframe Decisions:** Highlight potential gains rather than focusing on losses.
- **Celebrate Risk-Taking:** Reward calculated risks and learning from failure.

LAW OF THE INSTRUMENT

Definition: Overrelying on familiar tools or methods.

MITIGATION STRATEGIES

- **Encourage Learning:** Provide training in alternative approaches.
- **Foster Open Communication:** Allow teams to challenge current practices.

IN-GROUP BIAS

Definition: Favoring one's own group over others.

MITIGATION STRATEGIES

- **Encourage Collaboration:** Promote cross-team initiatives.
- **Standardize Evaluations:** Use objective criteria for promotions and rewards.

ILLUSION OF VALIDITY

Definition: Overestimating judgment accuracy despite unpredictability.

MITIGATION STRATEGIES

- **Promote Humility:** Emphasize the role of uncertainty in outcomes.
- **Evaluate Performance Regularly:** Use systematic reviews to assess decisions objectively.

HYPERBOLIC DISCOUNTING

Definition: Preferring smaller, immediate rewards over larger, delayed ones.

MITIGATION STRATEGIES

- **Visualize Future Benefits:** Use scenarios to make long-term rewards tangible.
- **Set Short-Term Goals:** Break larger goals into smaller, achievable steps.

HINDSIGHT BIAS

Definition: Overestimating the predictability of past events.

MITIGATION STRATEGIES

- **Document Decisions:** Record assumptions and rationale to clarify hindsight.
- **Encourage Diverse Perspectives:** Use varied viewpoints to challenge oversimplified narratives.

HARD-EASY EFFECT

Definition: Overestimating ability for hard tasks and underestimating it for easy ones.

MITIGATION STRATEGIES

- **Collaborate on Estimates:** Combine input from multiple team members.
- **Adopt Agile Methods:** Use iterative approaches to refine estimates.

HALO EFFECT

Definition: Letting positive impressions in one area create a positive impression of the whole.

- **Provide Unbiased Feedback:** Encourage objective reviews of new initiatives.
- **Offer Trials:** Allow hands-on experiences to evaluate merits independently.

FUNCTIONAL FIXEDNESS

Definition: Failing to see alternative uses for tools or concepts.

MITIGATION STRATEGIES

- **Encourage Creative Thinking:** Facilitate brainstorming sessions to explore new ideas.
- **Use Cross-Functional Teams:** Introduce diverse perspectives to challenge conventional uses.

Note that Chapter 9 covers eight additional biases, including anchoring bias, authority bias, availability bias, confirmation bias, groupthink, overconfidence bias, sunk-cost fallacy, and zero-risk bias. This appendix was primarily sourced from the Uncertainty Project.[157]

---

157 "Biases," The Uncertainty Project, accessed May 4, 2024, https://www.theuncertaintyproject.org/blueprint/biases.

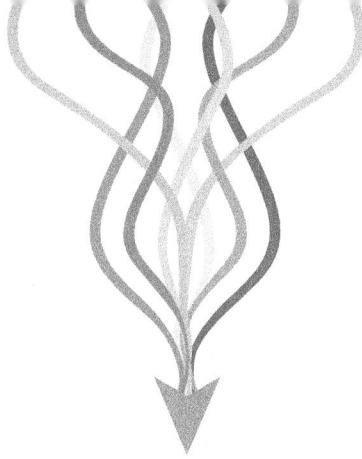

APPENDIX H

INSIGHTS INDEX

Envision your organization has contextualized decisions and linked them to strategy, goals, outcomes, and work. Additionally, your organization can run analytics on this context graph over multiple years and across any combination of division, product, region, team, work, and time. Now, consider the following insights but through the lens of a much deeper understanding of the context, trends, and predicted outcomes.

CEO

- Revenue Growth Rate
- Net Profit Margin
- Customer Retention Rate
- Employee Engagement Score
- Market Share
- Earnings Before Interest, Taxes, Depreciation, and Amortization (EBITDA)
- Strategic Initiative Progress

- Total Addressable Market (TAM) Penetration
- Operating Cash Flow
- Customer Net Promoter Score (NPS)
- Organizational Alignment Index
- Competitive Benchmark Index
- Innovation Pipeline Growth
- Cost of Customer Acquisition (CAC)
- Return on Investment (ROI) Across Portfolios

COO

- Operational Efficiency Ratio
- Average Order-Fulfillment Time
- Supply-Chain Reliability Index
- Cost Per Unit (CPU)
- Workforce Utilization Rate
- Process Automation Percentage
- Downtime-Hours/Impact Analysis
- Inventory Turnover Ratio
- First-Time Quality Rate
- Customer Complaint Resolution Time

CFO

- Revenue Versus Forecast Variance
- EBITDA Margin
- Free Cash Flow (FCF)
- Budget Variance Analysis
- Debt-to-Equity Ratio
- ROI
- Cost of Capital
- Gross-Margin Trends
- Accounts-Receivable Turnover
- Financial Risk Score

CRO (REVENUE)

- Pipeline Coverage Ratio
- Sales Conversion Rate
- CAC
- Monthly Recurring Revenue (MRR)
- Average Deal Size
- Sales-Cycle Length
- Churn Rate
- Cross-Sell/Upsell Revenue Percentage
- Sales Forecast Accuracy
- Customer Retention Rate

CSO (STRATEGY)

- Strategic Initiative Progress Score
- Time-to-Market for Strategic Initiatives
- Competitive Intelligence Index
- Scenario Planning Effectiveness
- Long-Term Growth Projection
- Organizational Agility Index
- Goal Achievement Rate
- Risk-Mitigation Score
- Resource Allocation Efficiency
- Market-Trend Alignment

CPO (PRODUCT)

- Product Revenue Growth Rate
- Customer Retention Rate by Product
- NPS by Product
- Churn Rate by Product
- Product Development Cycle Time
- Roadmap Delivery Accuracy
- Feature Utilization Rate

- Innovation Pipeline Contribution
- Market Share by Product
- Customer Satisfaction Index by Product
- Active User Growth Rate
- Time-to-Market for New Features
- Product Profitability Margins
- Adoption Rate of New Features
- Customer Feedback Integration Rate
- Average Time to Resolve Product Bugs
- Research and Development (R&D) Investment Efficiency
- Cross-Functional Team Alignment Score
- Feature Prioritization Alignment with Strategy
- Competitive Benchmarking by Product
- Usage Analytics for Key Features
- Retention Impact of New Features
- Lifetime Value (LTV) by Product
- Product Portfolio ROI
- Cost of Product Development by Feature
- Customer Requests Fulfillment Rate
- Market Penetration Rate of Products
- Feedback-Loop Efficiency (Customer to Product Team)
- Strategic-Roadmap Alignment Score
- Product-Support Ticket Trends

CMO

- Customer Segmentation Accuracy
- Campaign ROI
- Customer Acquisition Cost by Channel
- Brand Awareness Score
- Website Traffic to Lead Ratio
- Content Engagement Rate
- Marketing Qualified Leads (MQLs)
- Cost Per Lead (CPL)

- Social Media Share of Voice
- Email Open/Click-Through Rates

CPO (PEOPLE/HR)

- Employee Retention Rate
- Hiring Time-to-Fill
- Training ROI
- Diversity and Inclusion Index
- Internal Promotion Rate
- Employee Net Promoter Score (eNPS)
- Absenteeism Rate
- Succession-Planning Readiness
- Engagement-Survey Participation
- Compensation Benchmarking Data

CIO

- System Uptime Percentage
- IT Budget Utilization
- Cybersecurity Threat Resolution Time
- Technology Adoption Rate
- IT Project Delivery On-Time Rate
- Shadow IT Occurrence Rate
- Data Breach Incidents
- Help-Desk Resolution Time
- Software ROI Analysis
- Cloud Utilization Percentage

CTO

- Innovation Cycle Time
- Code-Deployment Frequency
- Technical Debt Ratio

- R&D Investment Efficiency
- Bug-Resolution Time
- Product Uptime Percentage
- Developer Productivity Index
- Security Vulnerability Mitigation Rate
- System Scalability Score
- Technical Roadmap Alignment

BUSINESS UNIT LEADERS

- Unit-Level Revenue Growth
- Profit-and-Loss Accountability Metrics
- Customer-Satisfaction Score
- Localized Market Share
- Talent Retention in Unit
- Goal Completion Rate
- Team Engagement Index
- Operational Cost Efficiency
- Customer-Feedback Analysis
- Competitive Position in Unit's Market

HEAD OF PRODUCT

- Product Adoption Rate
- Market Fit Score
- Roadmap Delivery On-Time Rate
- Customer-Feedback Integration Rate
- Innovation Contribution to Revenue
- Churn Impact Per Product
- Average Time-to-Ship Features
- Feature Utilization Rate
- Active-User Growth Rate
- Product ROI

PORTFOLIO MANAGER

- Portfolio ROI
- Project Prioritization Score
- Resource Allocation Efficiency
- Risk-Adjusted Return Metrics
- Portfolio Alignment with Strategy
- Capacity Utilization Score
- Budget Compliance Rate
- Time-to-Benefit for Investments
- Program Risk Ratings
- Stakeholder Satisfaction Index

PROGRAM MANAGERS

- Milestone Completion Rate
- Scope-Creep Percentage
- Program Risk-Mitigation Score
- Cross-Dependency Management Efficiency
- Deliverable Acceptance Rate
- Budget Variance Per Program
- Time-to-Value for Programs
- Stakeholder Feedback Rating
- Project Interdependencies Risk
- Change Request Count

PRODUCT MANAGERS

- Feature Adoption Rate
- Customer-Feedback Integration Score
- Roadmap Completion Percentage
- Feature Prioritization Alignment
- Product–Market Fit Index
- Competitive Product Benchmarking
- Bugs-Per-Release Count

- Release Timeliness
- Product Usage Analytics
- Customer Satisfaction Specific to Product

ENGINEERING MANAGERS

- Team Velocity Metrics
- Code-Quality Index
- Sprint Completion Rate
- Technical Debt Management
- Developer Retention Rate
- Average Bug-Fix Time
- Collaboration Efficiency Index
- Onboarding Time for New Engineers
- CI/CD Pipeline Efficiency
- Peer-Review Quality Score

INSIGHTS IMPROVED BY HISTORICAL CONTEXT

Below is a sample list:

- Alignment of goals to strategy
- Alignment of work to strategic goals
- Behavior, customer needs, and trends
- Business continuity under various risk scenarios
- Competition and market positioning
- Contingency planning based on different scenarios
- Crisis management
- Development opportunities
- Flow metrics
- Investment portfolio recommendations
- Market opportunities
- Possible future scenarios
- Portfolio optimization and diversification

- Quantifying and prioritizing risks
- Resource allocation and operational efficiency
- Risks associated with different investments
- Risk identification and assessment
- Risk-mitigation monitoring
- Strategies for investment risk mitigation
- Strategies to minimize risk

DIFFICULT INSIGHTS TO CAPTURE

Organizational memory, in conjunction with a context graph, enables continuous visibility into new or traditionally challenging insights that can improve operational efficiency and strategic advantage, such as:

- Bias identification and reduction measures
- Change impact on risk
- Change impact on dependency
- Change impact on finance
- Change impact on proximity
- Change impact on work
- Change pattern recognition
- Decision blast radius
- Decision routing optimization
- Decision velocity
- Decision prioritization and escalation
- Estimation efficiency
- Hypothesis forecasting
- Hypothesis management
- Lessons learned from past decisions
- Performance indicators
- Predictive models for forecasting outcomes of decisions
- Prioritization recommendations
- Transformation benchmarking

- Transformation force multipliers
- Transformation sentiment tracking
- Velocity measurement
- Wargaming scenarios
- And many more

Organizational memory enables a fuller understanding of the correlation of one change in the business to the rest of the business. This capability can create tremendous potential to facilitate better strategic decisions.

ACKNOWLEDGMENTS

This book is the result of countless collaborations, shared ideas, and collective efforts to challenge what's possible.

I am deeply grateful to my wife, Lexi, whose encouragement gave me the courage to take bold risks as an entrepreneur, and to my parents, who instilled in me the values of hard work and persistence. To my mentors and colleagues—Hunter Nelson, Greg Stock, Tim Cooper, Barry O'Reilly, Doug Cogan, PV Boccasam, and Cameron Deatsch—your insights and guidance have profoundly shaped my journey.

A special debt of gratitude goes to my brilliant co-founders at Dotwork and AgileCraft: Kyle Byrd, Shak Patel, and Rick Cobb. Without your partnership, none of this would have been possible.

I also want to thank my editors and publishers, along with John May and John Cutler, for helping refine my ideas and bring this book to life. Finally, to the early readers of this manuscript—your invaluable feedback guided me through the challenges of getting this book to market as a first-time author.

www.ingramcontent.com/pod-product-compliance
Lightning Source LLC
Chambersburg PA
CBHW071539210326
41597CB00019B/3048